Recommended by L

TOP

SHOPS, RESTAURANTS, ARTS & NIGHTLIFE

MANCHESTER

Guide Book 2020

The Most Recommended Places
in Manchester

MANCHESTER

GUIDE BOOK

2020

SHOPS, RESTAURANTS, ATTRACTIONS & NIGHTLIFE

MANCHESTER GUIDE BOOK 2020
Shops, Restaurants, Arts, Entertainment and Nightlife

© Rebecca R. Queen, 2020
© E.G.P. Editorial, 2020

ISBN-13: 9781083073440

I N D E X

MANCHESTER GUIDEBOOK 2020

Shops, Restaurants, Arts, Entertainment and Nightlife

*This directory is dedicated to Manchester Business Owners and Managers
who provide the experience that the locals and tourists enjoy.
Thanks you very much for all that you do and thank for being the "People Choice".*

*Thanks to everyone that posts their reviews online and
the amazing reviews sites that make our life easier.*

*The places listed in this book are the most positively reviewed
and recommended by locals and travelers from around the world.*

*Thank you for your time and enjoy the directory that is
designed with locals and tourist in mind!*

TOP 500 SHOPS

The Most Recommended by Locals & Trevelers

(From #1 to #500)

#1
Manchester Craft
Category: Arts & Crafts
Average price: Modest
Area: Northern Quarter
Address: 17 Oak St
Manchester M4 5JD, UK
Phone: 0161 832 4274

#2
Afflecks
Category: Antiques, Vintage, Jewelry
Average price: Modest
Area: Northern Quarter
Address: 52 Church Street
Manchester M4 1PW, UK
Phone: 0161 839 0718

#3
Selfridges & Co
Category: Department Store
Average price: Expensive
Area: City Centre
Address: 1 Exchange Square Central
Manchester M3 1BD, UK
Phone: +44 870 837 7377

#4
Fred Aldous Art, Craft and Hobby Suppliers
Category: Art Supplies, Fabric Store, Cards & Stationery
Average price: Modest
Area: Northern Quarter
Address: 37 Lever Street
Manchester M1 1LW, UK
Phone: 0161 236 4224

#5
Retro Rehab
Category: Used, Vintage, Women's Clothing
Average price: Modest
Area: Northern Quarter
Address: 91 Oldham Street
Manchester M4 1LW, UK
Phone: 0161 839 2050

#6
Museum of Science & Industry
Category: Museum, Art Gallery
Average price: Inexpensive
Area: Castlefield
Address: Liverpool Road
Manchester M3 4FP, UK
Phone: 0161 832 2244

#7
Manchester Arndale
Category: Shopping Center
Average price: Modest
Area: City Centre
Address: Market Street
Manchester M4 3AQ, UK
Phone: 0161 833 9851

#8
Piccadilly Records
Category: Music & DVDs, Vinyl Records
Average price: Modest
Area: Northern Quarter
Address: 53 Oldham Street
Manchester M1 1JR, UK
Phone: 0161 839 8008

#9
Primark
Category: Women's Clothing, Men's Clothing, Baby Gear & Furniture
Average price: Inexpensive
Area: City Centre
Address: 106-122 Market Street
Manchester M1 1WA, UK
Phone: 0161 923 4772

#10
Magma
Category: Bookstore, Comic Books, Cards & Stationery
Average price: Modest
Area: Northern Quarter
Address: 22 Oldham Street
Manchester M1 1JN, UK
Phone: 0161 236 8778

#11
Forbidden Planet
Category: Bookstore
Average price: Modest
Area: Northern Quarter
Address: 65 Oldham Street
Manchester M1 1JR, UK
Phone: 0161 839 4777

#12
Oklahoma
Category: Coffee & Tea, Cards & Stationery, Breakfast & Brunch
Average price: Modest
Area: Northern Quarter
Address: 74-76 High Street
Manchester M4 1ES, UK
Phone: 0161 834 1136

#13
Aldi
Category: Electronics, Grocery
Average price: Inexpensive
Area: Northern Quarter
Address: 67-71 Market Street
Manchester M4 2EA, UK
Phone: +44 844 406 8800

#14
Oi Polloi
Category: Accessories, Sports Wear,
Men's Clothing
Average price: Expensive
Area: Northern Quarter
Address: 63 Thomas Street
Manchester M4 1LQ, UK
Phone: 0161 831 7870

#15
Venus Flowers
Category: Florist
Average price: Expensive
Area: Oxford Road Corridor
Address: 95 Oxford Street
Manchester M1 6ET, UK
Phone: 0161 228 7000

#16
Cow
Category: Women's Clothing,
Used, Vintage
Average price: Modest
Area: Gay Village
Address: Parker Street
Manchester M1 4BD, UK
Phone: +44 844 504 0400

#17
H.Blyth & Co
Category: Art Supplies
Average price: Modest
Area: Northern Quarter
Address: 1 Stevenson Square
Manchester M1 1DN, UK
Phone: 0161 236 1302

#18
Empire Exchange
Category: Bookstore, Antiques
Average price: Modest
Area: Northern Quarter
Address: 1 Newton St
Manchester M1 1HW, UK
Phone: 0161 236 4445

#19
Rockers England
Category: Fashion
Average price: Modest
Area: Northern Quarter
Address: 89 Oldham Street
Manchester M4 1LF, UK
Phone: 0161 839 9202

#20
Paperchase
Category: Cards & Stationery,
Art Supplies
Average price: Expensive
Area: City Centre
Address: 14 Bank House
Manchester M1 1PX, UK
Phone: 0161 835 9935

#21
Manchester Museum
Category: Museum, Art Gallery
Average price: Inexpensive
Area: Oxford Road Corridor
Address: Oxford Road
Manchester M13 9PL, UK
Phone: 0161 275 2634

#22
Forsyth Brothers
Category: Musical Instruments,
Music & DVDs
Average price: Modest
Area: City Centre
Address: 126 Deansgate
Manchester M3 2GR, UK
Phone: 0161 834 3281

#23
Agent Provocateur
Category: Lingerie
Average price: Exclusive
Area: City Centre
Address: 81 King Street
Manchester M2 4AH, UK
Phone: 0161 833 3735

#24
Debenhams
Category: Department Store
Average price: Modest
Area: Northern Quarter
Address: 123 Market Street
Manchester M60 1, UK
Phone: +44 844 561 6161

#25
Blackwell's
Category: Bookstore
Average price: Expensive
Area: Oxford Road Corridor
Address: Precinct Center
Manchester M13 9RN, UK
Phone: 0161 274 3331

#26
Abakhan
Category: Fabric Store
Average price: Modest
Area: Northern Quarter
Address: 111-115 Oldham St
Manchester M4 1LN, UK
Phone: 0161 839 3229

#27
Clarks
Category: Shoe Store
Average price: Modest
Area: City Centre
Address: 47 Market Street
Manchester M1 1WR, UK
Phone: +44 844 499 1789

#28
H&M
Category: Accessories,
Men's Clothing, Women's Clothing
Average price: Inexpensive
Area: City Centre
Address: 58-70 Market Street
Manchester M1 1PN, UK
Phone: 0161 836 2800

#29
Apple
Category: Electronics, Computers
Average price: Expensive
Area: City Centre
Address: Unit 23 New Canon Street Mall
Manchester M4 3AJ, UK
Phone: 0161 216 4570

#30
Thunder Egg
Category: Women's Clothing,
Flowers & Gifts
Average price: Expensive
Area: Piccadilly
Address: 22 Oldham Street
Manchester M1 1JN, UK
Phone: 0161 235 0606

#31
Boots
Category: Pharmacy,
Cosmetics & Beauty Supply
Average price: Modest
Area: City Centre
Address: 32 Market Street
Manchester M2 1PL, UK
Phone: 0161 832 6533

#32
Edinburgh Bicycle Co-operative
Category: Bikes
Average price: Expensive
Area: Oxford Road Corridor, Rusholme
Address: 7 Wilmslow Road
Manchester M14 5FT, UK
Phone: 0161 257 3897

#33
Junk Shop
Category: Used, Vintage
Average price: Modest
Area: West Didsbury
Address: 174 Burton Road
Manchester M20 1LH, UK
Phone: 0161 238 8517

#34
Chorlton Bookshop
Category: Bookstore
Average price: Modest
Area: Chorlton
Address: 506-508 Wilbraham Rd
Manchester M21 9AW, UK
Phone: 0161 881 6374

#35
Quality Save
Category: Discount Store
Average price: Inexpensive
Area: City Centre
Address: Piccadilly Plaza
Manchester M1 4AJ, UK
Phone: 0161 228 3031

#36
Kingbee Records
Category: Music & DVDs
Average price: Modest
Area: Chorlton
Address: 519 Wilbraham Road
Manchester M21 0UF, UK
Phone: 0161 860 4762

#37
Seen Opticians
Category: Optometrists,
Eyewear & Opticians
Area: City Centre
Address: 6 St Anns Arcade
Manchester M2 7HN, UK
Phone: 0161 835 2324

#38
Manchester Buddhist Centre
Category: Buddhist Temple,
Bookstore, Yoga
Area: Northern Quarter
Address: 16-20 Turner St
Manchester M4 1DZ, UK
Phone: 0161 834 9232

#39
Sew In
Category: Arts & Crafts
Average price: Modest
Area: Didsbury Village
Address: 741 Wilmslow Road
Manchester M20 6RN, UK
Phone: 0161 445 5861

#40
Poundland
Category: Department Store
Average price: Inexpensive
Area: City Centre
Address: Lower Floor
Manchester M1 1WR, UK
Phone: 0161 839 9870

#41
Richard Goodall Gallery
Category: Art Gallery
Average price: Expensive
Area: Northern Quarter
Address: 59 Thomas Street
Manchester M4 1NA, UK
Phone: 0161 832 3435

#42
Ken Foster's Cycle Logic
Category: Bikes
Average price: Modest
Area: Chorlton
Address: 374-376 Barlow Moor Rd
Manchester M21 8AZ, UK
Phone: 0161 881 7160

#43
Paramount Books
Category: Bookstore, Comic Books
Average price: Modest
Area: City Centre
Address: 25-27 Shudehill
Manchester M4 2AF, UK
Phone: 0161 834 9509

#44
Belly Button Design
Category: Cards & Stationery, Jewelry
Average price: Modest
Area: West Didsbury
Address: 240 Burton Road
Manchester M20 2LW, UK
Phone: 0161 434 4236

#45
Busy Bee Toy Shop
Category: Toy Store
Average price: Modest
Area: Chorlton
Address: 517 Wilbraham Road
Manchester M21 0UF, UK
Phone: 0161 881 5838

#46
Marks & Spencer
Category: Department Store
Average price: Expensive
Area: City Centre
Address: 7 Market Street
Manchester M1 1WT, UK
Phone: 0161 831 7341

#47
TK Maxx
Category: Fashion
Average price: Modest
Area: City Centre
Address: 106-122 Market Street
Manchester M1 1WA, UK
Phone: 0161 236 1885

#48
Harvey Nichols & Co
Category: Department Store
Average price: Exclusive
Area: City Centre
Address: 21 New Cathedral Street
Manchester M1 1AD, UK
Phone: 0161 828 8888

#49
Harriet & Dee
Category: Flowers & Gifts
Average price: Expensive
Area: Didsbury Village
Address: 8 Warburton Street
Manchester M20 6WA, UK
Phone: 0161 438 2500

#50
Urban Outfitters
Category: Department Store
Average price: Expensive
Area: City Centre
Address: 42-43 Market Street
Manchester M1 1WR, UK
Phone: 0161 817 6640

#51
Monkey Puzzle Toys
Category: Toy Store
Area: Chorlton
Address: 93 Manchester Rd
Manchester M21 9GA, UK
Phone: 0161 862 0100

#52
**Centre for Chinese
Contemporary Art**
Category: Art Gallery, Arts & Crafts
Average price: Inexpensive
Area: Northern Quarter
Address: 7 Thomas Street
Manchester M4 1EU, UK
Phone: 0161 832 7271

#53
Travelling Man
Category: Toy Store, Hobby Shop,
Comic Books
Average price: Modest
Area: Northern Quarter
Address: 4 Dale Street
Manchester M1 1JW, UK
Phone: 0161 237 1877

#54
Zara
Category: Accessories,
Men's Clothing, Women's Clothing
Average price: Modest
Area: City Centre
Address: New Cathedral St
Manchester M1 4AD, UK
Phone: 0161 831 0940

#55
Northern Flower
Category: Florist
Average price: Expensive
Area: Northern Quarter
Address: 58 Tib St
Manchester M4 1LG, UK
Phone: 0161 832 7731

#56
Schuh
Category: Shoe Store, Leather Goods
Average price: Expensive
Area: City Centre
Address: 31 Market Street
Manchester M1 1WR, UK
Phone: 0161 834 6521

#57
Levenshulme Antiques Village
Category: Antiques, Arts & Crafts
Average price: Modest
Area: Levenshulme
Address: 965 Stockport Road
Manchester M19 3NP, UK
Phone: 0161 225 7025

#58
Junk
Category: Women's Clothing
Average price: Expensive
Area: Northern Quarter
Address: 2 Dale Street
Manchester M1 1JW, UK
Phone: 0161 238 8517

#59
Johnny Roadhouse
Category: Musical Instruments
Average price: Modest
Area: Oxford Road Corridor
Address: 123 Oxford Rd
Manchester M1 7DU, UK
Phone: 0161 273 1000

#60
Argos
Category: Department Store
Average price: Modest
Area: City Centre
Address: R10-R19 Unit
Manchester M4 3AT, UK
Phone: +44 845 165 7661

#61
Beatin' Rhythm Records
Category: Music & DVDs
Average price: Modest
Area: Northern Quarter
Address: 42 Tib Street
Manchester M4 1LA, UK
Phone: 0161 834 7783

#62
Richard Goodall Gallery
Category: Art Gallery, Museum
Average price: Modest
Area: Northern Quarter
Address: 103 High Street
Manchester M4 1HQ, UK
Phone: 0161 834 3330

#63
CUBE
Category: Art Gallery
Area: Oxford Road Corridor
Address: 113-115 Portland Street
Manchester M1 6DW, UK
Phone: 0161 237 5525

#64
Blossom
Category: Florist
Average price: Modest
Area: Chorlton
Address: 97
Manchester Road
Manchester M21 9GA, UK
Phone: 0161 881 4567

#65
University of Manchester Student Union Shop
Category: Office Equipment,
Convenience Store
Average price: Inexpensive
Area: Oxford Road Corridor
Address: Oxford Road
Manchester M13 9PR, UK
Phone: 0161 275 2936

#66
Oxfam
Category: Thrift Store
Average price: Inexpensive
Area: Oxford Road Corridor
Address: 300-302 Oxford Road
Manchester M13 9NS, UK
Phone: 0161 273 2019

#67
Sainsbury's
Category: Grocery, Fashion,
Beer, Wine & Spirits
Average price: Modest
Area: Ordsall
Address: 100 Regent Rd
Manchester M5 4QU, UK
Phone: 0161 839 2441

#68
Richer Sounds
Category: Electronics
Average price: Modest
Area: Castlefield
Address: 268 Deansgate
Manchester M3 4JB, UK
Phone: +44 33 3900 0086

#69
Sainsbury's
Category: Grocery, Fashion,
Beer, Wine & Spirits
Average price: Inexpensive
Area: Fallowfield
Address: 347 Wilmslow Road
Manchester M14 6SS, UK
Phone: 0161 224 4778

#70
Oxfam
Category: Bookstore, Thrift Store
Average price: Modest
Area: Didsbury Village
Address: 778 Wilmslow Road
Manchester M20 2DR, UK
Phone: 0161 434 5380

#71
Didsbury Village Bookshop
Category: Bookstore
Average price: Modest
Area: Didsbury Village
Address: 47 Barlow More Road
Manchester M20 6TW, UK
Phone: 0161 438 0211

#72
Manchester French Christmas Market
Category: Shopping Center
Average price: Inexpensive
Area: City Centre
Address: King St
Manchester M2 4, UK
Phone: 0161 234 7356

#73
Rolex Books & Music Shop
Category: Bookstore, Shopping Center,
Personal Shopping
Average price: Inexpensive
Area: Rusholme
Address: 81-83 Wilmslow Road
Manchester M14 5SU, UK
Phone: 0161 225 4448

#74
Wowie Zowie!
Category: Furniture Store,
Music & DVDs
Average price: Modest
Area: Chorlton
Address: 107
Manchester Road
Manchester M21 9GA, UK
Phone: 0161 860 6470

#75
Size?
Category: Shoe Store
Average price: Expensive
Area: City Centre
Address: 18 Market Street
Manchester M1 1PT, UK
Phone: 0161 839 8086

#76
Attic Fancy Dress
Category: Costumes, Jewelry
Average price: Inexpensive
Area: Northern Quarter
Address: 52 Church Street
Manchester M4 1PW, UK
Phone: 0161 832 3839

#77
Islington Mill
Category: Music Venues, Art Gallery
Average price: Modest
Area: Salford University Campus
Address: James St
Manchester M3 5HW, UK
Phone: +44 7947 649896

#78
Twenty Twenty Two
Category: Bar, Art Gallery, Music Venues
Average price: Modest
Area: Northern Quarter
Address: 20 Dale Street
Manchester M1 1EZ, UK
Phone: 0161 237 9360

#79
Bodycare Health & Beauty
Category: Cosmetics & Beauty Supply
Average price: Inexpensive
Area: City Centre
Address: Arndale Center
Manchester M4 2EA, UK
Phone: 0161 839 3973

#80
Vivienne Westwood
Category: Women's Clothing
Average price: Expensive
Area: City Centre
Address: 47 Spring Garden King Street
Manchester M2 2BG, UK
Phone: 0161 835 2121

#81
Brazilian Waxing Company
Category: Cosmetics & Beauty Supply
Area: City Centre
Address: 7 Cheapside
Manchester M2 4WG, UK
Phone: +44 20 8123 4332

#82
Levi's
Category: Leather Goods,
Men's Clothing, Women's Clothing
Average price: Expensive
Area: City Centre
Address: Arndale Center
Manchester M4 3AQ, UK
Phone: 0161 833 4979

#83
L'Occitane
Category: Cosmetics & Beauty Supply
Average price: Expensive
Area: City Centre
Address: 10 King Street
Manchester M2 6AG, UK
Phone: 0161 839 3216

#84
Sports Direct
Category: Sporting Goods
Average price: Inexpensive
Area: City Centre
Address: Arndale Ctr
Manchester M4 2HU, UK
Phone: +44 870 838 7162

#85
Edwards Of Manchester
Category: Shoe Store
Average price: Expensive
Area: City Centre
Address: 61 Deansgate
Manchester M3 2BW, UK
Phone: 0161 834 1339

#86
Foot Asylum
Category: Shoe Store
Average price: Modest
Area: City Centre
Address: L1/L2 Arndale Centre
Manchester M4 2HU, UK
Phone: 0161 839 5407

#87
French Connection
Category: Accessories,
Women's Clothing
Average price: Expensive
Area: City Centre
Address: 2-4 Exchange Square
Manchester M2 7HA, UK
Phone: 0161 835 1727

#88
Oasis
Category: Women's Clothing
Average price: Expensive
Area: City Centre
Address: Upper Level
Manchester M1, UK
Phone: 0161 831 9967

#89
Original Levi Store
Category: Fashion
Area: Altrincham
Address: 156 Regent Cresent
Manchester M17 8AP, UK
Phone: 0161 746 8800

#90
Loop!
Category: Cards & Stationery
Average price: Expensive
Area: Chorlton
Address: 66 Beech Road
Manchester M21 9EG, UK
Phone: 0161 882 0801

#91
Mango
Category: Women's Clothing
Average price: Expensive
Area: City Centre
Address: 48-50 Market Street
Manchester M1 1PW, UK
Phone: 0161 835 9100

#92
Foot Locker
Category: Shoe Store
Average price: Modest
Area: Northern Quarter
Address: 49 Market Street
Manchester M1 1WR, UK
Phone: 0161 819 5990

#93
PAD
Category: Flowers & Gifts, Home Decor
Average price: Modest
Area: Chorlton
Address: 105 Manchester Road
Manchester M21 9GA, UK
Phone: 0161 881 0088

#94
Levenshulme Market
Category: Shopping Center
Average price: Inexpensive
Area: Levenshulme
Address: Stockport Road
Manchester M19 3AB, UK
Phone: +44 7853 266598

#95
Pound Empire
Category: Discount Store
Average price: Inexpensive
Area: Piccadilly
Address: 12 Piccadilly
Manchester M1 3AN, UK
Phone: 0161 923 4609

#96
Me & Yu
Category: Accessories
Average price: Modest
Area: Northern Quarter
Address: 52 Church Street
Manchester M4 1PW, UK
Phone: 0161 839 0399

#97
RIBA Bookshop
Category: Bookstore
Average price: Modest
Area: Oxford Road Corridor
Address: 113-115 Portland Street
Manchester M1 6DW, UK
Phone: 0161 236 7691

#98
Longsight Market
Category: Shopping Center
Average price: Inexpensive
Area: Longsight
Address: Dickenson Road
Manchester M13 0WG, UK
Phone: 0161 225 9859

#99
The Disney Store
Category: Toy Store
Average price: Expensive
Area: City Centre
Address: Unit 22
Manchester M4 3AJ, UK
Phone: 0161 832 2492

#100
The Cook Shop
Category: Kitchen & Bath
Average price: Modest
Address: Arndale Centre
Manchester M1 1XY, UK
Phone: +44 7814 796228

#101
Easytel UK
Category: Mobile Phones, Computers
Average price: Inexpensive
Area: Rusholme
Address: 8 Wilmslow Road
Manchester M14 5TP, UK
Phone: 0161 224 8600

#102
Clas Ohlson
Category: Hardware Store, Appliances
Average price: Modest
Area: City Centre
Address: Manchester Arndale
Manchester M4 3AQ, UK
Phone: 0161 832 7375

#103
Pop Boutique
Category: Antiques, Jewelry,
Used, Vintage
Average price: Modest
Area: Northern Quarter
Address: 34-36 Oldham Street
Manchester M1 1JN, UK
Phone: 0161 236 5797

#104
Build-A-Bear Workshop
Category: Toy Store
Average price: Expensive
Area: City Centre
Address: Unit 36, Halle Square
Manchester M4 3AQ, UK
Phone: 0161 839 4308

#105
East
Category: Women's Clothing,
Jewelry, Accessories
Average price: Expensive
Area: City Centre
Address: 18a The Triangle
Manchester M4 3TR, UK
Phone: 0161 839 5102

#106
Kiku Boutique
Category: Lingerie, Bridal
Average price: Modest
Area: Northern Quarter
Address: 100 Tib Street
Manchester M4 1LR, UK
Phone: 0161 819 5031

#107
Tutzy News
Category: Newspapers & Magazines
Average price: Inexpensive
Area: City Centre
Address: Piccadilly Plaza
Manchester M1 4AJ, UK
Phone: 0161 236 9763

#108
The Gap
Category: Men's Clothing, Women's
Clothing, Children's Clothing
Average price: Expensive
Area: City Centre
Address: 30 St Ann Street
Manchester M2 7LF, UK
Phone: 0161 835 4110

#109
The Works
Category: Arts & Crafts, Books,
Mags, Music & Video
Average price: Inexpensive
Area: City Centre
Address: Arndale Center
Manchester M4 3AQ, UK
Phone: 0161 835 2297

#110
Den Furniture
Category: Furniture Store
Average price: Exclusive
Area: Northern Quarter
Address: 42-44 Oldham Street
Manchester M4 1LE, UK
Phone: 0161 236 1112

#111
The Black Sheep Store
Category: Shoe Store, Sports Wear,
Outdoor Gear
Average price: Modest
Area: Northern Quarter
Address: 59 Church Street
Manchester M4 1PD, UK
Phone: 0161 839 9313

#112
Waterstones
Category: Coffee & Tea, Bookstore,
Newspapers & Magazines
Average price: Modest
Area: City Centre
Address: Arndale Center
Manchester M4 3AQ, UK
Phone: 0161 832 8563

#113
Timberland
Category: Shoe Store, Men's Clothing
Average price: Exclusive
Area: City Centre
Address: 40-42 King Street
Manchester M2 6BA, UK
Phone: 0161 834 6643

#114
Swatch
Category: Watches
Average price: Modest
Area: City Centre
Address: Market Street
Manchester M2 1NP, UK
Phone: 0161 832 0755

#115
Elm Interiors
Category: Home & Garden,
Cards & Stationery
Average price: Expensive
Area: Didsbury Village
Address: 766 Wilmslow Road
Manchester M20 2DR, UK
Phone: 0161 448 8551

#116
Steranko Fashion Shop
Category: Fashion
Average price: Modest
Area: West Didsbury
Address: 172 Burton Road
Manchester M20 1LH, UK
Phone: 0161 448 0108

#117
Castlefield Artisan Market
Category: Farmers Market,
Used, Vintage
Average price: Modest
Area: Castlefield
Address: Duke Street
Manchester M3 4NF, UK
Phone: +44 7826 465673

#118
W H Lung Cash & Carry
Category: Wholesale Store,
Specialty Food, Chinese
Average price: Modest
Area: Oxford Road Corridor
Address: 97 Upper Brook Street
Manchester M13 9TX, UK
Phone: 0161 274 3177

#119
Vintage Vogue
Category: Jewelry, Used, Vintage
Average price: Expensive
Area: Chorlton
Address: 390 Barlow Moor Road
Manchester M21 8BH, UK
Phone: 0161 881 7150

#120
Diesel
Category: Men's Clothing,
Women's Clothing, Swimwear
Average price: Expensive
Area: City Centre
Address: 74 King Street
Manchester M2 4NJ, UK
Phone: 0161 839 8868

#121
Joy
Category: Fashion, Flowers & Gifts
Average price: Exclusive
Area: City Centre
Address: 37 Hanging Ditch
Manchester M4 3TR, UK
Phone: 0161 832 9823

#122
Schuh
Category: Shoe Store
Average price: Modest
Area: Rusholme
Address: 138 Regent Cresent
Manchester M17 8AA, UK
Phone: 0161 202 9044

#123
The Perfume Shop
Category: Cosmetics & Beauty Supply
Average price: Modest
Area: City Centre
Address: 9a Arndale Ctr
Manchester M4 2EA, UK
Phone: 0161 819 1700

#124
Esprit
Category: Fashion
Average price: Modest
Area: City Centre
Address: 33 Market Street
Manchester M1 1WR, UK
Phone: 0161 214 5170

#125
New Cross Army Surplus Military Kit
Category: Sporting Goods,
Men's Clothing, Women's Clothing
Average price: Modest
Area: Northern Quarter
Address: 25-27 Tib Street
Manchester M4 1LX, UK
Phone: 0161 832 9683

#126
Lipsy
Category: Women's Clothing
Average price: Modest
Area: City Centre
Address: Arndale Ctr
Manchester M4 3AB, UK
Phone: 0161 837 7021

#127
The Co-operative Food
Category: Grocery, Tobacco Shop, Beer,
Wine & Spirits
Average price: Expensive
Area: Chorlton
Address: 599-601 Wilbraham Road
Manchester M21 9AN, UK
Phone: 0161 881 8211

#128
Wanderland Boutique
Category: Women's Clothing
Average price: Expensive
Area: Salford University Campus
Address: 52 Church Street
Manchester M4 1, UK
Phone: 0161 236 2379

#129
Sally Hair & Beauty Supplies
Category: Cosmetics & Beauty Supply
Area: City Centre
Address: 16 The Mall Arndale Centre
Manchester M4 3AD, UK
Phone: 0161 865 2252

#130
Ran
Category: Shoe Store, Men's Clothing
Average price: Modest
Area: City Centre
Address: 8 St Anns Arcade
Manchester M2 7HW, UK
Phone: 0161 832 9650

#131
The Bead Shop
Category: Jewelry, Arts & Crafts
Average price: Inexpensive
Area: Northern Quarter
Address: 52 Church Street
Manchester M4 1PW, UK
Phone: 0161 833 9950

#132
Elysia
Category: Men's Clothing,
Women's Clothing
Area: Salford University Campus
Address: 52 Church Street
Manchester M4 1, UK
Phone: 0161 839 7820

#133
Cotswold Outdoor
Category: Outdoor Gear,
Men's Clothing, Accessories
Area: Oxford Road Corridor
Address: 6a Oxford Road
Manchester M1 5QA, UK
Phone: 0161 236 4123

#134
Ryman Stationery
Category: Office Equipment
Average price: Modest
Area: City Centre
Address: 85 Halle Mall
Manchester M4 2HU, UK
Phone: 0161 834 6566

#135
Aldo
Category: Shoe Store
Average price: Expensive
Area: City Centre
Address: Arndale Ctr
Manchester M4 3AQ, UK
Phone: 0161 832 3754

#136
Pottery Corner
Category: Arts & Crafts
Average price: Modest
Area: Chorlton
Address: 34 Beech Road
Manchester M21 9EL, UK
Phone: 0161 882 0010

#137
Castle Gallery
Category: Art Gallery
Average price: Exclusive
Area: City Centre
Address: 75 Deansgate
Manchester M2 7, UK
Phone: 0161 839 3800

#138
Fossil
Category: Watches
Average price: Expensive
Area: City Centre
Address: Arndale Centre
Manchester M4 3AQ, UK
Phone: 0161 838 9010

#139
Mashed
Category: Men's Clothing, Outdoor Gear
Area: Northern Quarter
Address: 52 Church Street
Manchester M4 1PW, UK
Phone: 0161 839 4692

#140
Sweatshop
Category: Sporting Goods
Average price: Expensive
Area: City Centre
Address: Manchester Arndale Center
Manchester M4 3AQ, UK
Phone: +44 845 217 7587

#141
Ark
Category: Accessories, Men's Clothing,
Women's Clothing
Average price: Modest
Area: City Centre
Address: Unit L36
Manchester M4 3AQ, UK
Phone: 0161 832 2774

#142
House of Fraser
Category: Department Store,
Men's Clothing, Women's Clothing
Average price: Expensive
Area: City Centre
Address: 92-96 Deansgate
Manchester M3 2QG, UK
Phone: 0161 832 3414

#143
Alankar
Category: Women's Clothing, Bridal
Average price: Expensive
Area: Rusholme
Address: 46 - 48 Wilmslow Road
Manchester M14 5TQ, UK
Phone: 0161 256 3780

#144
All In One Garden Centre
Category: Nurseries & Gardening
Average price: Exclusive
Area: Oldham
Address: Rochdale Road
Manchester M24 2RB, UK
Phone: +44 1706 711711

#145
Monsoon
Category: Fashion
Average price: Modest
Area: Altrincham
Address: 72a Regent CR
Manchester M17 8AR, UK
Phone: 0161 747 8954

#146
Next
Category: Women's Clothing,
Men's Clothing, Furniture Store
Average price: Expensive
Area: City Centre
Address: 100 Corporation Street
Manchester M4 3AJ, UK
Phone: +44 844 844 5523

#147
All Saints
Category: Men's Clothing,
Women's Clothing
Average price: Expensive
Area: City Centre
Address: 45 Market Street
Manchester M1 1WR, UK
Phone: 0161 817 4820

#148
Gamestation
Category: Books, Mags, Music & Video
Average price: Inexpensive
Area: City Centre
Address: 180a Arndale Centre
Manchester M4 2HU, UK
Phone: 0161 833 1982

#149
WH Smith
Category: Bookstore, Cards & Stationery,
Newspapers & Magazines
Average price: Modest
Area: Piccadilly
Address: Piccadilly Station
Manchester M1 2PB, UK
Phone: 0161 236 5919

#150
Jilanis Newsagents
Category: Newspapers & Magazines
Average price: Inexpensive
Area: Rusholme
Address: 173 Wilmslow Road
Manchester M14 5AP, UK
Phone: 0161 256 4490

#151
Novus Contemporary Art
Category: Art Gallery
Average price: Modest
Area: West Didsbury
Address: Burton Road
Manchester M20 2LW, UK
Phone: 0161 438 3888

#152
Dr Hermans
Category: Tobacco Shop
Average price: Modest
Area: Northern Quarter
Address: 57 Church Street
Manchester M4 1PD, UK
Phone: 0161 834 1130

#153
The Deli on Burton Road
Category: Department Store, Sandwiches
Average price: Expensive
Area: West Didsbury
Address: BUrton Road
Manchester M20 1LH, UK
Phone: 0161 445 2912

#154
Staples
Category: Electronics, Office Equipment
Area: City Centre
Address: 118-124 Deansgate
Manchester M3 2GB, UK
Phone: 0161 827 3490

#155
Burton
Category: Men's Clothing,
Leather Goods, Accessories
Average price: Modest
Area: City Centre
Address: 99-101 Arndale Center
Manchester M4 3AB, UK
Phone: 0161 839 3201

#156
Grosvenor Supermarket
Category: Grocery, Tobacco Shop
Average price: Inexpensive
Area: Oxford Road Corridor
Address: 133a Grosvenor Street
Manchester M1 7HE, UK
Phone: 0161 273 8050

#157
Evans
Category: Women's Clothing
Average price: Modest
Area: City Centre
Address: 99-101 Arndale Centre
Manchester M4 3AB, UK
Phone: +44 845 121 4516

#158
Muse
Category: Jewelry
Average price: Inexpensive
Area: City Centre
Address: Lower Level
Manchester M1, UK
Phone: 0161 833 4183

#159
Lookey Newsagents
Category: Newspapers & Magazines
Average price: Modest
Area: Gay Village
Address: 76 Sackville Street
Manchester M1 3NJ, UK
Phone: 0161 273 4655

#160
Hugo Boss
Category: Men's Clothing
Average price: Exclusive
Area: City Centre
Address: 16-18 King Street
Manchester M2 6AG, UK
Phone: 0161 831 9548

#161
Dunnes
Category: Home & Garden, Fashion
Area: Ordsall
Address: Regent Retail Park
Manchester M5 4DE, UK
Phone: 0161 831 7444

#162
Millets
Category: Outdoor Gear, Sports Wear
Average price: Modest
Area: City Centre
Address: 49 Arndale Ctr
Manchester M4 2HU, UK
Phone: 0161 832 7547

#163
Carhartt
Category: Women's Clothing,
Men's Clothing
Average price: Modest
Area: Northern Quarter
Address: 59-61 Oldham Street
Manchester M1 1JR, UK
Phone: 0161 831 9488

#164
B & Q
Category: Hardware Store
Average price: Modest
Area: East Didsbury
Address: Kingsway
Manchester M19 1BB, UK
Phone: 0161 257 2839

#165
Mothercare
Category: Children's Clothing,
Baby Gear & Furniture, Toy Store
Average price: Modest
Area: Ancoats, Petersfield
Address: Great Ancoats Street
Manchester M4 6DL, UK
Phone: 0161 274 3818

#166
World Of Islam
Category: Bookstore
Area: Rusholme
Address: 211 Wilmslow Road
Manchester M14 5AG, UK
Phone: 0161 256 3232

#167
Long Tall Sally
Category: Fashion
Average price: Modest
Area: City Centre
Address: 16 South King Street
Manchester M2 6DW, UK
Phone: 0161 839 0425

#168
Pop-up
Category: Fashion
Area: Salford University Campus
Address: 52 Church Street
Manchester M4 1, UK
Phone: 0161 839 0718

#169
Hmv Manchester
Category: Books, Mags, Music & Video
Average price: Modest
Area: Northern Quarter
Address: 90 - 100 Market Street
Manchester M1 1PD, UK
Phone: 0161 834 8550

#170
Manchester Book Market
Category: Bookstore
Area: City Centre
Address: St Ann's Square
Manchester M2 7, UK
Phone: 0161 234735

#171
NOTE Skateboard Shop
Category: Sporting Goods
Average price: Modest
Area: Northern Quarter
Address: 34 Tib Street
Manchester M4 1LA, UK
Phone: 0161 839 7077

#172
Incognito Gallery
Category: Art Gallery
Average price: Modest
Area: Northern Quarter
Address: 5 Stevenson Square
Manchester M1 1DN, UK
Phone: 0161 228 7999

#173
Nokia Retail
Category: Mobile Phones
Average price: Inexpensive
Area: City Centre
Address: 35 Market St
Manchester M1 1WR, UK
Phone: 0161 834 7107

#174
Ali's DIY
Category: Hardware Store
Average price: Inexpensive
Area: Longsight
Address: 167 Dickenson Road
Manchester M13 0YN, UK
Phone: 0161 256 4500

#175
Nevisport
Category: Outdoor Gear
Average price: Expensive
Area: Spinningfields
Address: 188 - 192 Deansgate
Manchester M3 3ND, UK
Phone: 0161 839 9880

#176
Knock - Ireland
Category: Bookstore,
Religious Organization
Average price: Modest
Area: City Centre
Address: 101 Deansgate
Manchester M60 8, UK
Phone: 0161 819 2558

#177
Pen Shop
Category: Jewelry, Office Equipment
Average price: Expensive
Area: City Centre
Address: 54 King Street
Manchester M2 4LY, UK
Phone: 0161 839 3966

#178
Bang & Olufsen
Category: Electronics, Music & DVDs
Average price: Exclusive
Area: City Centre
Address: Unit 4 55 King Street
Manchester M2 4LQ, UK
Phone: 0161 832 6159

#179
Whistles
Category: Women's Clothing
Average price: Expensive
Area: City Centre
Address: 55 King Street
Manchester M2 4LQ, UK
Phone: 0161 839 5399

#180
Aston's Of Manchester
Category: Tobacco Shop
Average price: Modest
Area: City Centre
Address: 12 Royal Exchange Arcade
Manchester M2 7EA, UK
Phone: 0161 832 7895

#181
Adidas
Category: Sports Wear, Men's Clothing
Average price: Expensive
Area: City Centre
Address: 52-56 Market Street
Manchester M1 1PW, UK
Phone: 0161 832 6745

#182
Ridelow
Category: Bikes, Fashion
Area: Northern Quarter
Address: 27-29 Church Street
Manchester M4 1PE, UK
Phone: 0161 834 5788

#183
Milner & Webb
Category: Antiques
Area: Northern Quarter
Address: 52 Church Street
Manchester M4 1PW, UK
Phone: 0161 839 0718

#184
Lomography Store
Category: Photographers,
Photography Store & Services
Average price: Expensive
Area: Northern Quarter
Address: 20 Oldham Street
Manchester M1 1JN, UK
Phone: 0161 228 2360

#185
Vox Pop Music
Category: Music & DVDs
Average price: Modest
Area: Northern Quarter
Address: 53-55 Thomas Street
Manchester M4 1NA, UK
Phone: 0161 832 3233

#186
Aspecto
Category: Women's Clothing,
Men's Clothing, Shoe Store
Average price: Expensive
Area: City Centre
Address: The Triangle Exchange Square
Manchester M4 3TR, UK
Phone: 0161 839 1196

#187
Russell & Bromley
Category: Shoe Store
Average price: Expensive
Address: St Anns Place
Manchester M2 7LP, UK
Phone: 0161 834 3131

#188
Grin
Category: Flowers & Gifts
Average price: Inexpensive
Area: Northern Quarter
Address: 52 Church Street
Manchester M4 1PW, UK
Phone: 0161 839 6392

#189
The Gallery Café
Category: Coffee & Tea, Art Gallery
Average price: Modest
Area: Chinatown
Address: Mosley Street
Manchester M2 3JL, UK
Phone: 0161 235 8888

#190
GNC
Category: Sporting Goods
Area: City Centre
Address: 174 Arndale Centre
Manchester M4 2HU, UK
Phone: 0161 819 2201

#191
Dune Footwear
Category: Shoe Store
Average price: Expensive
Area: City Centre
Address: Arndale House
Manchester M4 3AQ, UK
Phone: 0161 832 4021

#192
Waterside Arts Centre
Category: Art Gallery, Performing Arts
Average price: Modest
Area: Sale
Address: 1 Waterside Plaza
Manchester M33 7ZF, UK
Phone: 0161 912 5616

#193
British Red Cross
Category: Thrift Store
Average price: Inexpensive
Area: Chorlton
Address: 21 Chorlton Place
Manchester M21 9AQ, UK
Phone: 0161 881 5249

#194
Didsbury Eyecare
Category: Eyewear & Opticians
Area: Didsbury Village
Address: 717 Wilmslow Rd
Manchester M20 6WF, UK
Phone: 0161 445 7668

#195
Modern Army Store
Category: Outdoor Gear, Active Life
Average price: Inexpensive
Area: Chorlton
Address: 488 Wilbraham Rd
Manchester M21 9AS, UK
Phone: 0161 881 6858

#196
Manchester Superstore
Category: Wholesale Store,
Grocery, Meat Shop
Area: Longsight
Address: 536-538 Stockport Road
Manchester M12 4JJ, UK
Phone: 0161 224 3441

#197
Lloyds News
Category: Convenience Store,
Tobacco Shop
Average price: Inexpensive
Area: Didsbury Village
Address: 232 Wilmslow Rd
Manchester M20 2, UK
Phone: 0161 224 2174

#198
Miss Selfridge
Category: Women's Clothing, Accessories
Average price: Expensive
Area: City Centre
Address: 74 Market St
Manchester M1 1PN, UK
Phone: 0161 834 3924

#199
Boots
Category: Pharmacy,
Cosmetics & Beauty Supply
Average price: Expensive
Area: Northern Quarter
Address: 11-13 Piccadilly
Manchester M1 1LY, UK
Phone: 0161 834 8244

#200
**Wesley Community
Furniture Project**
Category: Furniture Store
Average price: Inexpensive
Area: Rusholme
Address: 56-58 Lloyd St S
Manchester M14 7HT, UK
Phone: 0161 226 9051

#201
Euronews
Category: Tobacco Shop, Convenience
Store, Newspapers & Magazines
Average price: Inexpensive
Area: City Centre
Address: Piccadilly Garden
Manchester M2 3BA, UK
Phone: 0161 236 0319

#202
Lush
Category: Cosmetics & Beauty Supply
Average price: Modest
Area: Ancoats, Petersfield
Address: Arndale Ctr
Manchester M4 3QA, UK
Phone: 0161 832 3294

#203
Moda In Pelle
Category: Shoe Store, Leather Goods
Average price: Modest
Area: City Centre
Address: 4 Market St
Manchester M1 1PT, UK
Phone: 0161 839 5072

#204
Cafe Society Clothing
Category: Fashion
Average price: Modest
Area: Northern Quarter
Address: 35-39 Oldham Street
Manchester M1 1JG, UK
Phone: 0161 839 1195

#205
Inman's
Category: Newspapers & Magazines
Average price: Modest
Area: Didsbury Village
Address: 105-107 Lapwing Lane
Manchester M20 6UR, UK
Phone: 0161 446 2464

#206
Currys
Category: Electronics, Appliances
Average price: Modest
Area: Ancoats, Petersfield
Address: Great Ancoats Street
Manchester M4 6DL, UK
Phone: +44 870 609 7494

#207
Bismi Jewellers
Category: Jewelry
Average price: Exclusive
Area: Rusholme
Address: 99 Wilmslow Road
Manchester M14 5SU, UK
Phone: 0161 256 3599

#208
Clone Zone
Category: Fashion, Adult
Average price: Expensive
Area: Gay Village
Address: 36-38 Sackville St
Manchester M1 3WA, UK
Phone: 0161 236 1398

#209
Blacks
Category: Outdoor Gear, Sports Wear
Average price: Expensive
Area: Spinningfields
Address: 200 Deansgate
Manchester M3 3NN, UK
Phone: 0161 833 0349

#210
Lakeland
Category: Leather Goods,
Men's Clothing, Women's Clothing
Average price: Modest
Area: City Centre
Address: 14 St Ann's Square
Manchester M2 7HQ, UK
Phone: 0161 831 7103

#211
Blue Inc
Category: Men's Clothing
Average price: Inexpensive
Area: City Centre
Address: 31 Market Street
Manchester M1 1WR, UK
Phone: 0161 832 3866

#212
Panic Posters
Category: Hobby Shop, Home & Garden
Area: Salford University Campus
Address: 52 Church Street
Manchester M4 1, UK
Phone: 0161 833 0667

#213
Topman
Category: Men's Clothing, Shoe Store
Average price: Modest
Area: City Centre
Address: 19 Market St
Manchester M1 1WR, UK
Phone: 0161 839 6940

#214
Cyberdog Fashion Shop
Category: Fashion
Average price: Inexpensive
Area: Northern Quarter
Address: Afflecks Arcade
Manchester M1 1JG, UK
Phone: 0161 833 2177

#215
Metro Convenience Store
Category: Tobacco Shop, Wine & Spirits
Average price: Inexpensive
Area: Oxford Road Corridor
Address: 131 Oxford Rd
Manchester M1 7DY, UK
Phone: 0161 273 8777

#216
MenKind
Category: Gifts & Gadgets
Average price: Modest
Area: City Centre
Address: The Arndale
Manchester M4 3AQ, UK
Phone: +44 1384 7796

#217
Superdrug
Category: Cosmetics & Beauty Supply
Average price: Modest
Area: City Centre
Address: Arndale Ctr
Manchester M4 3AQ, UK
Phone: 0161 839 0581

#218
Finlays
Category: Newspapers & Magazines,
Tobacco Shop
Area: Oxford Road Corridor
Address: 26 Precinct Centre
Manchester M13 9RN, UK
Phone: 0161 273 6133

#219
Nood
Category: Women's Clothing
Average price: Modest
Area: Chorlton
Address: 36 Beech Road
Manchester M21 9EL, UK
Phone: 0161 860 0461

#220
T La Art and Gallery Shop
Category: Arts & Crafts, Gift Shop
Average price: Inexpensive
Area: Chinatown
Address: 16 Nicholas St
Manchester M1 4, UK
Phone: 0161 236 2333

#221
Monsoon
Category: Fashion
Average price: Expensive
Area: City Centre
Address: King St
Manchester M2 6AW, UK
Phone: 0161 834 3236

#222
Jake Shoes
Category: Shoe Store
Average price: Modest
Area: City Centre
Address: Arndale Centre
Manchester M4 3AQ, UK
Phone: 0161 833 9799

#223
Model Zone
Category: Hobby Shop, Toy Store
Average price: Modest
Area: Spinningfields
Address: 209 Deansgate
Manchester M3 3NW, UK
Phone: 0161 834 3972

#224
North Face Ellis Brigham
Category: Climbing, Outdoor Gear
Average price: Expensive
Area: Spinningfields
Address: 211 Deansgate
Manchester M3 3NW, UK
Phone: 0161 834 7278

#225
Cotswold
Category: Outdoor Gear, Sports Wear
Average price: Modest
Area: City Centre
Address: Unit 2 118 - 124 Deansgate
Manchester M3 2GQ, UK
Phone: 0161 839 9255

#226
Nike
Category: Sports Wear
Average price: Expensive
Area: City Centre
Address: 39 Market Street
Manchester M1 1WR, UK
Phone: 0161 819 2333

#227
Ernest Jones
Category: Jewelry
Average price: Expensive
Area: City Centre
Address: 97 Arndale Centre
Manchester M4 3AB, UK
Phone: 0161 839 7040

#228
Goldsmiths Jewellers
Category: Jewelry, Flowers & Gifts
Average price: Exclusive
Area: City Centre
Address: 87 Arndale Centre
Manchester M4 2HU, UK
Phone: 0161 839 1584

#229
The Carphone Warehouse
Category: Mobile Phones
Average price: Modest
Area: City Centre
Address: 181 Arndale Centre
Manchester M4 2HU, UK
Phone: +44 870 168 2532

#230
Nicholas
Category: Tobacco Shop,
Beer, Wine & Spirits
Area: Spinningfields
Address: 8 Barton Arcade
Manchester M3 2BW, UK
Phone: 0161 834 7328

#231
Generation Pop
Category: Art Gallery
Area: City Centre
Address: E3 New York Street
Manchester M1 4BD, UK
Phone: 0161 848 0880

#232
Bank Fashion
Category: Women's Clothing,
Men's Clothing
Average price: Modest
Area: City Centre
Address: Unit L38
Manchester M4 3AQ, UK
Phone: 0161 831 7500

#233
Clampdown Records
Category: Music & DVDs
Average price: Modest
Area: Northern Quarter
Address: 9-11 Paton St
Manchester M1 2BA, UK
Phone: 0161 237 5932

#234
Manchester Framing Co
Category: Framing
Average price: Modest
Area: Northern Quarter
Address: 68 Tib Street
Manchester M4 1LG, UK
Phone: 0161 835 2600

#235
Soundbase Megastore
Category: Electronics, Vinyl Records
Average price: Modest
Area: Northern Quarter
Address: 64 Oldham Street
Manchester M4 1LE, UK
Phone: 0161 238 8727

#236
Renegade Marmalade
Category: Women's Clothing,
Men's Clothing
Average price: Expensive
Area: City Centre
Address: 7 St James Square
Manchester M2 6XX, UK
Phone: 0161 834 5733

#237
G T Blagg
Category: Hardware Store
Area: West Didsbury
Address: 146 Burton Rd
Manchester M20 1LH, UK
Phone: 0161 445 4113

#238
Longboon Pharmacy
Category: Pharmacy
Average price: Modest
Area: Rusholme
Address: 181 Wilmslow Road
Manchester M14 5AP, UK
Phone: 0161 224 5510

#239
Oxfam
Category: Thrift Store
Area: Chorlton
Address: 494 Wilbraham Road
Manchester M21 9AS, UK
Phone: 0161 861 0108

#240
Mcqueen Fashion Shop
Category: Fashion
Average price: Expensive
Area: Chorlton
Address: 54 Beech Road
Manchester M21 9EG, UK
Phone: 0161 881 4718

#241
Hurricane Gift Shop
Category: Flowers & Gifts
Average price: Modest
Area: Chorlton
Address: 115 Beech Road
Manchester M21 9EQ, UK
Phone: 0161 881 8813

#242
Red 5
Category: Flowers & Gifts,
Hobby Shop, Toy Store
Area: City Centre
Address: 48 Barbirolli Mall
Manchester M4 3AQ, UK
Phone: 0161 835 1300

#243
Frog Furniture
Category: Furniture Store
Average price: Modest
Area: West Didsbury
Address: 168 Burton Road
Manchester M20 1LH, UK
Phone: 0161 448 9566

#244
The Bike Room
Category: Bikes
Area: Castlefield
Address: 274 Deansgate
Manchester M3 4JB, UK
Phone: 0161 870 8195

#245
Espionage Manchester
Category: Performing Arts, Florist
Area: Spinningfields
Address: Quay Street
Manchester M3, UK
Phone: +44 7502 000072

#246
Elite Dress Agency
Category: Accessories,
Women's Clothing, Used, Vintage
Area: City Centre
Address: 35 King St W
Manchester M3 2PW, UK
Phone: 0161 832 3670

#247
Planet Shop The
Category: Women's Clothing
Average price: Modest
Area: City Centre
Address: 34-36 King Street
Manchester M2 6AZ, UK
Phone: 0161 839 6225

#248
Charles Tyrwhitt
Category: Men's Clothing
Average price: Modest
Area: City Centre
Address: 30 King St
Manchester M2 6AZ, UK
Phone: 0161 833 0504

#249
Vivienne Westwood Anglomania
Category: Women's Clothing, Accessories
Average price: Expensive
Area: City Centre
Address: 47 Spring Garden
Manchester M3 3BN, UK
Phone: 0161 835 2228

#250
Calvin Klein
Category: Fashion
Average price: Expensive
Area: City Centre
Address: 37 Hanging Ditch
Manchester M4 4BG, UK
Phone: 0161 839 7910

#251
Manchester Spring Market
Category: Local Flavor, Shopping
Area: City Centre
Address: St Ann's Square
Manchester M2 7DH, UK
Phone: 0161 234 7356

#252
Stephens Photo Centre
Category: Photography Store & Services
Average price: Expensive
Area: City Centre
Address: Unit 19a Barton Arcade
Manchester M3 2BJ, UK
Phone: 0161 834 7754

#253
Porcelanosa
Category: Kitchen & Bath
Area: Castlefield
Address: Water Street
Manchester M3 4JU, UK
Phone: 0161 817 3300

#254
Alfred E Mutter
Category: Jewelry
Area: Northern Quarter
Address: 33 Thomas Street
Manchester M4 1NA, UK
Phone: 0161 832 7147

#255
Tiny's Tipple
Category: Home Decor
Average price: Expensive
Area: Northern Quarter
Address: 12 Hilton Street
Manchester M1 1JF, UK
Phone: 0161 236 1412

#256
The Mustard Tree
Category: Thrift Store
Average price: Inexpensive
Area: Ancoats, Petersfield
Address: 110 Oldham Rd
Manchester M4 5AG, UK
Phone: 0161 228 7331

#257
Fat Face
Category: Fashion
Average price: Expensive
Area: City Centre
Address: 8-10 Exchange St
Manchester M2 7HA, UK
Phone: 0161 833 1544

#258
The Carphone Warehouse
Category: Mobile Phones
Area: City Centre
Address: 26 Market Street
Manchester M1 1PW, UK
Phone: +44 870 168 2393

#259
Topshop
Category: Fashion
Average price: Expensive
Area: City Centre
Address: 74 Market Street
Manchester M1 1, UK
Phone: 0161 834 3924

#260
G-Star Raw Store
Category: Men's Clothing,
Women's Clothing
Average price: Expensive
Area: City Centre
Address: Unit U1 Arndale Centre
Manchester M4 3QA, UK
Phone: 0161 839 2299

#261
The Brass Teacher
Category: Musical Instruments
Average price: Inexpensive
Area: Levenshulme
Address: 77 Osborne Road
Manchester M19 2DZ, UK
Phone: +44 7930 517864

#262
Conrad Office & Art
Category: Art Supplies
Average price: Modest
Area: Chorlton
Address: 567 Wilbraham Rd
Manchester M21 0AE, UK
Phone: 0161 881 4076

#263
**Michele Jones Wedding
Photography**
Category: Wedding Planning,
Photography Store & Services
Area: Didsbury Village
Address: 11 The Beeches Mews
Manchester M20 2PF, UK
Phone: 0161 448 1080

#264
The Flower Lounge
Category: Florist
Average price: Modest
Area: West Didsbury
Address: 98 Barlow Moor Road
Manchester M20 2PN, UK
Phone: 0161 446 2556

#265
Build A Bear Workshop
Category: Toy Store
Average price: Modest
Area: Rusholme
Address: 26 Regent Crescent
Manchester M14 7, UK
Phone: 0161 749 4791

#266
Giddy Goat Toys
Category: Toy Store
Area: Didsbury Village
Address: 2 Albert Hill Street
Manchester M20 6RF, UK
Phone: 0161 445 1097

#267
Living Flowers
Category: Florist
Average price: Exclusive
Area: West Didsbury
Address: 232 Burton Rd
Manchester M20 2LW, UK
Phone: +44 7970 448675

#268
BHS
Category: Department Store
Average price: Inexpensive
Area: City Centre
Address: 57 Market St
Manchester M1 1WN, UK
Phone: 0161 834 1151

#269
Cornerhouse Bookshop
Category: Bookstore
Average price: Modest
Area: Oxford Road Corridor
Address: 70 Oxford Street
Manchester M1 5NH, UK
Phone: 0161 200 1500

#270
Maliks
Category: Tobacco Shop,
Convenience Store
Average price: Inexpensive
Area: Oxford Road Corridor
Address: 66 Hathersage Road
Manchester M13 0FN, UK
Phone: 0161 224 2005

#271
Phillip Stoner the Jeweller
Category: Jewelry
Average price: Exclusive
Area: Oldham
Address: Unit G20 The Avenue
Manchester M3 3HF, UK
Phone: 0161 833 1751

#272
Star News Office Licence
Category: Newspapers & Magazines
Average price: Inexpensive
Area: Rusholme
Address: 165 Wilmslow Road
Manchester M14 5AP, UK
Phone: 0161 249 0188

#273
Hidden Corner
Category: Women's Clothing,
Costumes, Adult
Average price: Modest
Area: City Centre
Address: Arndale Centre
Manchester M4 3AQ, UK
Phone: 0161 839 2118

#274
Accessorize
Category: Accessories,
Women's Clothing
Average price: Modest
Area: Piccadilly
Address: Unit 10 Piccadilly Station
Manchester M1 2BN, UK
Phone: 0161 236 0199

#275
Jack & Jones, Vero Moda
Category: Fashion
Area: City Centre
Address: 93 Halle Mall
Manchester M4 3AQ, UK
Phone: 0161 828 3000

#276
Superdrug
Category: Pharmacy, Cosmetics
Average price: Modest
Area: Northern Quarter
Address: 7-9 Piccadilly
Manchester M1 1LZ, UK
Phone: 0161 834 6091

#277
Oxfam Originals
Category: Used, Vintage
Average price: Modest
Area: Northern Quarter
Address: 51 Oldham Street
Manchester M1 1JR, UK
Phone: 0161 839 3160

#278
Diamond Telecom
Category: Computers, Mobile Phones
Area: Rusholme
Address: 53 Wilmslow Road
Manchester M14 5TB, UK
Phone: 0161 257 2450

#279
Superstar Extra
Category: Videos & Video Game Rental,
Beer, Wine & Spirits
Average price: Modest
Area: Rusholme
Address: 57-59 Wilmslow Road
Manchester M14 5TB, UK
Phone: 0161 225 9729

#280
Aftabs Convenience Store
Category: Tobacco Shop, Grocery,
Convenience Store
Area: Oxford Road Corridor
Address: 1 Bonsall St
Manchester M15 6DR, UK
Phone: 0161 868 0614

#281
Marks & Spencer
Category: Department Store
Area: Ancoats, Petersfield
Address: Great Ancoats Street
Manchester M4 6DE, UK
Phone: 0161 236 7672

#282
Slaters
Category: Men's Clothing
Area: City Centre
Address: 1 Brown Street
Manchester M2 1DA, UK
Phone: 0161 819 6680

#283
Abacus
Category: Jewelry
Area: Salford University Campus
Address: 52 Church St
Manchester M4 1, UK
Phone: 0161 832 9300

#284
Specsavers
Category: Eyewear & Opticians
Area: City Centre
Address: 84 Arndale Ctr
Manchester M4 2HU, UK
Phone: 0161 834 6665

#285
Church Street Market
Category: Grocery, Fashion
Average price: Modest
Area: Northern Quarter
Address: Church St
Manchester M4 1, UK
Phone: 0161 832 3552

#286
Kraak
Category: Art Gallery, Music Venues
Average price: Modest
Area: Northern Quarter
Address: 11 Stevenson Square
Manchester M1 1DB, UK
Phone: +44 7855 939129

#287
Berwick Electronics
Category: Appliances
Average price: Modest
Area: Northern Quarter
Address: 53 Tib Street
Manchester M4 1LS, UK
Phone: 0161 834 4416

#288
Boardmans Teleflora
Category: Florist
Area: Oxford Road Corridor
Address: 296 Oxford Road
Manchester M13 9NS, UK
Phone: 0161 273 4582

#289
Argos
Category: Department Store
Average price: Modest
Area: Rusholme
Address: Arndale Centre
Manchester M32 9BA, UK
Phone: +44 845 165 7215

#290
Up & Running
Category: Sporting Goods, Shoe Store
Address: 32 Hanging Ditch
Manchester M4 3TR, UK
Phone: 0161 832 8338

#291
Beaverbrooks
Category: Jewelry, Flowers & Gifts
Average price: Modest
Area: City Centre
Address: 86 Arndale Centre
Manchester M4 2HU, UK
Phone: 0161 834 4904

#292
Adidas
Category: Sports Wear, Shoe Store
Average price: Expensive
Area: City Centre
Address: Unit 24 Arndale Ctr
Manchester M4 3AJ, UK
Phone: 0161 833 0902

#293
Orange
Category: Mobile Phones
Average price: Expensive
Area: City Centre
Address: Arndale Ctr
Manchester M4 3AQ, UK
Phone: +44 870 376 3385

#294
The Hilton Aqua Emporium
Category: Appliances, Pet Store
Average price: Modest
Area: Northern Quarter
Address: 5a Hilton Street
Manchester M4 1LP, UK
Phone: 0161 839 5757

#295
Fanboy 3
Category: Hobby Shop
Average price: Modest
Area: Northern Quarter
Address: 17 Newton Street
Manchester M1 1FZ, UK
Phone: 0161 247 7735

#296
Topshop
Category: Shoe Store, Accessories
Average price: Expensive
Area: City Centre
Address: Arndale Ctr
Manchester M4 3AQ, UK
Phone: 0161 615 8660

#297
Pastiche
Category: Women's Clothing
Average price: Expensive
Area: Oxford Road Corridor
Address: 34 Halle Square
Manchester M4 2HU, UK
Phone: 0161 834 3146

#298
GameXchange
Category: Computers
Area: Rusholme
Address: Arndale Ctr
Manchester M32 9BB, UK
Phone: 0161 864 3444

#299
General Store
Category: Women's Clothing,
Accessories, Men's Clothing
Average price: Expensive
Area: City Centre
Address: 7 Barton Arcade
Manchester M3 2BW, UK
Phone: 0161 839 3864

#300
3 Store
Category: Mobile Phones
Average price: Expensive
Area: City Centre
Address: 27 Market St
Manchester M2 7, UK
Phone: 0161 832 8489

#301
Sole Trader
Category: Shoe Store
Average price: Modest
Area: City Centre
Address: Unit 21
Manchester M4 3AQ, UK
Phone: 0161 839 2442

#302
Miss Selfridge
Category: Women's Clothing
Average price: Modest
Area: City Centre
Address: Market Street
Manchester M1 1PN, UK
Phone: 0161 834 3924

#303
New Look
Category: Fashion
Average price: Inexpensive
Area: City Centre
Address: Arndale Ctr
Manchester M4 2HU, UK
Phone: 0161 214 0880

#304
Jeffery-West
Category: Shoe Store
Area: Spinningfields
Address: 1 Barton Arcade
Manchester M3 2BB, UK
Phone: 0161 835 9284

#305
Boots
Category: Pharmacy,
Cosmetics & Beauty Supply
Average price: Modest
Area: Piccadilly
Address: Unit 5 Manchester 2BN, UK
Phone: 0161 228 2059

#306
Fopp
Category: Music & DVDs,
Vinyl Records, Bookstore
Average price: Inexpensive
Area: City Centre
Address: 19 Brown Street
Manchester M2 1DA, UK
Phone: 0161 830 7630

#307
Lahore Store
Category: Convenience Store
Average price: Inexpensive
Area: Longsight
Address: 32 Laindon Road
Manchester M14 5DP, UK
Phone: 0161 224 4208

#308
PDSA
Category: Thrift Store
Area: Chorlton
Address: 460 Wilbraham Road
Manchester M21 0AG, UK
Phone: 0161 860 4004

#309
Lloyds Pharmacy
Category: Pharmacy
Average price: Inexpensive
Area: Fallowfield
Address: 228 Wilmslow Road
Manchester M14 6LE, UK
Phone: 0161 224 7782

#310
IKEA
Category: Furniture Store
Average price: Modest
Area: Ashton Under Lyne
Address: Wellington Road
Manchester OL6 7TE, UK
Phone: +44 845 355 2186

#311
Poshu
Category: Shoe Store, Accessories
Area: City Centre
Address: 5 Police Street
Manchester M2 6, UK
Phone: 0161 819 2444

#312
Shuropody
Category: Shoe Store
Average price: Modest
Area: City Centre
Address: 49 Deansgate
Manchester M3 2, UK
Phone: 0161 834 8570

#313
Office Sale Shop
Category: Shoe Store
Area: City Centre
Address: 3 St Anne's Square
Manchester M2 7LP, UK
Phone: 0161 832 7337

#314
Molton Brown
Category: Cosmetics & Beauty Supply
Average price: Expensive
Area: City Centre
Address: 7 St Ann's Square
Manchester M2 7EF, UK
Phone: 0161 873 8018

#315
Games Workshop
Category: Hobby Shop, Toy Store
Area: City Centre
Address: Unit R35 Arndale Center
Manchester M4 3AT, UK
Phone: 0161 834 6871

#316
Invicta Studio
Category: Photographers,
Electronics, Personal Shopping
Area: Oxford Road Corridor
Address: 83 Oxford Street
Manchester M1 6EG, UK
Phone: 0161 236 4644

#317
Vom Fass
Category: Flowers & Gifts
Average price: Expensive
Area: City Centre
Address: Exchange Square
Manchester M3 1BD, UK
Phone: +44 800 123400

#318
Knickerbox
Category: Lingerie
Average price: Modest
Area: City Centre
Address: Arndale Centre
Manchester M4 2HU, UK
Phone: 0161 831 9797

#319
Coast
Category: Accessories,
Women's Clothing
Average price: Expensive
Area: City Centre
Address:
Manchester Arndale
Manchester M60 1TA, UK
Phone: 0161 832 6341

#320
Chase Music
Category: Musical Instruments
Area: Northern Quarter
Address: 58 Oldham Street
Manchester M4 1LE, UK
Phone: 0161 236 6794

#321
Extreme Largeness
Category: Jewelry, Accessories,
Women's Clothing
Area: City Centre
Address: 52 Church Street
Manchester M4 1PW, UK
Phone: 0161 839 0595

#322
Baylis & Knight
Category: Women's Clothing
Area: Northern Quarter
Address: 301 Aflex Palace
Manchester M4 1PW, UK
Phone: 0161 881 8002

#323
WH Smith
Category: Books, Mags, Music & Video
Average price: Modest
Area: City Centre
Address: Store 5
Manchester M4 2HU, UK
Phone: 0161 834 8300

#324
Lacoste
Category: Men's Clothing,
Women's Clothing
Average price: Modest
Area: Ancoats, Petersfield
Address: 4 New Cathedral Street
Manchester M4 1AD, UK
Phone: 0161 834 9559

#325
Morrison's Local
Category: Shopping, Food
Area: Oxford Road Corridor
Address: 60 Grafton Street
Manchester M13 9NU, UK
Phone: 0161 274 4095

#326
B&M Bargains
Category: Outlet Store
Area: Chorlton
Address: 595-597 Wilbraham Road
Manchester M21 9AJ, UK
Phone: 0161 881 6860

#327
Maplin Electronics
Category: Electronics, Computers
Average price: Expensive
Area: Oxford Road Corridor
Address: 8 Oxford Road
Manchester M1 5QA, UK
Phone: 0161 236 0281

#328
Ellis Brigham Mountain Equipment
Category: Outdoor Gear
Average price: Expensive
Area: Spinningfields
Address: 211 Deansgate
Manchester M3 3NW, UK
Phone: 0161 839 8468

#329
Mulberry
Category: Women's Clothing
Average price: Exclusive
Area: City Centre
Address: 62 King Street
Manchester M2 4ND, UK
Phone: 0161 839 3333

#330
Tommy Hilfiger
Category: Men's Clothing
Average price: Expensive
Area: City Centre
Address: 51 King St
Manchester M2 7AZ, UK
Phone: 0161 831 7364

#331
Phones 4U
Category: Mobile Phones
Average price: Modest
Area: City Centre
Address: 72 Market St
Manchester M1 1PN, UK
Phone: 0161 831 9103

#332
The Fragrance Shop
Category: Cosmetics & Beauty Supply
Average price: Modest
Area: City Centre
Address: 60D Cromford Ct
Manchester M4 2HU, UK
Phone: 0161 833 1723

#333
The Card Factory
Category: Cards & Stationery
Average price: Modest
Area: City Centre
Address: 58 Arndale Centre
Manchester M4 3AB, UK
Phone: 0161 834 1080

#334
United Footwear
Category: Shoe Store
Average price: Inexpensive
Area: Northern Quarter
Address: 68-70 Oldham Street
Manchester M4 1LE, UK
Phone: 0161 228 1706

#335
Walia News
Category: Newspapers & Magazines
Average price: Inexpensive
Area: Northern Quarter
Address: Church Street
Manchester M4 1PW, UK
Phone: 0161 839 6450

#336
Superdry
Category: Men's Clothing,
Women's Clothing
Average price: Expensive
Area: City Centre
Address: Arndale Centre
Manchester M4 3AQ, UK
Phone: 0161 832 2774

#337
Currys Digital
Category: Electronics, Computers,
Office Equipment
Average price: Modest
Area: City Centre
Address: 165 Halle Mall
Manchester M4 3AB, UK
Phone: +44 844 561 6263

#338
A & A Pharmacy
Category: Pharmacy
Average price: Modest
Area: Rusholme
Address: 58 Wilmslow Road
Manchester M14 5AL, UK
Phone: 0161 224 8501

#339
Crocs
Category: Shoe Store
Average price: Modest
Area: City Centre
Address: Arndale Centre
Manchester M4 3AJ, UK
Phone: 0161 832 8178

#340
Cushion Couture
Category: Home Decor
Average price: Modest
Address: Unit 94-96 Halle Mall
Manchester M4 3AB, UK
Phone: 0161 839 7934

#341
BodyActive
Category: Sporting Goods
Area: Fallowfield
Address: 74 Mosley St
Manchester M2 3LW, UK
Phone: 0161 228 0898

#342
French Connection
Category: Accessories,
Women's Clothing
Average price: Modest
Area: Altrincham
Address: 125 Regent Crescent
Manchester M17 8AR, UK
Phone: 0161 746 8396

#343
Anand Fashions
Category: Shoe Store,
Women's Clothing
Area: Fallowfield
Address: 219 Wilmslow Road
Manchester M14 5AG, UK
Phone: 0161 256 0026

#344
Medlock
Category: Convenience Store
Average price: Inexpensive
Area: Oxford Road Corridor
Address: 74 Hathersage Road
Manchester M13 0FN, UK
Phone: 0161 224 1909

#345
The International 3
Category: Art Gallery
Area: Piccadilly
Address: 8 Fairfield St
Manchester M1 2, UK
Phone: 0161 237 3336

#346
Chaal Shoes 4 You
Category: Shoe Store
Average price: Modest
Area: Rusholme
Address: 126 Wilmslow Road
Manchester M14 5AH, UK
Phone: 0161 225 4411

#347
Pound Choice Plus
Category: Hardware Store, Discount Store
Average price: Inexpensive
Area: Levenshulme
Address: Stockport Road
Manchester M19 3AW, UK
Phone: 0161 224 7666

#348
Legends
Category: Framing
Average price: Modest
Area: Rochdale
Address: 4 Royal Exchange Arcade
Manchester M1, UK
Phone: +44 7754 812290

#349
Simon Green at Rankin Styles Interiors
Category: Furniture Store
Average price: Modest
Area: Spinningfields, City Centre
Address: 64 Bridge Street
Manchester M3 3BN, UK
Phone: 0161 839 6662

#350
Nomad Travel & Outdoor
Category: Outdoor Gear
Area: Spinningfields, City Centre
Address: 66-68 Bridge St
Manchester M3 3RJ, UK
Phone: 0161 832 2134

#351
Audio T
Category: Electronics
Average price: Expensive
Area: City Centre
Address: 63 Bridge Street
Manchester M3 3BQ, UK
Phone: 0161 839 8869

#352
T M Lewin
Category: Fashion
Average price: Modest
Area: City Centre
Address: 44 King Street
Manchester M2 6BA, UK
Phone: 0161 835 1330

#353
Fred Perry
Category: Fashion
Average price: Modest
Area: City Centre
Address: 11 Police Street
Manchester M2 7LQ, UK
Phone: 0161 832 9874

#354
Jones Bootmaker
Category: Shoe Store
Average price: Modest
Area: City Centre
Address: 47 King Street
Manchester M2 7AY, UK
Phone: +44 845 602 8168

#355
Jack Wills
Category: Men's Clothing,
Women's Clothing
Area: City Centre
Address: 35 King Street
Manchester M2 7AT, UK
Phone: 0161 831 9508

#356
The Crombie Store
Category: Women's Clothing,
Men's Clothing
Average price: Modest
Area: City Centre
Address: 33 King St
Manchester M2 6AA, UK
Phone: 0161 832 8977

#357
Dkny
Category: Fashion
Average price: Expensive
Area: City Centre
Address: 76-80 King Street
Manchester M2 4NH, UK
Phone: 0161 819 1048

#358
Nicholas Jones Bespoke
Category: Women's Clothing,
Men's Clothing, Sewing & Alterations
Average price: Exclusive
Area: City Centre
Address: 10 St Anns Arcade
Manchester M2 7HW, UK
Phone: +44 845 459 0161

#359
Oilily
Category: Children's Clothing
Area: City Centre
Address: Barton Arcade
Manchester M3 2BB, UK
Phone: 0161 839 2832

#360
Wildings Photo & Video Centre
Category: Photography Store & Services
Area: City Centre
Address: 47 Deansgate
Manchester M3 2AY, UK
Phone: 0161 832 2656

#361
Hervia Bazaar
Category: Women's Clothing,
Accessories, Men's Clothing
Area: City Centre
Address: 40 Spring Garden
Manchester M2 1EN, UK
Phone: 0161 835 2777

#362
Huk
Category: Fashion
Area: Salford University Campus
Address: 52 Church Street
Manchester M4 1, UK
Phone: 0161 834 1340

#363
Dorothy Perkins
Category: Women's Clothing
Area: City Centre
Address: 99-101 Arndale Centre
Manchester M4 3AB, UK
Phone: 0161 839 0426

#364
Chisholm Hunter
Category: Jewelry
Area: City Centre
Address: 60 Arndale Center
Manchester M4 3AB, UK
Phone: 0161 833 3859

#365
Top Shop / Top Man
Category: Men's Clothing
Area: City Centre
Address: 23-31 Market Street
Manchester M1 1WR, UK
Phone: 0161 834 5793

#366
D&A
Category: Eyewear & Opticians
Average price: Expensive
Area: City Centre
Address: Unit 55 Arndale Centre
Manchester M4 2HU, UK
Phone: 0161 865 1306

#367
Flower Style Manchester
Category: Florist
Average price: Modest
Area: Spinningfields
Address: Quay Street
Manchester M3 3JZ, UK
Phone: 0161 834 4044

#368
Eduardo Pelle
Category: Accessories
Area: City Centre
Address: The Triangle
Manchester M4 3TR, UK
Phone: 0161 832 8908

#369
Manchester French Market
Category: Local Flavor
Average price: Modest
Area: City Centre
Address: St Ann's Square
Manchester M2 7DH, UK
Phone: 0161 234 7356

#370
Entertainment Trader
Category: Pawn Shop
Area: Northern Quarter
Address: 50-56 High Street
Manchester M4 1ED, UK
Phone: 0161 831 9697

#371
Ellis Brigham
Category: Sporting Goods
Average price: Exclusive
Area: Castlefield
Address: Duke Street
Manchester M3 4NF, UK
Phone: 0161 833 0746

#372
Capes Dunn & Co
Category: Antiques
Average price: Exclusive
Area: Oxford Road Corridor
Address: 38 Charles Street
Manchester M1 7DB, UK
Phone: 0161 273 1911

#373
Scarce Clothing
Category: Men's Clothing
Area: Northern Quarter
Address: 16 Oldham Street
Manchester M1 1JQ, UK
Phone: 0161 236 2659

#374
Clark Brothers
Category: Office Equipment,
Arts & Crafts
Average price: Modest
Area: Northern Quarter
Address: 34-36 Thomas Street
Manchester M4 1ER, UK
Phone: 0161 834 5880

#375
G W Lofthouse
Category: Engraver,
Trophies and Medals
Average price: Modest
Area: Northern Quarter, City Centre
Address: 44 Shudehill
Manchester M4 4AA, UK
Phone: 0161 834 4562

#376
Beauty With In
Category: Gift Shop,
Cosmetics & Beauty Supply
Area: Northern Quarter
Address: Manchester M1 1HW, UK
Phone: +44 843 289 2941

#377
Bags Of Flavor
Category: Shoe Store,
Men's Clothing, Used, Vintage
Average price: Expensive
Area: Northern Quarter
Address: 55 Oldham St
Manchester M1 1JR, UK
Phone: 0161 834 6166

#378
Nell
Category: Women's Clothing
Area: Northern Quarter
Address: 17 Oak Street
Manchester M4 5JD, UK
Phone: +44 7855 752088

#379
T Shirt Xpress
Category: Fashion
Area: Northern Quarter
Address: 93 Oldham Street
Manchester M4 1LW, UK
Phone: 0161 839 5668

#380
Big In Amsterdam
Category: Music & DVDs, Adult
Area: Northern Quarter
Address: 78 Tib Street
Manchester M4 1LG, UK
Phone: 0161 833 4135

#381
Flannels Clearance
Category: Accessories,
Men's Clothing, Women's Clothing
Area: Spinningfields
Address: The Avenue
Manchester M3 3FL, UK
Phone: 0161 837 6292

#382
Urban Suite
Category: Furniture Store
Average price: Expensive
Area: Northern Quarter
Address: 2 New George Street
Manchester M4 4AE, UK
Phone: 0161 831 9966

#383
Nua
Category: Adult
Average price: Modest
Area: Northern Quarter
Address: 49 Tib Street
Manchester M4 1LS, UK
Phone: 0161 839 5580

#384
Strawberri Peach
Category: Fashion
Average price: Modest
Area: Northern Quarter
Address: 52 Church Street
Manchester M4 1PW, UK
Phone: 0161 839 1110

#385
Cherry Cherry Clothing
Category: Women's Clothing
Area: Northern Quarter
Address: 52 Church Street
Manchester M4 1PW, UK
Phone: 0161 839 0718

#386
Purl City Yarns
Category: Knitting Supplies
Area: Northern Quarter
Address: 62 Port Street
Manchester M1 2EQ, UK
Phone: 0161 425 3864

#387
The Black Sheep Store
Category: Sporting Goods,
Men's Clothing
Area: Ancoats, Petersfield
Address: 28 Mason Street
Manchester M4 5EY, UK
Phone: 0161 834 7974

#388
Celebrate!
Category: Cards & Stationery
Area: City Centre
Address: Manchester Arndale
Manchester M4 3AQ, UK
Phone: 0161 833 9851

#389
RcMods
Category: Hobby Shop
Area: City Centre
Address: The Triangle
Manchester M4 3TR, UK
Phone: 0161 839 6090

#390
Vanisha's Design Boutique
Category: Women's Clothing, Accessories
Area: City Centre
Address: 52 Church Street
Manchester M4 1, UK
Phone: +44 7864 094466

#391
Bicycle Boutique
Category: Bike Rental, Bikes
Area: Oxford Road Corridor
Address: Hillcourt St
Manchester M1 7HU, UK
Phone: 0161 273 7801

#392
The Carphone Warehouse
Category: Mobile Phones, Electronics
Area: Oxford Road Corridor
Address: 99 Oxford Road
Manchester M1 7EL, UK
Phone: +44 870 168 2851

#393
Reiss Menswear
Category: Men's Clothing,
Women's Clothing
Average price: Expensive
Area: Rusholme
Address: 159 Regent Crescent
Manchester M17 8AR, UK
Phone: 0161 746 8700

#394
Scope
Category: Thrift Store
Area: Levenshulme
Address: 386 Dickenson Road
Manchester M13 0WQ, UK
Phone: 0161 224 2062

#395
British Red Cross
Category: Thrift Store
Area: Chorlton
Address: 611 Wilbraham Road
Manchester M21 9AN, UK
Phone: 0161 860 6965

#396
Franny & Filer
Category: Jewelry
Area: Chorlton
Address: 70 Beech Road
Manchester M21 9EG, UK
Phone: 0161 881 4912

#397
C & W Etchells
Category: Newspapers & Magazines
Area: Chorlton
Address: 44 Beech Road
Manchester M21 9EL, UK
Phone: 0161 881 1764

#398
Creative Recycling
Category: Art Gallery
Area: Chorlton
Address: 40 Beech Road
Manchester M21 9EL, UK
Phone: 0161 881 4422

#399
Kiss My Feet
Category: Shoe Store
Area: Chorlton
Address: 93 Beech Road
Manchester M21 9EQ, UK
Phone: 0161 860 4800

#400
Joypad Video Games
Category: Computers,
Videos & Video Game Rental
Area: Chorlton
Address: 444 Barlow Moor Road
Manchester M21 0BQ, UK
Phone: 0161 861 0909

#401
Manchester Car Audio
Category: Automotive, Electronics
Average price: Expensive
Area: Levenshulme
Address: 850 Stockport Road
Manchester M19 3AH, UK
Phone: 0161 225 2222

#402
Everest DIY Store
Category: Hardware Store
Average price: Inexpensive
Area: Levenshulme
Address: 854-856 Stockport Road
Manchester M19 3AH, UK
Phone: 0161 249 0999

#403
Carpeteria
Category: Home Decor
Area: Levenshulme
Address: 787 Stockport Road
Manchester M19 3DL, UK
Phone: 0161 224 1628

#404
Ladybarn News
Category: Newspapers & Magazines
Area: Ladybarn
Address: 106 Mauldeth Road
Manchester M14 6SQ, UK
Phone: 0161 445 4039

#405
St. Ann's Hospice
Category: Thrift Store
Area: Ladybarn
Address: 124 Mauldeth Rd W
Manchester M14 6, UK
Phone: 0161 448 9977

#406
St. Ann's Hospice
Category: Furniture Store
Area: Ladybarn
Address: 128 Mauldeth Road
Manchester M14 6SQ, UK
Phone: 0161 445 7990

#407
Sue Ryder Care
Category: Thrift Store
Area: Ladybarn
Address: 103 Mauldeth Road
Manchester M14 6SR, UK
Phone: 0161 248 0522

#408
Stella's Wedding Dresses
Category: Bridal, Flowers & Gifts
Area: West Didsbury
Address: 116 Burton Road
Manchester M20 1LP, UK
Phone: 0161 445 4646

#409
Frames
Category: Framing
Area: West Didsbury
Address: 33 Lawping Ln
Manchester M20 2NT, UK
Phone: 0161 445 2354

#410
The White Closet
Category: Women's Clothing
Area: West Didsbury
Address: 204 Burton Rd
Manchester M20 2LW, UK
Phone: 0161 445 5678

#411
Sterling Pharmacy
Category: Pharmacy
Area: Didsbury Village
Address: 103 Lapwing Lane
Manchester M20 6UR, UK
Phone: 0161 445 3753

#412
Wendy J Levy Contemporary Art
Category: Art Gallery
Area: Didsbury Village
Address: 17 Warburton Street
Manchester M20 6WA, UK
Phone: 0161 446 4880

#413
Dunelm
Category: Furniture Store
Area: Bolton
Address: Green Street
Manchester M26 3ED, UK
Phone: 0161 724 1004

#414
Radley & Co
Category: Accessories, Leather Goods
Average price: Exclusive
Area: City Centre
Address: 8 New Cathedral St
Manchester M1 1AD, UK
Phone: 0161 834 0531

#415
River Island
Category: Fashion, Jewelry
Average price: Modest
Area: City Centre
Address: 92 Arndale Ctr
Manchester M4 3AB, UK
Phone: 0161 834 2268

#416
Swagger Menswear
Category: Men's Clothing
Average price: Expensive
Area: Northern Quarter
Address: 93 Piccadilly
Manchester M1 2DA, UK
Phone: 0161 236 0388

#417
JD Sports
Category: Sporting Goods,
Shoe Store, Men's Clothing
Average price: Expensive
Area: City Centre
Address: 16-18 Barbirolli Mall
Manchester M4 3AB, UK
Phone: 0161 819 5221

#418
H Samuel
Category: Jewelry
Area: City Centre
Address: 7-7A Upper Level
Manchester M4 2EA, UK
Phone: 0161 835 1317

#419
Delia's Florist
Category: Florist
Average price: Modest
Area: Chorlton
Address: 289 Barlow Moor Road
Manchester M21 7GH, UK
Phone: 0161 445 1279

#420
Boots
Category: Pharmacy,
Cosmetics & Beauty Supply
Average price: Modest
Address: 39-43 King St
Manchester M2 7AT, UK
Phone: 0161 834 8315

#421
THREE Mobile
Category: Mobile Phones
Area: City Centre
Address: 24 St Ann's Square
Manchester M2 7JB, UK
Phone: 0161 839 1744

#422
Twilight Salons
Category: Hair Salons,
Cosmetics & Beauty Supply
Average price: Modest
Area: Northern Quarter
Address: 5 Kelvin Street
Manchester M4 1ET, UK
Phone: 0161 833 0249

#423
No Angel
Category: Women's Clothing
Area: Northern Quarter
Address: 20 Oldham St
Manchester M1 1JN, UK
Phone: 0161 236 8982

#424
Aleef
Category: Newspapers & Magazines,
Convenience Store
Average price: Inexpensive
Area: Northern Quarter
Address: 1a High Street
Manchester M4 1QB, UK
Phone: 0161 832 9739

#425
JD Sports
Category: Sporting Goods
Average price: Modest
Area: Piccadilly
Address: Great Ancoats Street
Manchester M4 6DJ, UK
Phone: 0161 273 5637

#426
Ryman Stationery
Category: Office Equipment
Area: Oxford Road Corridor
Address: Oxford Road
Manchester M13 9RN, UK
Phone: 0161 272 7060

#427
Get Connected
Category: Mobile Phones
Area: Oxford Road Corridor
Address: 342 Oxford Road
Manchester M13 9NG, UK
Phone: 0161 273 5000

#428
Bond
Category: Women's Clothing
Average price: Modest
Area: West Didsbury
Address: 130 Burton Rd
Manchester M20 1JQ, UK
Phone: 0161 434 5434

#429
The Picture House
Category: Framing
Area: Didsbury Village
Address: 47 Barlow Moor Road
Manchester M20 6TW, UK
Phone: +44 7738 068030

#430
Jenny Jones
Category: Jewelry
Average price: Modest
Area: Rochdale
Address: 9 Royal Exchange Arcade
Manchester M2 7EA, UK
Phone: 0161 839 0102

#431
**Erica and Edwards
Diamond Specialist**
Category: Jewelry
Average price: Expensive
Area: Rochdale
Address: Royal Exchange Arcade
Manchester M2 7EA, UK
Phone: 0161 831 9937

#432
Photo Studio
Category: Photography Store & Services
Average price: Inexpensive
Area: Rusholme
Address: 69 Wilmslow Road
Manchester M14 5TB, UK
Phone: 0161 257 0010

#433
Fancy Jewellers
Category: Jewelry
Average price: Expensive
Area: Rusholme
Address: 85 Wilmslow Road
Manchester M14 5SU, UK
Phone: 0161 224 0589

#434
Bravissimo
Category: Lingerie
Average price: Expensive
Area: City Centre
Address: Exchange Square
Manchester M3 1BD, UK
Phone: 0161 839 7050

#435
H&M
Category: Fashion, Jewelry
Average price: Modest
Area: City Centre
Address: 90 Halle Mall
Manchester M4 2HU, UK
Phone: 0161 214 1130

#436
Waterstones
Category: Bookstore, Coffee & Tea
Average price: Modest
Area: City Centre
Address: 91 Deansgate
Manchester M3 2BW, UK
Phone: 0161 837 3000

#437
All Saints
Category: Department Store
Average price: Exclusive
Area: City Centre
Address: Exchange Square
Manchester M3 1BD, UK
Phone: 0161 838 0566

#438
Berketex Brides
Category: Bridal, Flowers & Gifts
Average price: Modest
Area: City Centre
Address: Marsden Way Arndale Centre
Manchester M4 3AQ, UK
Phone: 0161 839 6781

#439
Cameolord
Category: Pharmacy
Average price: Modest
Area: Chinatown
Address: 7 Oxford Street
Manchester M1 4PB, UK
Phone: 0161 236 1445

#440
Toys 'R' Us
Category: Toy Store, Electronics, Furniture
Average price: Expensive
Area: Piccadilly
Address: Great Ancoats Street
Manchester M4 6DJ, UK
Phone: 0161 272 6515

#441
Office
Category: Shoe Store, Leather Goods
Average price: Modest
Area: City Centre
Address: 3 St Ann's Place
Manchester M2 7LP, UK
Phone: 0161 834 3804

#442
Wave Contemporary Jewellery
Category: Jewelry, Watches
Average price: Modest
Area: City Centre
Address: 16-18 Royal Exchange
Manchester M2 7EA, UK
Phone: 0161 832 9868

#443
Deichman Shoes UK
Category: Shoe Store
Average price: Modest
Area: City Centre
Address: 37 Arndale Centre
Manchester M4 2HU, UK
Phone: 0161 834 5752

#444
UGG Australia
Category: Shoe Store
Average price: Expensive
Area: City Centre
Address: 3 New Cathedral Street
Manchester M1 1AD, UK
Phone: 0161 839 7956

#445
WH Smith
Category: Bookstore
Average price: Modest
Area: City Centre
Address: 2 Victoria Station Approach
Manchester M3 1NY, UK
Phone: 0161 834 5591

#446
Aleef Newsagents
Category: Newspapers & Magazines
Average price: Modest
Area: City Centre
Address: Unit K9 Arndale Centre
Manchester M4 3AT, UK
Phone: 0161 834 7400

#447
No Angel
Category: Women's Clothing
Average price: Modest
Area: Northern Quarter
Address: 52 Church St
Manchester M4 1PW, UK
Phone: 0161 834 7379

#448
Gold Centre
Category: Jewelry, Flowers & Gifts
Average price: Inexpensive
Area: City Centre
Address: Arndale Centre
Manchester M4 3AD, UK
Phone: 0161 835 3933

#449
Dr & Herbs
Category: Pharmacy
Area: Gay Village
Address: Arndale Centre
Manchester M1, UK
Phone: 0161 831 7688

#450
O2
Category: Mobile Phones
Average price: Modest
Area: City Centre
Address: Upper Level
Manchester M1, UK
Phone: 0161 834 3681

#451
The Vestry
Category: Women's Clothing
Average price: Modest
Area: Longsight
Address: Manchester Arndale Centre
Manchester M1, UK
Phone: 0161 819 2492

#452
Chorlton Family Photography
Category: Photographers,
Photography Store & Services
Area: Chorlton
Address: Chorlton
Manchester M21 9NW, UK
Phone: +44 7735 479490

#453
Tesco
Category: Department Store
Area: Levenshulme
Address: 998-990 Stockport Road
Manchester M19 3NN, UK
Phone: +44 845 671 9386

#454
Aleef Newsagents
Category: Newspapers & Magazines
Average price: Inexpensive
Area: Spinningfields, City Centre
Address: 76 Bridge Street
Manchester M3 2RJ, UK
Phone: 0161 236 5049

#455
Advanced Photo
Category: Photography Store & Services
Average price: Modest
Area: City Centre
Address: 25 John Dalton Street
Manchester M2 6FW, UK
Phone: 0161 839 8838

#456
Wrapped In Leather
Category: Leather Goods
Average price: Expensive
Area: City Centre
Address: 43 King St W
Manchester M3 2PW, UK
Phone: 0161 834 9629

#457
Boodles
Category: Jewelry
Average price: Exclusive
Area: City Centre
Address: 1 King Street
Manchester M2 6AW, UK
Phone: 0161 833 9000

#458
Oasis
Category: Women's Clothing
Area: City Centre
Address: 50 King Street
Manchester M2 4LY, UK
Phone: 0161 839 4735

#459
Christopher James
Category: Jewelry
Area: City Centre
Address: 7 - 9 St Ann Street
Manchester M2 7LG, UK
Phone: 0161 819 1213

#460
3 Store
Category: Mobile Phones
Area: City Centre
Address: 24 St Ann's Square
Manchester M2 7JB, UK
Phone: 0161 839 1744

#461
High & Mighty
Category: Men's Clothing,
Personal Shopping
Area: City Centre
Address: 55 King Street
Manchester M1 1PX, UK
Phone: 0161 834 7367

#462
Crumpler
Category: Luggage, Accessories
Area: City Centre
Address: 18 Cross Street
Manchester M2 7AE, UK
Phone: 0161 832 9997

#463
Jacobs
Category: Photography Store & Services
Average price: Expensive
Area: City Centre
Address: 16 Cross Street
Manchester M2 7AE, UK
Phone: 0161 834 7500

#464
The Whisky Shop
Category: Whisky Specialist
Average price: Exclusive
Area: City Centre
Address: 3 Exchange Street
Manchester M2 7EE, UK
Phone: 0161 832 6110

#465
Aleef
Category: Newspapers & Magazines,
Convenience Store
Area: Oxford Road Corridor
Address: 91-93 Oxford Street
Manchester M1 6ET, UK
Phone: 0161 228 7420

#466
O2
Category: Mobile Phones
Area: City Centre
Address: Unit 168
Manchester M4 2HU, UK
Phone: 0161 834 3681

#467
Tokyo Royale
Category: Fashion
Area: Salford University Campus
Address: 52 Church Street
Manchester M4 1, UK
Phone: 0161 834 3661

#468
Wilkinson
Category: Department Store
Average price: Inexpensive
Area: City Centre
Address: 65-66 The Mall
Manchester M24 4EL, UK
Phone: 0161 655 3814

#469
Withy Grove Store
Category: Office Equipment
Area: City Centre
Address: 35-39 Withy Grove
Manchester M4 2BJ, UK
Phone: 0161 834 0044

#470
Ted Baker
Category: Accessories,
Men's Clothing, Women's Clothing
Average price: Modest
Area: City Centre
Address: 6 New Cathedral Street
Manchester M1 1AD, UK
Phone: 0161 834 8332

#471
Louis Vuitton
Category: Luggage, Italian,
Leather Goods
Average price: Modest
Address: Exchange Sq
Manchester M3 1BD, UK
Phone: 0161 828 0400

#472
Shudehill Book Centre
Category: Bookstore, Adult
Average price: Modest
Area: Northern Quarter
Address: 34 Shudehill
Manchester M4 1EZ, UK
Phone: 0161 839 0376

#473
Central Radio
Category: Electronics
Average price: Expensive
Area: Northern Quarter
Address: 30-32 Shudehill
Manchester M4 1EZ, UK
Phone: 0161 834 6700

#474
Vision Express
Category: Eyewear & Opticians
Average price: Modest
Area: City Centre
Address: 52 Arndale Centre
Manchester M4 2HU, UK
Phone: 0161 832 8855

#475
Marhaba Newsagents
Category: Newspapers & Magazines, Convenience Store
Average price: Inexpensive
Area: Northern Quarter
Address: 47 Piccadilly
Manchester M1 2AP, UK
Phone: 0161 236 7526

#476
Fanboy Three
Category: Computers, Toy Store
Average price: Modest
Area: Northern Quarter
Address: 17 Newton Street
Manchester M1 1FZ, UK
Phone: 0161 247 7735

#477
A.L.M Traders
Category: Newspapers & Magazines
Average price: Inexpensive
Area: Northern Quarter
Address: 62 Oldham Street
Manchester M4 1LE, UK
Phone: 0161 236 9590

#478
Scarce Clothing
Category: Men's Clothing
Area: Northern Quarter
Address: 4 Afflecks Arcade
Manchester M1 1JG, UK
Phone: 0161 819 1114

#479
Rohan
Category: Outdoor Gear
Area: City Centre
Address: 8-10 Acresfield
Manchester M2 7HA, UK
Phone: 0161 832 6272

#480
Sports Direct
Category: Sporting Goods
Area: Salford University Campus
Address: Old Field Rd
Manchester M5 4BT, UK
Phone: +44 870 333 9544

#481
Dojo Ecoshop
Category: Home Decor
Average price: Modest
Area: Ancoats, Petersfield
Address: 38 Mason St
Manchester M4 5EZ, UK
Phone: 0161 834 5432

#482
Cards Galore
Category: Cards & Stationery
Average price: Modest
Area: Piccadilly
Address: Unit 12
Manchester M1 2BN, UK
Phone: 0161 236 0337

#483
Rowfers
Category: Fashion
Average price: Modest
Area: Northern Quarter
Address: 52 Church St
Manchester M4 1PW, UK
Phone: 0161 833 4640

#484
Faith Pharmacy
Category: Pharmacy
Area: Oxford Road Corridor
Address: 59 Booth St West
Manchester M15 6PQ, UK
Phone: 0161 232 8044

#485
Kurt Geiger
Category: Shoe Store
Area: Ancoats, Petersfield
Address: Kendals
Manchester M60 3AU, UK
Phone: +44 844 800 3744

#486
Superdrug
Category: Cosmetics & Beauty Supply, Pharmacy
Area: Oxford Road Corridor
Address: Oxford Road
Manchester M13 9RN, UK
Phone: 0161 249 3816

#487
Unicorn Home Furnishings
Category: Furniture Store
Average price: Modest
Area: Longsight
Address: 525 Stockport Road
Manchester M12 4JH, UK
Phone: 0161 248 9595

#488
Uptown Girl
Category: Fashion
Area: Longsight
Address: 555 Stockport Road
Manchester M12 4JH, UK
Phone: 0161 256 2400

#489
Boots
Category: Pharmacy,
Cosmetics & Beauty Supply
Area: Chorlton
Address: 20-22 Chorlton Place
Manchester M21 9AQ, UK
Phone: 0161 881 1121

#490
Max Spielmann
Category: Photography Store & Services
Area: Chorlton
Address: 436 Barlow Moor Road
Manchester M21 0AB, UK
Phone: +44 870 750 5626

#491
Joseph Gleave & Son
Category: Hardware Store
Area: Chorlton
Address: 995 Chester Road
Manchester M32 0NB, UK
Phone: 0161 865 6025

#492
Lighthouse Charity Shop
Category: Thrift Store
Area: Chorlton
Address: 364 Barlow Moor Rd
Manchester M21 8AZ, UK
Phone: 0161 786 1440

#493
Jean Genie
Category: Children's Clothing,
Men's Clothing, Women's Clothing
Average price: Modest
Area: Chorlton
Address: 97 Beech Rd
Manchester M21 9, UK
Phone: 0161 860 4976

#494
Sound Studio
Category: Automotive, Electronics
Average price: Expensive
Area: Levenshulme
Address: 848 Stockport Road
Manchester M19 3AW, UK
Phone: 0161 256 1939

#495
Photo Express
Category: Photography Store & Services,
Video/Film Production
Area: Levenshulme
Address: 900 Stockport Road
Manchester M19 3AD, UK
Phone: 0161 257 0500

#496
B Kemp
Category: Newspapers & Magazines
Area: West Didsbury
Address: 542 Wilmslow Road
Manchester M20 4BY, UK
Phone: 0161 445 4346

#497
Sifters Records
Category: Music & DVDs
Average price: Modest
Area: East Didsbury
Address: 177 Fog Ln
Manchester M20 6FJ, UK
Phone: 0161 445 8697

#498
Andrew Graham Shoes
Category: Shoe Store
Average price: Modest
Area: Didsbury Village
Address: 673 Wilmslow Rd
Manchester M20 6RA, UK
Phone: 0161 445 8243

#499
Cancer Research UK
Category: Thrift Store
Area: Didsbury Village
Address: 800 Wilmslow Road
Manchester M20 6UH, UK
Phone: 0161 445 1182

#500
Fonda
Category: Women's Clothing,
Men's Clothing
Average price: Expensive
Area: Didsbury Village
Address: 677 Wilmslow Road
Manchester M20 6RA, UK
Phone: 0161 446 1177

TOP 500 RESTAURANTS

The Most Recommended by Locals & Trevelers

(From #1 to #500)

#1
Barbakan Delicatessen
Cuisines: Bakery, Desserts, Deli
Average price: £11-25
Area: Chorlton
Address: 67-71 Manchester Road
Manchester M21 9PW
Phone: 0161 881 7053

#2
The Marble Arch
Cuisines: Pub, Gastropub
Average price: £11-25
Area: Ancoats, Petersfield
Address: 73 Rochdale Road
Manchester M4 4HY
Phone: 0161 832 5914

#3
Cornerhouse
Cuisines: Cinema, Bar, Cafe
Average price: £11-25
Area: Oxford Road Corridor
Address: 70 Oxford Street
Manchester M1 5NH
Phone: 0161 200 1500

#4
Mughli
Cuisines: Indian, Pakistani
Average price: £11-25
Area: Rusholme
Address: 30 Wilmslow Road
Manchester M14 5TQ
Phone: 0161 248 0900

#5
Gaucho Grill
Cuisines: Argentine
Average price: £26-45
Address: 2a St Marys Street
Manchester M3 2LB
Phone: 0161 833 4333

#6
Katsouris Deli
Cuisines: Deli, Sandwiches
Average price: Under £10
Area: City Centre
Address: 113 Deansgate
Manchester M3 2BQ
Phone: 0161 937 0010

#7
Home Sweet Home
Cuisines: American, Coffee & Tea,
Breakfast & Brunch
Average price: £11-25
Area: Northern Quarter
Address: 49-51 Edge Street
Manchester M4 1HE
Phone: 0161 244 9424

#8
Akbar's
Cuisines: Indian
Average price: £11-25
Area: Castlefield
Address: 73-83 Liverpool Road
Manchester M3 4NQ
Phone: 0161 834 8444

#9
Sinclair's Oyster Bar
Cuisines: Pub, British
Average price: Under £10
Area: City Centre
Address: 2 Cathedral Gates
Manchester M3 1SW
Phone: 0161 834 0430

#10
Croma
Cuisines: Pizza, Italian
Average price: £11-25
Area: City Centre
Address: 1 Clarence Street
Manchester M2 4DE
Phone: 0161 237 9799

#11
Pi
Cuisines: British, Pub
Average price: £11-25
Area: Chorlton
Address: 99 Manchester Road
Manchester M21 9GA
Phone: 0161 882 0000

#12
Try Thai
Cuisines: Thai
Average price: £11-25
Area: Chinatown
Address: 52 Faulkner Street
Manchester M1 4FH
Phone: 0161 228 1822

#13
Grill On The Alley
Cuisines: Lounge, British, Gastropub
Average price: £26-45
Address: 5 Ridgefield
Manchester M2 6EG
Phone: 0161 833 3465

#14
Yuzu
Cuisines: Japanese
Average price: £11-25
Area: Chinatown
Address: 39 Faulkner Street
Manchester M1 4EE
Phone: 0161 236 4159

#15
Teacup
Cuisines: Coffee & Tea, Tea Room,
Breakfast & Brunch
Average price: £11-25
Area: Northern Quarter
Address: 53-55 Thomas Street
Manchester M4 1NA
Phone: 0161 832 3233

#16
The Deaf Institute
Cuisines: Burgers, Lounge
Average price: £11-25
Area: Oxford Road Corridor
Address: 135 Grosvenor Street
Manchester M1 7HE
Phone: 0161 276 9350

#17
Fuzion
Cuisines: Japanese, Asian Fusion, Thai
Average price: £11-25
Area: Fallowfield
Address: 264 Wilmslow Road
Manchester M14 6JR
Phone: 0161 248 6688

#18
Seoul Kimchi
Cuisines: Korean, Japanese
Average price: £11-25
Area: Oxford Road Corridor
Address: 275 Upper Brook Street
Manchester M13 0HR
Phone: 0161 273 5556

#19
Chaophraya
Cuisines: Thai, Bar
Average price: £26-45
Address: Chapel Walks Manchester
Manchester M2 1HN
Phone: 0161 832 8342

#20
Knott Bar
Cuisines: Pub, British, Burgers
Average price: £11-25
Area: Castlefield
Address: 374 Deansgate
Manchester M3 4LY
Phone: 0161 839 9229

#21
Trof
Cuisines: Bar, British
Average price: £11-25
Area: City Centre
Address: 6-8 Thomas Street
Manchester M4 1EU
Phone: 0161 833 3197

#22
SoLIta
Cuisines: Barbeque, Burgers, American
Average price: £11-25
Area: Northern Quarter
Address: 37 Turner Street
Manchester M4 1DW
Phone: 0161 839 2200

#23
The Didsbury
Cuisines: Bar, Gastropub
Average price: £11-25
Address: 852 Wilmslow Road
Manchester M20 2SG
Phone: 0161 445 5389

#24
Sam's Chop House
Cuisines: British, Pub
Average price: £11-25
Area: City Centre
Address: Blackpool Hold
Manchester M2 1HN
Phone: 0161 834 3210

#25
Greens
Cuisines: Vegetarian
Average price: £11-25
Area: West Didsbury
Address: 43 Lapwing Lane
Manchester M20 2NT
Phone: 0161 434 4259

#26
Caspian
Cuisines: Fast Food, Takeaway,
Middle Eastern
Average price: Under £10
Area: Rusholme
Address: 61-63 Wilmslow Road
Manchester M14 5TB
Phone: 0161 225 1057

#27
Dough
Cuisines: Pizza, Italian
Average price: £11-25
Area: Northern Quarter
Address: 75-77 High Street
Manchester M4 1FS
Phone: 0161 834 9411

#28
Thyme Out Delicatessen
Cuisines: Deli, Breakfast & Brunch
Average price: Under £10
Area: West Didsbury
Address: 147 Nell Lane
Manchester M20 2LG
Phone: 0161 434 8686

#29
Soup Kitchen
Cuisines: Bar, Cafe, Sandwiches
Average price: £11-25
Area: Northern Quarter
Address: 31-33 Spear Street
Manchester M1 1DF
Phone: 0161 236 5100

#30
Tampopo
Cuisines: Asian Fusion,
Vietnamese, Thai
Average price: £11-25
Area: City Centre
Address: 38 Exchange Sq Unit 2
Manchester M4 3TR
Phone: 0161 839 6484

#31
Sweet Mandarin
Cuisines: Chinese, Specialty Food
Average price: £26-45
Area: Northern Quarter
Address: 19 Copperas Street
Manchester M4 1HS
Phone: 0161 832 8848

#32
Mr Thomas's Chop House
Cuisines: British, Pub
Average price: £26-45
Area: City Centre
Address: 52 Cross Street
Manchester M2 7AR
Phone: 0161 832 2245

#33
El Rincon de Rafa
Cuisines: Spanish, Basque
Average price: £11-25
Area: Castlefield
Address: 244 Deansgate
Manchester M3 4BQ
Phone: 0161 839 8819

#34
BrewDog Manchester
Cuisines: Pub, Burgers, Barbeque
Average price: £11-25
Address: 35 Peter Street
Manchester M2 5BG
Phone: 0161 832 9038

#35
Don Giovanni's
Cuisines: Italian, Bar, Pizza
Average price: £11-25
Address: 11 Oxford Street
Manchester M1 5AN
Phone: 0161 228 2482

#36
The Ox
Cuisines: Hotel, Gastropub, Bar
Average price: £26-45
Area: Castlefield
Address: Liverpool Road
Manchester M3 4NQ
Phone: 0161 839 7740

#37
Ning
Cuisines: Thai, Malaysian, Asian Fusion
Average price: £11-25
Area: Ancoats, Petersfield
Address: 92 Oldham Street
Manchester M4 1LJ
Phone: 0844 414 5484

#38
Phetpailin
Cuisines: Thai
Average price: £11-25
Area: Chinatown
Address: 46 George Street
Manchester M1 4HF
Phone: 0161 228 6500

#39
Wings
Cuisines: Chinese, Bar
Average price: £26-45
Address: 1 Lincoln Square
Manchester M2 5LN
Phone: 0161 834 9000

#40
Falafel
Cuisines: Falafel
Average price: Under £10
Area: Rusholme
Address: Wilmslow Road
Manchester M14 5TG
Phone: 0161 256 1372

#41
San Carlo Cicchetti
Cuisines: Tapas, Italian,
Breakfast & Brunch
Average price: £26-45
Area: City Centre
Address: 40-42 King Street W
Manchester M3 2QG
Phone: 0161 839 2233

#42
The Old Wellington
Cuisines: Gastropub, Pub, British
Average price: £11-25
Area: City Centre
Address: 4 Cathedral Gates
Manchester M3 1SW
Phone: 0161 839 5179

#43
Nawaab
Cuisines: Indian, Pakistani
Average price: £11-25
Area: Levenshulme
Address: 1008 Stockport Road
Manchester M19 3WN
Phone: 0161 224 6969

#44
Kro Bar
Cuisines: Pub, European
Average price: £11-25
Area: Oxford Road Corridor
Address: 325 Oxford Road
Manchester M13 9PG
Phone: 0161 274 3100

#45
Gorilla
Cuisines: Cafe, Breakfast & Brunch
Average price: £11-25
Address: 54-56 Whitworth Street West
Manchester M1 5WW
Phone: 0161 407 0301

#46
This & That
Cuisines: Indian
Average price: Under £10
Area: Northern Quarter
Address: 3 Soap Street
Manchester M4 1EW
Phone: 0161 832 4971

#47
The Northern Quarter
Cuisines: British
Average price: £11-25
Area: Northern Quarter
Address: 108 High Street
Manchester M4 1HT
Phone: 0161 832 7115

#48
Dukes 92
Cuisines: Pub, British
Average price: £11-25
Area: Castlefield
Address: 18 Castle Street
Manchester M3 4LZ
Phone: 0161 839 3522

#49
Wagamama
Cuisines: Chinese, Japanese, Soup
Average price: £11-25
Area: City Centre
Address: 1 Print Works
Manchester M4 2BS
Phone: 0161 839 5916

#50
The Rice Bowl
Cuisines: Chinese
Average price: £11-25
Area: City Centre
Address: 33a Cross Street
Manchester M2 1NL
Phone: 0161 832 9033

#51
Room
Cuisines: Bar, European
Average price: £26-45
Area: City Centre
Address: 81 King Street
Manchester M2 4AH
Phone: 0161 839 2005

#52
Herbi Vores
Cuisines: Vegetarian, Coffee & Tea
Average price: Under £10
Area: Oxford Road Corridor
Address: Burlington Street
Manchester M13 9PL
Phone: 0161 275 2408

#53
Michael Caines Restaurant
Cuisines: British, Champagne Bar
Average price: £26-45
Area: Piccadilly
Address: 107 Piccadilly
Manchester M1 2DB
Phone: 0161 200 5678

#54
Trove
Cuisines: Bakery, Breakfast & Brunch
Average price: Under £10
Area: Levenshulme
Address: 1032 Stockport Road
Manchester M19 3EX
Phone: 0161 224 8588

#55
Vermilion
Cuisines: Thai, Lounge
Average price: £26-45
Address: Hulme Hall Lane
Manchester M40 8AD
Phone: 0161 202 0055

#56
Oklahoma
Cuisines: Coffee & Tea,
Breakfast & Brunch
Average price: £11-25
Area: Northern Quarter
Address: 74-76 High Street
Manchester M4 1ES
Phone: 0161 834 1136

#57
English Lounge
Cuisines: Pub, British, Burgers
Average price: £11-25
Area: Northern Quarter
Address: 64-66 High Street
Manchester M4 1EA
Phone: 0161 832 4824

#58
Red Chilli
Cuisines: Chinese
Average price: £11-25
Area: Chinatown
Address: 70 Portland Street
Manchester M1 4GU
Phone: 0161 236 2888

#59
Kosmos Taverna
Cuisines: Greek
Average price: £11-25
Area: Fallowfield
Address: 248 Wilmslow Road
Manchester M14 6LD
Phone: 0161 225 9106

#60
Yakisoba
Cuisines: Asian Fusion, Japanese, Thai
Average price: £11-25
Area: Chorlton
Address: 360 Barlow Moor Road
Manchester M21 8AZ
Phone: 0161 862 0888

#61
The Alchemist
Cuisines: British, European, Cocktail Bar
Average price: £26-45
Area: Spinningfields
Address: 3 Hardman Street
Manchester M3 3HF
Phone: 0161 817 2950

#62
Battered Cod
Cuisines: Fish & Chips
Average price: Under £10
Area: Fallowfield
Address: 1 Ladybarn Lane
Manchester M14 6NQ
Phone: 0161 224 2379

#63
Saints & Scholars
Cuisines: British
Average price: £11-25
Area: Didsbury Village
Address: 694 Wilmslow Road
Manchester M20 2DN
Phone: 0161 448 2457

#64
Odder Bar
Cuisines: Bar, Breakfast & Brunch
Average price: £11-25
Area: Oxford Road Corridor
Address: 14 Oxford Road
Manchester M1 5QA
Phone: 0161 238 9132

#65
Dimitri's
Cuisines: Greek, Tapas Bar
Average price: £11-25
Area: Castlefield
Address: Campfield Arcade
Manchester M3 4FN
Phone: 0161 839 3319

#66
I Am Pho
Cuisines: Vietnamese
Average price: Under £10
Area: Chinatown
Address: 44 George Street
Manchester M1 4HF
Phone: 0161 236 1230

#67
Luck Lust Liquor & Burn
Cuisines: Mexican
Average price: £11-25
Area: Northern Quarter
Address: 100-102 High Street
Manchester M4 1HP
Phone: 0161 244 9425

#68
Lime Tree
Cuisines: British
Average price: Above £46
Area: West Didsbury
Address: 8 Lapwing Lane
Manchester M20 2WS
Phone: 0161 445 1217

#69
The Woodstock
Cuisines: Pub, Gastropub
Average price: £11-25
Area: Didsbury Village
Address: 139 Barlow Moor Road
Manchester M20 2DY
Phone: 0161 448 7951

#70
La Viña
Cuisines: Spanish, Tapas
Average price: £11-25
Area: City Centre
Address: 105-107 Deansgate
Manchester M3 2BQ
Phone: 0161 835 3144

#71
Red's True Barbecue
Cuisines: Barbeque, Burgers, American
Average price: £11-25
Address: 22 Lloyd Street
Manchester M2 5WA
Phone: 0161 820 9140

#72
Retro Bar
Cuisines: Breakfast & Brunch, Dive Bar
Average price: Under £10
Area: Gay Village
Address: 78 Sackville Street
Manchester M1 3NJ
Phone: 0161 274 4892

#73
Sapporo Teppanyaki
Cuisines: Japanese, Sushi Bar
Average price: £26-45
Area: Castlefield
Address: 91-93 Liverpool Road
Manchester M3 4JN

#74
Panama Hatty's
Cuisines: European, Mexican
Average price: £11-25
Area: City Centre
Address: 43a Brown Street
Manchester M2 2JJ
Phone: 0161 832 8688

#75
Cachumba
Cuisines: Cafe
Average price: £11-25
Area: West Didsbury
Address: 220 Burton Road
Manchester M20 2LW
Phone: 0161 445 2479

#76
Gemini Café
Cuisines: Breakfast & Brunch, Pizza
Average price: Under £10
Area: Oxford Road Corridor
Address: 328-330 Oxford Road
Manchester M13 9NG
Phone: 0161 272 7723

#77
Isinglass English Dining Room
Cuisines: European, British
Average price: £26-45
Address: 46 Flixton Road
Manchester M41 5AB
Phone: 0161 749 8400

#78
Tokyo Season
Cuisines: Japanese, Sushi Bar,
Asian Fusion
Average price: £11-25
Area: Chinatown
Address: 52 Portland Street
Manchester M1 4QU
Phone: 0161 236 7898

#79
Simple
Cuisines: British, American
Average price: £11-25
Area: Northern Quarter
Address: 44 Tib Street
Manchester M4 1LA
Phone: 0161 832 8764

#80
Habesha
Cuisines: Ethiopian, Halal, African
Average price: £11-25
Area: Gay Village
Address: 29-31 Sackville Street
Manchester M1 3LZ
Phone: 0161 228 7396

#81
The Gallery Café
Cuisines: Breakfast & Brunch
Average price: Under £10
Area: Oxford Road Corridor
Address: Oxford Road
Manchester M15 6ER
Phone: 0161 275 7497

#82
Dogs 'n' Dough
Cuisines: Hot Dogs, Pizza, American
Average price: £11-25
Area: City Centre
Address: 55 Cross Street
Manchester M2 4JN
Phone: 0161 834 3996

#83
Piccolino
Cuisines: Italian
Average price: £11-25
Address: 8 Clarence Street
Manchester M2 4DW
Phone: 0161 835 9860

#84
Bistro West 156
Cuisines: British
Average price: £26-45
Area: West Didsbury
Address: 156 Burton Rd
Manchester M20 1LH
Phone: 0161 445 1921

#85
Folk Café Bar
Cuisines: Bar, Cafe, Sandwiches
Average price: £11-25
Area: West Didsbury
Address: 169-171 Burton Road
Manchester M20 2LN
Phone: 0161 445 2912

#86
Little Yang Sing
Cuisines: Chinese
Average price: £26-45
Area: Chinatown
Address: 17 George Street
Manchester M1 4HE
Phone: 0161 228 7722

#87
The French By Simon Rogan
Cuisines: British
Average price: Above £46
Address: Peter Street
Manchester M60 2DS
Phone: 0161 236 3333

#88
Efes Taverna
Cuisines: Turkish, Bar
Average price: Under £10
Area: Oxford Road Corridor
Address: 46 Princess Street
Manchester M1 6HR
Phone: 0161 236 1824

#89
Tampopo
Cuisines: Asian Fusion, Japanese
Average price: £11-25
Address: 16 Albert Square
Manchester M2 5PF
Phone: 0161 819 1966

#90
Umami
Cuisines: Japanese, Sushi Bar
Average price: Under £10
Area: Oxford Road Corridor
Address: 149/153 Oxford Road
Manchester M1 1EE
Phone: 0161 273 2300

#91
The Friendship Inn
Cuisines: Pub, Coffee & Tea, British
Average price: £11-25
Area: Fallowfield
Address: 351-353 Wilmslow Road
Manchester M14 6XS
Phone: 0161 224 5758

#92
Turkish Delight
Cuisines: Turkish, Ethnic Food
Average price: £11-25
Area: Chorlton
Address: 573 Barlow Moor Road
Manchester M21 8AE
Phone: 0161 881 0503

#93
Slice Pizza & Bread Bar
Cuisines: Pizza, Fast Food, Takeaway
Average price: Under £10
Area: Northern Quarter
Address: Stevenson Square
Manchester M1 1JJ
Phone: 0161 236 9032

#94
Rice
Cuisines: Asian Fusion, Chinese,
Fast Food, Takeaway
Average price: Under £10
Area: Northern Quarter
Address: 1 Piccadilly Garden
Manchester M1 1RG
Phone: 0161 244 5540

#95
Rustica
Cuisines: Sandwiches, Cafe
Average price: Under £10
Area: Northern Quarter
Address: 7 Hilton Street
Manchester M1 2
Phone: 0161 835 3850

#96
Armenian Taverna
Cuisines: Middle Eastern
Average price: £11-25
Address: 3 Princess Street
Manchester M2 4DF
Phone: 0161 834 9025

#97
Punjab Tandoori
Cuisines: Indian, Fast Food, Takeaway
Average price: £11-25
Area: Rusholme
Address: 177 Wilmslow Road
Manchester M14 5AP
Phone: 0161 225 2960

#98
Christie's Bistro
Cuisines: French, Coffee & Tea
Average price: £11-25
Area: Oxford Road Corridor
Address: Oxford Road
Manchester M13 9PL
Phone: 0161 275 7702

#99
Blue Ginger
Cuisines: Chinese, Fast Food, Takeaway
Average price: Above £46
Area: Fallowfield
Address: 5a Wilbraham Road
Manchester M14 6JS
Phone: 0161 257 3184

#100
Piccolino
Cuisines: Italian
Average price: £26-45
Area: West Didsbury
Address: 6 Lapwing Lane
Manchester M20 2WS
Phone: 0161 434 7524

#101
Kro Piccadilly
Cuisines: Bar, European, British
Average price: £11-25
Area: Piccadilly
Address: 1 Piccadilly Garden
Manchester M1 1RG
Phone: 0161 244 5765

#102
Nandos Fallowfield
Cuisines: Portuguese
Average price: Above £46
Area: Fallowfield
Address: 351 Wilmslow Rd
Manchester M14 6SS
Phone: 0161 249 3972

#103
Fish Hut
Cuisines: Fish & Chips, Takeaway
Average price: Under £10
Area: Castlefield
Address: 27 Liverpool Road
Manchester M3 4NW
Phone: 0161 839 0957

#104
EastZEast
Cuisines: Indian
Average price: £11-25
Area: Oxford Road Corridor
Address: Princess Street
Manchester M1 7DG
Phone: 0161 244 5353

#105
EastZEast
Cuisines: Indian
Average price: £26-45
Area: City Centre
Address: Blackfriars Street
Manchester M3 5BQ
Phone: 0161 834 3500

#106
Kebabish
Cuisines: Fast Food, Takeaway
Average price: £11-25
Area: Rusholme
Address: 109 Wilmslow Road
Manchester M14 5AN
Phone: 0161 224 4994

#107
Southern 11
Cuisines: American, Barbeque, Burgers
Average price: £11-25
Area: Spinningfields
Address: Unit 26 3 Hardman Street
Manchester M3 3EB
Phone: 0161 832 0482

#108
Don Marco
Cuisines: Italian, Pizza
Average price: £11-25
Area: Castlefield
Address: 1 Campfield Avenue Arcade
Manchester M3 4FN
Phone: 0161 831 9130

#109
The Blue Pig
Cuisines: Bar, Persian/Iranian
Average price: £11-25
Area: Northern Quarter
Address: 69 High St Manchester
Manchester M4 1FS
Phone: 0161 832 0630

#110
Topkapi Palace
Cuisines: Turkish
Average price: £11-25
Address: 205 Deansgate
Manchester M3 3NW
Phone: 0161 832 9803

#111
Frankie & Benny's
Cuisines: American, Italian
Average price: £11-25
Area: City Centre
Address: 36 St Ann's Street
Manchester M2 7LE
Phone: 0161 835 2479

#112
Walrus
Cuisines: Lounge, Tapas
Average price: £11-25
Area: Northern Quarter
Address: 78-88 High Street
Manchester M4 1ES
Phone: 0161 828 8700

#113
Olive Delicatessen
Cuisines: Deli, Coffee & Tea
Average price: £11-25
Area: Gay Village
Address: 36-38 Whitworth Street
Manchester M1 3NR
Phone: 0161 236 2360

#114
Solomon Grundy
Cuisines: Bar, Breakfast & Brunch
Average price: £11-25
Address: 447 Wilmslow Rd
Manchester M20 4AN
Phone: 0161 7466 592069

#115
Caffeine & Co
Cuisines: Cafe, Coffee & Tea
Average price: Under £10
Area: City Centre
Address: 11 St James Square
Manchester M2 6WH
Phone: 07789 113334

#116
Bonbon Chocolate Boutique
Cuisines: Cafe, Chocolatiers
Average price: £11-25
Area: Northern Quarter
Address: 9 John Street
Manchester M4 1EQ
Phone: 0161 839 4416

#117
Pancho's Burritos
Cuisines: Mexican, Street Vendors
Average price: Under £10
Area: Northern Quarter, City Centre
Address: 49 High St
Manchester M4 3AH
Phone: 07947 976346

#118
On the Corner
Cuisines: Sandwiches, Cafe, Desserts
Average price: £11-25
Area: Chorlton
Address: 93 Beech Road
Manchester M21 9EQ
Phone: 0161 881 4841

#119
Moose Coffee
Cuisines: American, Coffee & Tea,
Breakfast & Brunch
Average price: £11-25
Area: City Centre
Address: 20 York Street
Manchester M2 3BB
Phone: 0161 228 7994

#120
Laughing Buddha
Cuisines: Chinese, Fast Food, Takeaway
Average price: £11-25
Area: Didsbury Village
Address: 782 Wilmslow Rd
Manchester M20 2DJ
Phone: 0871 963 2865

#121
Red Chilli Chinese Restaurant
Cuisines: Chinese
Average price: £11-25
Area: Oxford Road Corridor
Address: 403-419 Oxford Road
Manchester M13 9WL
Phone: 0161 273 1288

#122
Japan Deli/Little Samsi
Cuisines: Japanese, Sushi Bar,
Delicatessen
Average price: £11-25
Area: West Didsbury
Address: 521 Wilmslow Road
Manchester M20 4BA
Phone: 0161 445 9205

#123
Buzzrocks Caribbean Caterers
Cuisines: Caribbean
Average price: Under £10
Address: 166 Stretford Road
Manchester M15 5TL
Phone: 0161 227 7770

#124
Vnam
Cuisines: Vietnamese, Chinese, Thai
Average price: £11-25
Area: Ancoats, Petersfield
Address: 140 Oldham Road
Manchester M4 6BG
Phone: 0161 205 2700

#125
**Great Kathmandu Tandoori
Restaurant**
Cuisines: Indian, Pakistani
Average price: £11-25
Area: West Didsbury
Address: 140 Burton Road
Manchester M20 1JQ
Phone: 0161 445 2145

#126
Yang Sing
Cuisines: Chinese
Average price: £26-45
Address: 34 Princess Street
Manchester M1 4JY
Phone: 0161 236 2200

#127
La Tasca Restaurant
Cuisines: Spanish, Tapas
Average price: £11-25
Area: City Centre
Address: 76 Deansgate
Manchester M3 2FW
Phone: 0161 834 8234

#128
Albert's Shed
Cuisines: Italian, British, Gastropub
Average price: £26-45
Area: Castlefield
Address: 20 Castle Street
Manchester M3 4LZ
Phone: 0161 839 9818

#129
St. Petersburg
Cuisines: Russian, Greek
Average price: £11-25
Area: Gay Village
Address: 68 Sackville Street
Manchester M1 3NJ
Phone: 0161 236 6333

#130
The Albert Square Chop House
Cuisines: British, Pub
Average price: £26-45
Address: Albert Square
Manchester M2 5PF
Phone: 0161 834 1866

#131
Gordon's Kitchen
Cuisines: Chinese, Fast Food, Takeaway
Average price: Under £10
Address: 293 Chester Rd
Manchester M15 4EY
Phone: 0161 839 3836

#132
Rice
Cuisines: Fast Food, Takeaway, Asian
Fusion, Indonesian
Average price: £11-25
Area: Oxford Road Corridor
Address: Oxford Road
Manchester M1 5QS
Phone: 0161 237 1570

#133
Zinc Bar and Grill
Cuisines: British, Bar, American
Average price: £26-45
Area: City Centre
Address: The Triangle
Manchester M4 3TR
Phone: 0161 827 4200

#134
Lal Qila
Cuisines: Indian, Pakistani
Average price: £11-25
Area: Rusholme
Address: 123-127 Wilmslow Road
Manchester M14 5
Phone: 0161 224 9999

#135
The Rose Garden
Cuisines: British
Average price: Above £46
Area: West Didsbury
Address: 218 Burton Road
Manchester M20 2LW
Phone: 0161 478 0747

#136
The Grill on New York Street
Cuisines: Steakhouse, British
Average price: £26-45
Area: Chinatown, City Centre
Address: New York St
Manchester M1 4BD
Phone: 0161 238 9790

#137
Albert's
Cuisines: British
Average price: Above £46
Area: West Didsbury
Address: 120-122 Barlow Moor Road
Manchester M20 2PU
Phone: 0161 434 8289

#138
On The 8th Day
Cuisines: Health Food, Cafe
Average price: £11-25
Area: Oxford Road Corridor
Address: 111 Oxford Road
Manchester M1 7DU
Phone: 0161 273 4878

#139
Felicini
Cuisines: Italian, Wine Bar, Pizza
Average price: £11-25
Address: 60 Oxford Street
Manchester M1 5EE
Phone: 0161 228 6633

#140
**Beautiful British Butty
and Portland Plaice**
Cuisines: Takeaway, Fish & Chips
Average price: Under £10
Area: Chinatown
Address: 88 Portland Street
Manchester M1 4GX
Phone: 0161 237 1002

#141
Yadgar Cafe
Cuisines: Indian, Pakistani
Average price: Under £10
Area: Northern Quarter
Address: 71 Thomas Street
Manchester M4 1ES
Phone: 0161 831 7753

#142
Eastern Bloc Records
Cuisines: Music Venues, Cafe
Average price: £11-25
Area: Northern Quarter
Address: 5A Stevenson Square
Manchester M1 1DN
Phone: 0161 228 6555

#143
Hard Rock Cafe
Cuisines: American, Bar
Average price: £11-25
Area: City Centre
Address: 27 Withy Grove
Manchester M4 2BS
Phone: 0161 831 6700

#144
Nando's
Cuisines: Portuguese, Chicken Wings
Average price: £11-25
Area: Oxford Road Corridor
Address: 3 Chester Street
Manchester M1 5QS
Phone: 0161 236 5600

#145
Moonlight
Cuisines: Takeaway, Sweet Shop
Average price: Under £10
Area: Rusholme
Address: 75 Wilmslow Road
Manchester M14 5TB
Phone: 0161 248 9327

#146
Blue Ginger
Cuisines: Chinese, Fast Food, Takeaway
Average price: £11-25
Area: Oxford Road Corridor
Address: Chester Street
Manchester M1 5QS
Phone: 0161 235 0700

#147
Choice
Cuisines: British
Average price: £26-45
Area: Castlefield
Address: Castle Quay
Manchester M15 4NT
Phone: 0161 833 3400

#148
Revolucion De Cuba
Cuisines: Club, Cuban, Cocktail Bar
Average price: £26-45
Address: 11 Peter Street
Manchester M2 5QR
Phone: 0161 826 8266

#149
Velvet Bar & Restaurant
Cuisines: British, Lounge, Hotel
Average price: £11-25
Area: Gay Village
Address: 2 Canal Street
Manchester M1 3HE
Phone: 0161 236 9003

#150
Tai Wu
Cuisines: Chinese, Buffet
Average price: £11-25
Address: 44 Oxford Street
Manchester M1 5EJ
Phone: 0161 937 2853

#151
Eden Bar
Cuisines: British, Italian, Gastropub
Average price: £11-25
Area: Gay Village
Address: 3 Brazil Street
Manchester M1 3PJ
Phone: 0161 237 9852

#152
Sangam
Cuisines: Indian
Average price: £11-25
Area: Rusholme
Address: 9 Wilmslow Road
Manchester M14 5TB
Phone: 0161 225 9248

#153
Bluu
Cuisines: Lounge, British
Average price: £11-25
Area: Northern Quarter
Address: 85 High Street
Manchester M4 1BD
Phone: 0161 839 7195

#154
Black Dog Ballroom
Cuisines: Lounge, Snooker & Pool Hall
Average price: £11-25
Area: Northern Quarter
Address: 43 Oldham Street
Manchester M1 1JG
Phone: 0161 839 0664

#155
Kabana
Cuisines: Indian, Pakistani, Takeaway
Average price: Under £10
Area: Northern Quarter
Address: 52 Back Turner Street
Manchester M4 1FP
Phone: 0161 835 2447

#156
Pie and Ale
Cuisines: Specialty Food, British
Average price: £11-25
Area: Northern Quarter
Address: Lever Street
Manchester M1 1FN
Phone: 0161 228 1610

#157
Gusto
Cuisines: Italian, Bar
Average price: £11-25
Area: Didsbury Village
Address: 756 Wilmslow Road
Manchester M20 2DW
Phone: 0161 445 8209

#158
Australasia
Cuisines: Asian Fusion
Average price: £26-45
Area: Spinningfields
Address: 1 The Avenue
Manchester M3 3AP
Phone: 0161 831 0288

#159
The Bank
Cuisines: Pub, British
Average price: £11-25
Area: Chinatown, City Centre
Address: 57 Mosley Street
Manchester M2 3FF
Phone: 0872 107 7077

#160
Bem Brasil
Cuisines: Brazilian, Wine Bar
Average price: £26-45
Area: Northern Quarter
Address: 58 Lever Street
Manchester M1 1FJ
Phone: 0161 923 6888

#161
Wing's Dai Pai Dong
Cuisines: Asian Fusion, Takeaway
Average price: Under £10
Area: City Centre
Address: 49 High Street
Manchester M4 3AH
Phone: 0161 832 0088

#162
Lammars
Cuisines: Lounge, Tapas Bar
Average price: £11-25
Area: Northern Quarter
Address: 57 Hilton Street
Manchester M1 2EJ
Phone: 0161 237 9058

#163
Pizza Express
Cuisines: Pizza, Italian
Average price: £11-25
Area: City Centre
Address: 37 Hanging Ditch
Manchester M4 3TR
Phone: 0161 834 6130

#164
TGI Fridays
Cuisines: American
Average price: £26-45
Address: Cross Street
Manchester M33 7JR
Phone: 0161 962 2962

#165
The Footage
Cuisines: Pub, Burgers, Club
Average price: Under £10
Area: Oxford Road Corridor
Address: 137 Grosvenor Street
Manchester M1 7DZ
Phone: 0161 275 9164

#166
Barburrito
Cuisines: Mexican, Fast Food,
Takeaway, Food
Average price: Under £10
Area: City Centre
Address: 68 Deansgate
Manchester M3 2BW
Phone: 0161 839 1311

#167
Black Dog Ballroom NWS
Cuisines: Barbeque, Lounge,
Snooker & Pool Hall
Average price: £11-25
Area: Oxford Road Corridor
Address: 11-13 New Wakefield Street
Manchester M1 5NP
Phone: 0161 236 4899

#168
Barburrito
Cuisines: Mexican, Tex-Mex
Average price: Under £10
Address: 134 The Orient
Manchester M17 8EH
Phone: 0161 747 6165

#169
Koffee Pot
Cuisines: Cafe
Average price: £11-25
Area: Northern Quarter
Address: 21 Hilton Street
Manchester M1 1JJ

#170
The Waterhouse
Cuisines: Pub, British, Burgers
Average price: Under £10
Area: City Centre
Address: 67-71 Princess Street
Manchester M2 4EG
Phone: 0161 200 5380

#171
Persia Grill House
Cuisines: Persian/Iranian
Average price: £11-25
Area: Chorlton
Address: 255 Barlow Moor Road
Manchester M21 7GJ
Phone: 0161 860 6864

#172
Volta Eaterie & Bar
Cuisines: Gastropub, Pub
Average price: £26-45
Area: West Didsbury
Address: 167 Burton Rd
Manchester M20 2LN
Phone: 0161 448 8887

#173
Kingfisher Fish & Chips
Cuisines: Fish & Chips
Average price: Under £10
Area: Northern Quarter
Address: 43 Tib Street
Manchester M4 1LX
Phone: 0161 270 5806

#174
Moon
Cuisines: Indian
Average price: £11-25
Area: Didsbury Village
Address: 452 Wilmslow Road
Manchester M20 3BW
Phone: 0161 448 8700

#175
47 King Street West
Cuisines: Coffee & Tea, Sandwiches
Average price: £11-25
Area: City Centre
Address: 47 King Street West
Manchester M3 2PW
Phone: 0161 839 1929

#176
New Bilash Balti House
Cuisines: Indian, Pakistani
Average price: £11-25
Address: 555 Bolton Road
Manchester M27 8QT
Phone: 0161 728 5333

#177
Pacific
Cuisines: Chinese
Average price: £11-25
Area: Chinatown
Address: 58-60 George Street
Manchester M1 4HF
Phone: 0161 228 6668

#178
Lucha Libre
Cuisines: Mexican
Average price: £11-25
Address: Unit 4
Manchester M3 3HN
Phone: 0161 850 0629

#179
Carluccio's
Cuisines: Italian
Average price: £11-25
Area: Spinningfields
Address: 3 Hardman Square
Manchester M3 3EB
Phone: 0161 839 0623

#180
The Alchemist
Cuisines: American
Average price: £11-25
Area: Chinatown
Address: 1 New York Street
Manchester M1 4HD
Phone: 0161 228 3856

#181
Buffet City
Cuisines: Chinese, Buffet
Average price: Under £10
Area: Oxford Road Corridor
Address: 111 Portland Street
Manchester M1 6DN
Phone: 0161 228 3388

#182
Neighbourhood
Cuisines: American
Average price: £11-25
Area: Spinningfields
Address: Avenue North Manchester
Phone: 0161 832 6334

#183
Kim By The Sea
Cuisines: European,
Breakfast & Brunch, Bar
Average price: £11-25
Address: 49 Old Birley Street
Manchester M15 5RF
Phone: 0161 232 7667

#184
Fu's Chinese Restaurant Café
Cuisines: Chinese
Average price: £11-25
Area: Chinatown
Address: 56 Faulkner Street
Manchester M1 4FH
Phone: 0161 237 1444

#185
Thai Spice
Cuisines: Thai
Average price: £11-25
Area: Chorlton
Address: 66a Beech Road
Manchester M21 9EG
Phone: 0161 881 0400

#186
Nando's
Cuisines: Portuguese, Chicken Wings
Average price: £11-25
Area: Didsbury Village
Address: Wilmslow Road
Manchester M20 5PG
Phone: 0161 438 0054

#187
Giraffe
Cuisines: American
Average price: £11-25
Address: 136-138 The Orient
Manchester M17 8EQ
Phone: 0161 747 2100

#188
Restaurant Bar & Grill
Cuisines: British, European
Average price: £26-45
Area: City Centre
Address: 14 John Dalton Street
Manchester M2 6JP
Phone: 0161 839 1999

#189
Koh Samui
Cuisines: Thai
Average price: £11-25
Area: Chinatown
Address: 16 Princess St
Manchester M1 4NB
Phone: 0161 237 9511

#190
Tops
Cuisines: Buffet
Average price: £11-25
Area: Oxford Road Corridor
Address: 106 Portland Street
Manchester M1 4RJ
Phone: 0161 237 1000

#191
Puccini Pizzeria
Cuisines: Italian
Average price: £11-25
Address: 173 Chorley Road
Manchester M27 4AE
Phone: 0161 794 1847

#192
The Market Restaurant
Cuisines: British
Average price: £26-45
Area: Northern Quarter
Address: 104 High Street
Manchester M4 1HQ
Phone: 0161 834 3743

#193
Abdul's
Cuisines: Fast Food, Takeaway
Average price: £11-25
Area: Rusholme
Address: 121 Wilmslow Road
Manchester M14 5AN
Phone: 0161 256 2627

#194
The Rising Sun
Cuisines: Pub, British
Average price: Under £10
Address: 22 Queen Street
Manchester M2 5HX
Phone: 0161 834 1193

#195
Manchester 235
Cuisines: Gambling, Chinese, Bar
Average price: £26-45
Address: 2 Watson Street
Manchester M3 4LP
Phone: 0161 828 0300

#196
Bakery
Cuisines: Bakery, Wine Bar
Average price: £11-25
Area: Northern Quarter
Address: 43-45 Lever Street
Manchester M1 1FN
Phone: 0161 236 9014

#197
Babylon
Cuisines: Fast Food, Takeaway
Average price: Under £10
Area: Oxford Road Corridor
Address: 125 Oxford Road
Manchester M1 7DU
Phone: 0161 273 5680

#198
Umezushi
Cuisines: Japanese, Sushi Bar
Average price: £26-45
Area: City Centre
Address: Mirabel Street
Manchester M3 1PJ
Phone: 0161 832 1852

#199
Coriander
Cuisines: Indian
Average price: £11-25
Area: Chorlton
Address: 279 Barlow Moor Road
Manchester M21 7GH
Phone: 0161 881 7750

#200
Dosa Xpress
Cuisines: Indian
Average price: Under £10
Address: 19 Copson Street
Manchester M20 3HE
Phone: 0161 434 4494

#201
Frankie & Benny's UK
Cuisines: Italian
Average price: £11-25
Address: Wilmslow Road
Manchester M20 5PG
Phone: 0161 446 4140

#202
Corbieres
Cuisines: Wine Bar, Pizza, Dive Bar
Average price: Under £10
Area: City Centre
Address: 2 Half Moon Street
Manchester M2 7PB
Phone: 0161 834 3381

#203
Popolino
Cuisines: Pizza, Fast Food, Takeaway
Average price: Under £10
Area: Oxford Road Corridor
Address: 119 Oxford Road
Manchester M1 7DU
Phone: 0161 273 3335

#204
Rosso Restaurant
Cuisines: Italian, Cocktail Bar
Average price: £26-45
Area: City Centre
Address: 43 Spring Garden
Manchester M2 2BG
Phone: 0161 832 1400

#205
Tai Pan Restaurant
Cuisines: Chinese
Average price: £11-25
Area: Oxford Road Corridor
Address: 81-97 Upper Brook Street
Manchester M13 9TX
Phone: 0161 273 2798

#206
Rozafa
Cuisines: Greek, Mediterranean
Average price: £11-25
Area: City Centre
Address: 63 Princess Street
Manchester M2 4EQ
Phone: 0161 236 6389

#207
Al Faisal Tandoori
Cuisines: Indian, Pakistani, Takeaway
Average price: Under £10
Area: Northern Quarter
Address: 58 Thomas Street
Manchester M4 1EG
Phone: 0161 834 3266

#208
Café Istanbul
Cuisines: Turkish
Average price: £11-25
Area: Spinningfields, City Centre
Address: 79 Bridge Street
Manchester M3 2RH
Phone: 0161 833 9942

#209
North Star Piccadilly
Cuisines: Deli
Average price: Under £10
Area: Piccadilly
Address: 77 Dale Street
Manchester M1 2HG
Phone: 0161 237 9619

#210
Nando's
Cuisines: Portuguese, Chicken Wings
Average price: £26-45
Area: City Centre
Address: 27 Withy Grove
Manchester M4 2BS
Phone: 0161 832 0884

#211
Musicana Cafe
Cuisines: Cafe
Average price: £11-25
Area: Rusholme
Address: 10A Wilmslow Road
Manchester M14 5TP
Phone: 0161 225 1930

#212
Jamie's Italian
Cuisines: Italian
Average price: £26-45
Area: City Centre
Address: 100 King Street
Manchester M2 4WU
Phone: 0161 241 3901

#213
Nasi Lemak
Cuisines: Fast Food, Takeaway,
Malaysian, Chinese
Average price: £11-25
Area: Fallowfield
Address: 353 Wilmslow Road
Manchester M14 6XS
Phone: 0161 637 2752

#214
Azad Manzil
Cuisines: Indian, Pakistani
Average price: £11-25
Area: Chorlton
Address: 495 Barlow Moor Rd
Manchester M21 8AG
Phone: 0161 881 1021

#215
Rajdoot Restaurant
Cuisines: Indian, Pakistani
Average price: £11-25
Address: 18 Albert Square
Manchester M2 5PE
Phone: 0161 834 2176

#216
Pinchjo's
Cuisines: Spanish
Average price: £11-25
Area: West Didsbury
Address: 192 Burton Road
Manchester M20 1LH
Phone: 0161 434 2020

#217
Sanam Sweets Centre
Cuisines: Indian, Pakistani, Sweet Shop
Average price: £11-25
Area: Rusholme
Address: 169 Wilmslow Road
Manchester M14 5AP
Phone: 0161 224 3852

#218
W H Lung Cash & Carry
Cuisines: Chinese, Wholesalers
Average price: £11-25
Area: Oxford Road Corridor
Address: 97 Upper Brook Street
Manchester M13 9TX
Phone: 0161 274 3177

#219
Ithaca Manchester
Cuisines: Japanese
Average price: £26-45
Area: City Centre
Address: 36 John Dalton Street
Manchester M2 6LE
Phone: 0161 831 7409

#220
Janam Take Away Food Shop
Cuisines: Fast Food, Takeaway
Average price: Under £10
Area: Chinatown
Address: 78 Portland Street
Manchester M1 4QX
Phone: 0161 228 2485

#221
Pin-Up Bowling
Cuisines: Bowling Alley,
Desserts, Burgers
Average price: £11-25
Area: Spinningfields
Address: 1 Hardman Square
Manchester M3 3EB
Phone: 07585 890023

#222
Salvi's Mozzarella Bar
Cuisines: Delicatessen, Italian
Average price: £11-25
Area: City Centre
Address: Unit 22b
Manchester M4 3TR
Phone: 0161 222 8021

#223
Fresh Loaf
Cuisines: Fast Food, Takeaway,
Coffee & Tea
Average price: Under £10
Area: Northern Quarter
Address: 2 Central Buildings
Manchester M1 1JQ
Phone: 0161 228 7899

#224
Nafees Take Away Food Shop
Cuisines: Fast Food, Takeaway, Indian
Average price: Under £10
Area: Levenshulme
Address: 616 Stockport Road
Manchester M13 0RQ
Phone: 0161 225 6652

#225
Wok & Flame
Cuisines: Chinese, Fast Food, Takeaway
Average price: £11-25
Area: West Didsbury
Address: 206 Burton Road
Manchester M20 2LW
Phone: 0161 434 6318

#226
Dilshad Tandoori Restaurant
Cuisines: Ethiopian, Indian, Pakistani
Average price: £11-25
Address: 385 Hollinwood Avenue
Manchester M40 0JQ
Phone: 0161 681 2204

#227
Rosylee Tearoom
Cuisines: British, Coffee & Tea,
Breakfast & Brunch, Tea Room
Average price: £11-25
Area: Northern Quarter
Address: 11 Stevenson Square
Manchester M1 1DB
Phone: 0161 228 6629

#228
Moon Under Water
Cuisines: Pub, British
Average price: Under £10
Area: City Centre
Address: 68-74 Deansgate
Manchester M3 2FN
Phone: 0161 834 5882

#229
The Font
Cuisines: Lounge, Burgers
Average price: Under £10
Area: Fallowfield
Address: 236 Wilmslow Road
Manchester M14 6LE
Phone: 0161 248 4820

#230
Pizza Express
Cuisines: Pizza, Italian
Average price: £11-25
Address: 56 Peter Street
Manchester M2 3NQ
Phone: 0161 839 9300

#231
Sandinista
Cuisines: Tapas Bar, Lounge
Average price: £11-25
Area: City Centre
Address: 2 Old Bank Street
Manchester M2 7PF
Phone: 0161 832 9955

#232
Atlas Bar
Cuisines: Wine Bar, British,
Breakfast & Brunch
Average price: £11-25
Address: 376 Deansgate
Manchester M3 4LY
Phone: 0161 834 2124

#233
Saajan
Cuisines: Indian
Average price: Under £10
Area: Fallowfield
Address: 316 Wilmslow Road
Manchester M14 6XQ
Phone: 0161 248 4944

#234
Taco Bell
Cuisines: Mexican, Food Court,
Fast Food, Takeaway
Average price: Under £10
Area: City Centre
Address: Manchester Arndale Food Court
Manchester M4 3AQ

#235
Mary & Archie
Cuisines: British, Pub, Gastropub
Average price: £11-25
Area: West Didsbury
Address: 200 Burton Rd
Manchester M20 2LW
Phone: 0161 445 3130

#236
Paan House
Cuisines: Indian, Pakistani
Average price: £11-25
Address: 29 Ayres Road
Manchester M16 9WA
Phone: 0161 226 0518

#237
The Village Restaurant
Cuisines: Indian, Pakistani
Average price: £11-25
Area: Rusholme
Address: 97 Wilmslow Road
Manchester M14 5SU
Phone: 0161 225 2614

#238
Anand's Vegetarian Deli
Cuisines: Deli, Indian, Fast Food,
Takeaway
Average price: Under £10
Area: Rusholme
Address: 217 Wilmslow Road
Manchester M14 5AG
Phone: 0161 225 6742

#239
Hickson & Black's
Cuisines: Cheese Shop,
Butcher, Sandwiches
Average price: £26-45
Area: Chorlton
Address: 559 Barlow Moor Road
Manchester M21 8AN
Phone: 0161 881 2001

#240
The Whim Wham Cafe
Cuisines: Jazz & Blues, Bar, British
Average price: £11-25
Address: Arch 64 Whitworth Street West
Manchester M1 5WQ
Phone: 0161 236 0930

#241
Loco Express
Cuisines: Indian, Fast Food, Takeaway
Average price: £11-25
Area: Oxford Road Corridor
Address: 65 Arches Manchester M1 5WQ
Phone: 0161 237 3949

#242
Chunky Chicken
Cuisines: Fast Food, Takeaway
Average price: Under £10
Area: Rusholme
Address: 106 Wilmslow Road
Manchester M14 5AJ
Phone: 0161 248 9709

#243
Aladdin Restaurant
Cuisines: Middle Eastern
Average price: £11-25
Area: West Didsbury
Address: 529 Wilmslow Road
Manchester M20 4BA
Phone: 0161 434 8558

#244
Giovanni's Deli
Cuisines: Tea Room, Sandwiches
Average price: Under £10
Area: Gay Village
Address: 1 Pine Street
Manchester M1 4DY
Phone: 0161 228 7400

#245
International Society
Cuisines: University, Diner
Average price: Under £10
Area: Oxford Road Corridor
Address: 327 Oxford Road
Manchester M13 9PG
Phone: 0161 275 4959

#246
San Rocco
Cuisines: Italian, Mediterranean
Average price: £11-25
Address: 96 Bury Old Road
Manchester M8 5BW
Phone: 0161 795 5300

#247
Artisan
Cuisines: British
Average price: £11-25
Area: Spinningfields
Address: 22-28 Bridge Street
Manchester M3 3AB

#248
Dixy Chicken
Cuisines: Fast Food, Takeaway,
Chicken Wings
Average price: Under £10
Area: Fallowfield
Address: Wilbraham Road
Manchester M14 6JS
Phone: 0161 224 5577

#249
Paradise Take Away
Cuisines: Fast Food, Takeaway
Average price: Under £10
Area: Levenshulme
Address: 600 Stockport Road
Manchester M13 0RQ
Phone: 0161 225 1931

#250
Kukoos Street Food
Cuisines: Halal, Moroccan
Average price: Under £10
Area: Oxford Road Corridor
Address: 12A Oxford Road
Manchester M1 5QA
Phone: 0161 235 8536

#251
Chicken King
Cuisines: Fast Food, Takeaway,
Chicken Wings
Average price: Under £10
Area: Fallowfield
Address: 316 Wilmslow Road
Manchester M14 6
Phone: 0161 248 8989

#252
Panacea
Cuisines: Champagne Bar, British
Average price: Above £46
Area: City Centre
Address: 14 John Dalton St
Manchester M2 6JP
Phone: 0161 833 1111

#253
Continental
Cuisines: Fast Food, Takeaway
Average price: Under £10
Area: West Didsbury
Address: 127 Burton Road
Manchester M20 1JP
Phone: 0161 445 0560

#254
The Living Room
Cuisines: Wine Bar, British, Club
Average price: £26-45
Area: City Centre
Address: 80 Deansgate
Manchester M3 2ER
Phone: 0161 832 0083

#255
Grand Pacific
Cuisines: Asian Fusion, Bar
Average price: Above £46
Area: Oldham
Address: 1 The Avenue
Manchester M3 3AP
Phone: 0161 831 0288

#256
Harvey Nichols
Cuisines: British, Bar, Brasserie
Average price: Above £46
Area: City Centre
Address: 21 New Cathedral Street
Manchester M1 1AD
Phone: 0161 828 8898

#257
Zizzi's
Cuisines: Italian
Average price: £11-25
Area: Spinningfields
Address: Left Bank Spinningfields
Manchester M3 3AN
Phone: 0161 839 7984

#258
Patisserie Valerie
Cuisines: Bakery, French, Desserts
Average price: £26-45
Area: City Centre
Address: 2-4 St Ann Street
Manchester M2 7
Phone: 0161 839 9116

#259
The Bay Horse
Cuisines: Pub, Salad, Hot Dogs
Average price: £11-25
Area: Northern Quarter
Address: 35-37 Thomas Street
Manchester M4 1NA
Phone: 0161 661 1041

#260
Tampopo
Cuisines: Vietnamese, Thai
Average price: £11-25
Address: 135 The Orient
Manchester M17 8EH
Phone: 0161 747 8878

#261
Prohibition
Cuisines: Lounge, British
Average price: £11-25
Area: City Centre
Address: 2-10 St Mary's St
Manchester M3 2LB
Phone: 0161 831 9326

#262
Red Hot World Buffet
Cuisines: Buffet, Chinese, Indian
Average price: £11-25
Area: City Centre
Address: 48 Deansgate
Manchester M3 2EG
Phone: 0161 819 1240

#263
Hunters BBQ & Asian Take Away
Cuisines: American, Asian Fusion,
Fast Food, Takeaway
Average price: Under £10
Area: Northern Quarter
Address: 94 High Street
Manchester M4 1EF
Phone: 0161 839 5060

#264
Petra
Cuisines: Greek, Indian, Mediterranean
Average price: £11-25
Area: Oxford Road Corridor
Address: 267 Upper Brook Street
Manchester M13 0HR
Phone: 0161 274 4441

#265
Philpotts
Cuisines: Fast Food, Takeaway
Average price: £26-45
Area: Oxford Road Corridor
Address: 131 Portland Street
Manchester M1 4PY
Phone: 0161 923 6969

#266
Wetherspoons
Cuisines: Pub, British
Average price: £11-25
Area: Northern Quarter
Address: 49 Piccadilly
Manchester M1 2AP
Phone: 0161 236 9206

#267
The Piccadilly
Cuisines: British, Breakfast & Brunch
Average price: £11-25
Area: Northern Quarter
Address: 60 - 75 Piccadilly
Manchester M1 2BS
Phone: 0872 107 7077

#268
Frankie & Benny's
Cuisines: Italian
Average price: Above £46
Address: Trafford Centre
Manchester M17 8WW
Phone: 0161 747 1600

#269
Cafe Rouge
Cuisines: Cafe
Average price: £11-25
Address: 137 The Orient
Manchester M7 4TB
Phone: 0161 747 1927

#270
Woo Sang
Cuisines: Supermarket, Chinese
Average price: £11-25
Area: Chinatown
Address: 19-21 George Street
Manchester M1 4HE
Phone: 0161 236 4353

#271
Viet Shack
Cuisines: Vietnamese
Average price: Under £10
Area: Northern Quarter
Address: 49-61 High Street
Manchester M4

#272
Sweet Box
Cuisines: Sweet Shop, Juice Bar,
Ice Cream, Fast Food, Takeaway
Average price: £11-25
Area: Rusholme
Address: 155 - 157 Wilmslow Road
Manchester M14 5A
Phone: 0161 248 9760

#273
Sindhoor
Cuisines: Indian
Average price: £11-25
Address: 198-200 Mauldeth Rd
Manchester M19 1AJ
Phone: 0161 432 5246

#274
Cafe Rouge
Cuisines: Coffee & Tea, French
Average price: £26-45
Area: Didsbury Village
Address: 651 - 653 Unit D 651-653
Wilmslow Road
Manchester M20 6QZ
Phone: 0161 438 0444

#275
La Tasca
Cuisines: Spanish, Basque, Tapas
Average price: £11-25
Area: Didsbury Village
Address: Warburton Street
Manchester M20 6WA
Phone: 0161 438 0044

#276
Abergeldie Cafe
Cuisines: Coffee & Tea,
Fish & Chips, Pizza
Average price: £11-25
Area: Northern Quarter
Address: 40 Shudehill
Manchester M4 1EZ
Phone: 0161 834 5548

#277
Cuba Cafe
Cuisines: Cuban
Average price: £11-25
Area: Northern Quarter
Address: 43 Port St
Manchester M1 2EQ
Phone: 0161 236 3630

#278
Chilli Peri Chicken
Cuisines: Fast Food, Takeaway
Average price: Under £10
Area: Rusholme
Address: 120 Wilmslow Road
Manchester M14 5AH

#279
Sadaf Halaal
Cuisines: Fast Food, Takeaway
Average price: Under £10
Area: Rusholme
Address: 167 Wilmslow Road
Manchester M14 5AP
Phone: 0161 257 3557

#280
The Baths Supper Bar
Cuisines: Fish & Chips
Average price: £11-25
Area: Chorlton
Address: 113 Manchester Rd
Manchester M21 9PG
Phone: 0161 881 5104

#281
Treasure Pot
Cuisines: Chinese, Fast Food, Takeaway
Average price: £11-25
Area: Chorlton
Address: 101 Manchester Road
Manchester M21 9GA
Phone: 0161 881 3609

#282
Namaste Nepal
Cuisines: Himalayan/Nepalese, Indian
Average price: £26-45
Area: West Didsbury
Address: 164-166 Burton Road
Manchester M20 1LH
Phone: 0161 445 9060

#283
Persian Tasty Grill
Cuisines: Persian/Iranian
Average price: Under £10
Area: Levenshulme
Address: Stockport Road
Manchester M19 2

#284
Loaf
Cuisines: Wine Bar, British
Average price: Above £46
Address: Deansgate Locks
Manchester M1 5LH
Phone: 0161 819 5858

#285
Williams Sandwich Bar
Cuisines: Fast Food, Takeaway,
Coffee & Tea, Deli
Average price: Under £10
Area: Northern Quarter
Address: 45 Hilton Street
Manchester M1 2EF
Phone: 0161 236 1833

#286
Cedar Tree
Cuisines: British
Average price: £11-25
Area: Stockport
Address: 64 Middle Hillgate
Manchester SK1 3EH
Phone: 0161 480 0028

#287
Hadramout
Cuisines: Takeaway, Middle Eastern
Average price: £11-25
Area: Rusholme
Address: 1 Walmar Street East
Manchester M14 5SS
Phone: 0161 248 8843

#288
Thaikhun
Cuisines: Thai
Average price: £11-25
Area: Spinningfields
Address: 3 Hardman Street The Avenue
Manchester M3 3EB
Phone: 0161 819 2065

#289
Genting Club
Cuisines: Lounge, Sandwiches
Average price: £26-45
Area: Oxford Road Corridor
Address: 110 Portland Street
Manchester M1 4RL
Phone: 0161 228 0077

#290
Turtle Bay
Cuisines: Caribbean
Average price: £11-25
Area: Chinatown
Address: 33-35 Oxford St
Manchester M1 4BH

#291
Vivid Lounge
Cuisines: Coffee & Tea,
Sandwiches, Thai
Average price: £11-25
Area: Ancoats, Petersfield
Address: 149A Great Ancoats Street
Manchester M4 6DH
Phone: 0161 272 8474

#292
Bar San Juan
Cuisines: Spanish
Average price: £11-25
Area: Chorlton
Address: 56 Beech Road
Manchester M21 9EG
Phone: 0161 881 9259

#293
Jazera Charcoal Cuisine
Cuisines: Middle Eastern
Average price: Under £10
Area: Rusholme
Address: 22 Wilmslow Rd
Manchester M14 5TQ
Phone: 0161 257 3337

#294
Shahi Masala
Cuisines: Indian
Average price: £26-45
Area: Rusholme
Address: 16-18 Wilmslow Road
Manchester M14 5TQ
Phone: 0161 248 8344

#295
Zam Zam Tandoori
Cuisines: Indian, Fast Food, Takeaway
Average price: Under £10
Area: Chorlton
Address: 452 Wilborougham Road
Manchester M21 0AG
Phone: 0161 862 0999

#296
Canada Grill
Cuisines: Fast Food, Takeaway
Average price: Under £10
Area: Chorlton
Address: 613A Wilbraham Road
Manchester M21 9AN
Phone: 0161 881 1205

#297
Pinto's
Cuisines: Cafe, British
Average price: £11-25
Address: 3 Fairfax Road
Manchester M25
Phone: 0161 773 4774

#298
Armstrongs
Cuisines: Fish & Chips,
Fast Food, Takeaway
Average price: £11-25
Address: 486 Bury Old Road
Manchester M25 1NL
Phone: 0161 773 6023

#299
Ambiente
Cuisines: Spanish, Tapas Bar
Average price: £26-45
Address: 4b Worsley Road
Manchester M28 2NL
Phone: 0161 793 6003

#300
The Bar
Cuisines: Bar, British
Average price: £11-25
Area: Chorlton
Address: 533 Wilbraham Rd
Manchester M21 0UE
Phone: 0161 861 7576

#301
La Roma Restaurant
Cuisines: Italian
Average price: £11-25
Area: Bolton
Address: Ringley Road
Manchester M26 1GT
Phone: 01204 707932

#302
Tandle Hill Tavern
Cuisines: Pub, British
Average price: Under £10
Area: Oldham
Address: 14 Thornham Lane
Manchester M24 2SD
Phone: 01706 345297

#303
Chiquito
Cuisines: Mexican, Spanish
Average price: £11-25
Area: City Centre
Address: The Printworks
Manchester M4 2BS
Phone: 0161 830 1560

#304
The Slug & Lettuce
Cuisines: Wine Bar, Lounge, European
Average price: £11-25
Area: Spinningfields
Address: Left Bank Irwell Square
Manchester M3 3AN
Phone: 0845 126 2915

#305
By The Slice
Cuisines: Fast Food, Takeaway, Pizza
Average price: Under £10
Area: City Centre
Address: 2 Chapel Street
Manchester M3 7WJ
Phone: 0161 832 5553

#306
Bouzouki Restaurant
Cuisines: Greek, Mediterranean
Average price: £11-25
Area: Oxford Road Corridor
Address: 88 Princess Street
Manchester M1 6NG
Phone: 0161 236 9282

#307
Smoak Bar & Grill
Cuisines: Steakhouse
Average price: Above £46
Area: Piccadilly
Address: Smoak Bar & Grill at Malmaison
Manchester M1 1LZ
Phone: 0161 278 1000

#308
Baekdu
Cuisines: Korean
Average price: £11-25
Area: City Centre
Address: 77 Shudehill
Manchester M4 4AN
Phone: 0161 834 2227

#309
Subway
Cuisines: Sandwiches
Average price: Under £10
Area: Oxford Road Corridor
Address: 149 Oxford Road
Manchester M13 9DJ
Phone: 0161 273 8573

#310
Gemini Takeaway
Cuisines: Takeaway, Pizza, Chicken Wings
Average price: Under £10
Area: Oxford Road Corridor
Address: 308-310 Oxford Road
Manchester M13 9NS
Phone: 0161 273 3201

#311
Abdul's
Cuisines: Indian, Pakistani,
Fast Food, Takeaway
Average price: £11-25
Area: Oxford Road Corridor
Address: 133-135 Oxford Rd
Manchester M1 7DY
Phone: 0161 273 7339

#312
Byron
Cuisines: Burgers
Average price: £26-45
Address: 115 Deansgate
Manchester M3 2NW
Phone: 0161 832 1222

#313
The Paramount
Cuisines: Pub, Burgers
Average price: Under £10
Area: Oxford Road Corridor
Address: 33-35 Oxford Street
Manchester M1 4BH
Phone: 0161 233 1820

#314
The B Lounge
Cuisines: Pub, European
Average price: £11-25
Area: Piccadilly
Address: 97 Piccadilly
Manchester M1 2DB
Phone: 0161 236 4161

#315
Sanam Sweethouse
Cuisines: Indian, Pakistani, Sweet Shop
Average price: Under £10
Area: Rusholme
Address: 145-151 Wilmslow Road
Manchester M14 5AW
Phone: 0161 224 8824

#316
Noddys Take Away Food Shop
Cuisines: Fast Food, Takeaway
Average price: Under £10
Area: West Didsbury
Address: 573 Wilmslow Road
Manchester M20 3QH
Phone: 0161 434 7600

#317
Kashmiri Spice
Cuisines: Indian
Average price: Under £10
Address: 259 Kingsway
Manchester M19 1AN
Phone: 0161 442 3000

#318
Crazy Cow
Cuisines: Breakfast & Brunch
Average price: £11-25
Area: East Didsbury
Address: 837 Wilmslow Rd
Manchester M20 5WD
Phone: 0161 215 0325

#319
Couture Cafe Bar
Cuisines: Cafe, Coffee & Tea
Average price: £11-25
Area: Oxford Road Corridor
Address: 250 Oxford Road
Manchester M13 9PL
Phone: 0161 275 2675

#320
Changos Burrito Bar
Cuisines: Mexican
Average price: Under £10
Area: Oxford Road Corridor
Address: Oxford Street
Manchester M1 6FQ
Phone: 0161 228 2182

#321
Abduls
Cuisines: Fast Food, Takeaway
Average price: Under £10
Area: Fallowfield
Address: 318 Wilmslow Road
Manchester M14 6XQ
Phone: 0161 248 7573

#322
Croma
Cuisines: Pizza, Italian
Average price: £11-25
Area: Chorlton
Address: 500 Wilbraham Road
Manchester M21 9AP
Phone: 0161 881 1117

#323
Las Iguanas
Cuisines: Lounge, Latin American
Average price: £11-25
Area: City Centre
Address: 84 Deansgate
Manchester M3 2ER
Phone: 0161 819 2606

#324
Subway
Cuisines: Sandwiches
Average price: Under £10
Address: 49 Peter Street
Manchester M2 3NG
Phone: 0161 835 1982

#325
Swadesh
Cuisines: Indian
Average price: £11-25
Area: Chinatown
Address: 98 Portland Street
Manchester M1 4GX
Phone: 0161 236 1313

#326
Happy Seasons
Cuisines: Chinese
Average price: £11-25
Area: Chinatown
Address: 59 Faulkner Street
Manchester M1 4FF
Phone: 0161 236 7189

#327
Tusk
Cuisines: Burgers
Average price: £11-25
Area: Northern Quarter
Address: 78-88 High Street
Manchester M4 1ES
Phone: 0161 828 8700

#328
Saffron
Cuisines: Indian, Pakistani, Buffet
Average price: £11-25
Address: 107 Cheetham Hill Road
Manchester M8 8PY
Phone: 0161 834 1222

#329
KFC
Cuisines: American, Fast Food, Takeaway
Average price: Under £10
Area: Rusholme
Address: Arndale Centre
Manchester M1

#330
The Cod Father
Cuisines: Fish & Chips, British
Average price: Under £10
Area: Fallowfield
Address: 331 Wilmslow Road
Manchester M14 6NW
Phone: 0161 248 9719

#331
Lucky Star
Cuisines: Fast Food, Takeaway
Average price: £11-25
Address: 68 Mauldeth Rd W
Manchester M20 3FQ
Phone: 0161 434 6983

#332
Pacifica Cantonese
Cuisines: Chinese
Average price: £11-25
Address: 5-7 Church Road
Manchester M30 0DL
Phone: 0161 707 8828

#333
Langley Friery
Cuisines: Fish & Chips
Average price: Under £10
Address: 227 Wood Street
Manchester M24 5RA
Phone: 0161 653 6431

#334
Crazy Wendy's
Cuisines: Thai
Average price: £26-45
Area: West Didsbury
Address: 210 Burton Road
Manchester M20 2LW
Phone: 0161 445 5200

#335
Chopsticks Chinese Restaurant
Cuisines: Chinese, Fast Food, Takeaway
Average price: £11-25
Address: 161-169 Chorley Road
Manchester M27 4AE
Phone: 0161 727 9999

#336
Saigon Lotus
Cuisines: Vietnamese, Asian Fusion
Average price: Under £10
Area: Ancoats, Petersfield
Address: 146 Oldham Road
Manchester M4 6BG
Phone: 0161 914 6777

#337
Carluccio's
Cuisines: Italian
Average price: £11-25
Area: Piccadilly
Address: London Road Manchester M1

#338
Doops Coffee House
Cuisines: Coffee & Tea, Sandwiches
Average price: £11-25
Address: 63 Peter Street
Manchester M2 3
Phone: 0161 819 5678

#339
Atlas Shawarma
Cuisines: Fast Food, Takeaway,
Middle Eastern
Average price: Under £10
Area: Rusholme
Address: Manchester M14 5AH
Phone: 07874 675347

#340
Harry Ramsden's
Cuisines: British
Average price: £11-25
Area: Salford Quays
Address: Unit 5 Castlemore Retail Park
Manchester M16 0SN
Phone: 0161 873 8017

#341
Islamabad Grill
Cuisines: Indian
Average price: Under £10
Area: Rusholme
Address: 199-201 Wilmslow Road
Manchester M14 5AQ
Phone: 0161 257 3890

#342
The Post Box
Cuisines: Cafe
Average price: Under £10
Area: Chorlton
Address: 543 Wilbraham Road
Manchester M21 9PP
Phone: 0161 881 4853

#343
Olive & Thyme
Cuisines: Mediterranean
Average price: £26-45
Area: Chorlton
Address: 416-418 Barlow Moor Road
Manchester M21 8AD
Phone: 0161 881 6695

#344
Shans Takeaway
Cuisines: Fast Food, Takeaway
Average price: Under £10
Area: Fallowfield
Address: 312 Wilmslow Road
Manchester M14 6XQ
Phone: 0161 256 4358

#345
Peking Chef
Cuisines: Chinese
Average price: £11-25
Address: 208 Mauldeth Road
Manchester M19 1AJ

#346
University V Grills
Cuisines: Breakfast & Brunch, Greek
Average price: Under £10
Area: Oxford Road Corridor
Address: 12 Oxford Road
Manchester M13 9RN
Phone: 0161 273 2551

#347
Veggie Kitchen
Cuisines: British
Average price: Under £10
Area: Northern Quarter
Address: Piccadilly Garden
Manchester M1 1RG

#348
Mughal Taste
Cuisines: Indian, Pakistani
Average price: Under £10
Address: 53 Bury New Road
Manchester M8 8FX
Phone: 0161 832 0636

#349
Hong Kong Chippy
Cuisines: Fish & Chips
Average price: Under £10
Address: 149 Henrietta Street
Manchester M16 9PS
Phone: 0161 226 4083

#350
Delights
Cuisines: Halal
Average price: Under £10
Area: Rusholme
Address: 72 Wilmslow Road
Manchester M14 5AL
Phone: 0161 224 1555

#351
Jasmine
Cuisines: Arabian
Average price: £11-25
Area: Chorlton
Address: 569 Barlow Moor Road
Manchester M21 8AE
Phone: 0161 881 1442

#352
Zains Krispy Chicken
Cuisines: Fast Food, Takeaway
Average price: Under £10
Area: Rusholme
Address: 113 Wilmslow Rd
Manchester M14 5AN
Phone: 0161 224 4675

#353
Saajan
Cuisines: Indian
Average price: Under £10
Area: Rusholme
Address: 129 Wilmslow Road
Manchester M14 5AW
Phone: 0161 256 3070

#354
Karim's Orient Experience Restaurant
Cuisines: Asian Fusion
Average price: £26-45
Address: 382 Heywood Old Road
Manchester M24
Phone: 0161 653 6677

#355
Smiths
Cuisines: French
Average price: £11-25
Address: 1 Church Road
Manchester M30 0DL
Phone: 0161 788 7343

#356
Shiraz
Cuisines: Persian/Iranian
Average price: £11-25
Address: 299 Palatine Road
Manchester M22 4HH
Phone: 0161 945 8080

#357
Woodhouse Garden Inn
Cuisines: Pub, British
Average price: £26-45
Address: 48 Medlock Road
Manchester M35 9WN
Phone: 0161 681 3782

#358
Khan Saab
Cuisines: Indian, Pakistani
Average price: £11-25
Address: 117 Bury New Road
Manchester M45 6AA
Phone: 0161 766 2148

#359
Tung Fong
Cuisines: Chinese
Average price: £26-45
Address: 2 Worsley Road
Manchester M28 2NL
Phone: 0161 794 5331

#360
Shabaz Indian Take Away
Cuisines: Fast Food, Takeaway
Average price: £11-25
Address: 5 Rufford Parade
Manchester M45 8PL
Phone: 0161 796 1969

#361
Hills Traditional
Cuisines: Fish & Chips
Average price: Under £10
Area: Oldham
Address: 331 Oldham Road
Manchester M24 2DN
Phone: 0161 654 0299

#362
Spice House
Cuisines: Fast Food, Takeaway
Average price: £11-25
Address: 27 Spark Road
Manchester M23 1DQ
Phone: 0161 998 3080

#363
Spicy Hut Restaurant
Cuisines: Indian, Pakistani
Average price: £11-25
Area: Rusholme
Address: 35 Wilmslow Road
Manchester M14 5TB
Phone: 0161 248 6200

#364
Krunchy Fried Chicken
Cuisines: Fast Food, Takeaway
Average price: £11-25
Area: Rusholme
Address: 44, Wilmslow Road
Manchester M14 5TQ
Phone: 0161 256 3694

#365
Chico's Grill House
Cuisines: Fast Food, Takeaway
Average price: Under £10
Area: Longsight
Address: 185 Dickenson Road
Manchester M13 0YN
Phone: 0161 257 2576

#366
Ocean Treasure
Seafood Restaurant
Cuisines: Chinese
Average price: £26-45
Address: Greenside Way
Manchester M24 1SW
Phone: 0161 653 6688

#367
The Slug & Lettuce
Cuisines: British
Average price: £26-45
Area: City Centre
Address: 64-66 Deansgate
Manchester M3 2EN
Manchester M3 4
Phone: 0161 839 0985

#368
Siam Orchid
Cuisines: Thai, Karaoke
Average price: £11-25
Area: Chinatown
Address: 54 Portland Street
Manchester M1 4QU
Phone: 0161 236 1388

#369
Brasserie Chez Gerard
Cuisines: British, Moroccan, French
Average price: £26-45
Address: 2-10 Albert Square
Manchester M2 5
Phone: 0161 834 7633

#370
The Beijing
Cuisines: Chinese
Average price: Under £10
Area: Chinatown
Address: 48 Portland St
Manchester M1 4QU
Phone: 0161 228 0883

#371
Dockers
Cuisines: Fish & Chips
Average price: Under £10
Area: City Centre
Address: 27 Withy Grove
Manchester M4 2BS
Phone: 0161 773997

#372
TGI Fridays
Cuisines: American, Bar, Burgers
Average price: £11-25
Area: City Centre
Address: Cross Street
Manchester M2 7DH
Phone: 0844 692 8903

#373
YeoPan's
Cuisines: Chinese, Fast Food, Takeaway
Average price: £11-25
Area: Chorlton
Address: 522 Wilbraham Road
Manchester M21 9AW
Phone: 0161 881 6888

#374
All Star Lanes
Cuisines: Bowling Alley,
American, Cocktail Bar
Average price: £11-25
Address: 235 Deansgate
Manchester M3 4EN
Phone: 0161 871 3600

#375
Duttons Manchester
Cuisines: Gastropub
Average price: £11-25
Area: City Centre
Address: 2-10 Albert Square
Manchester M2
Phone: 0161 241 6839

#376
Kitchenette
Cuisines: British
Average price: £11-25
Address: 60 Oxford Street
Manchester M1 5EE
Phone: 0161 228 6633

#377
Philpotts
Cuisines: Sandwiches
Average price: Above £46
Address: Lowry House
Manchester M2 1FB
Phone: 0161 835 2111

#378
Krispy Chicken
Cuisines: Fast Food, Takeaway
Average price: Under £10
Area: Rusholme
Address: 113 Wilmslow Road
Manchester M14 5
Phone: 0161 224 4675

#379
McDonalds
Cuisines: Fast Food, Takeaway, American
Average price: Under £10
Address: 7 The Orient
Manchester M17 8EH

#380
Café Cilantro
Cuisines: Vegetarian
Average price: £11-25
Address: 52 Beech Rd
Manchester M21 9EG
Phone: 0871 961 4821

#381
Cheese Hamlet
Cuisines: Deli, Delicatessen
Average price: £11-25
Area: Didsbury Village
Address: 706 Wilmslow Road
Manchester M20 2DW
Phone: 0161 434 4781

#382
Palace Hotel
Cuisines: Hotel, British
Average price: £26-45
Area: Oxford Road Corridor
Address: Oxford Road
Manchester M60 7HA
Phone: 0161 288 1111

#383
Cafe Lloyd
Cuisines: Fish & Chips
Average price: £11-25
Address: 16 Lloyd St
Manchester M2 5ND
Phone: 0161 835 2073

#384
Per Tutti
Cuisines: Italian
Average price: £11-25
Area: Castlefield
Address: 3-11 Liverpool Road
Manchester M3 4NW
Phone: 0161 834 9741

#385
Papa G's
Cuisines: Greek
Average price: £11-25
Area: City Centre
Address: 27 Withy Grove
Manchester M4 2BS
Phone: 0161 834 8668

#386
Lass O'Gowrie
Cuisines: British, Pub
Average price: Under £10
Area: Gay Village
Address: 36 Charles Street
Manchester M1 7DB
Phone: 0161 273 6932

#387
Wood Wine & Deli
Cuisines: Wine Bar, Deli, Delicatessen
Average price: £11-25
Area: Northern Quarter
Address: 44 Tib Street
Manchester M4 1LA
Phone: 0161 478 7100

#388
Wing's
Cuisines: Chinese, Fast Food, Takeaway
Average price: Under £10
Area: City Centre
Address: Arndale Food Court
Manchester M4 3AQ
Phone: 0161 834 9000

#389
Subway
Cuisines: Fast Food, Takeaway
Average price: Under £10
Area: Longsight
Address: Manchester Arndale
Manchester M4 3AB
Phone: 04416 1835 9179

#390
Urban Spice
Cuisines: Fast Food, Takeaway
Average price: Under £10
Area: Oxford Road Corridor
Address: 70 Hathersage Road
Manchester M13 0FN
Phone: 0161 248 9773

#391
Fish Bait Fish Bar
Cuisines: Fish & Chips
Average price: Under £10
Area: West Didsbury
Address: 178 Burton Rd
Manchester M20 1LH
Phone: 0161 448 0128

#392
Due Fratelli
Cuisines: Fast Food, Takeaway
Average price: £11-25
Area: Chorlton
Address: 249 Barlow Moor Road
Manchester M21 7GJ
Phone: 0161 881 6444

#393
La Tasca
Cuisines: Spanish
Average price: £11-25
Address: Unit R7a The Trafford Centre
Manchester M17 8AA

#394
KFC
Cuisines: Fast Food, Takeaway,
Chicken Wings
Average price: £11-25
Address: 9 The Orient
Manchester M17 8EH
Phone: 0161 749 8012

#395
Cafe Greco
Cuisines: Italian, Sandwiches
Average price: Under £10
Area: City Centre
Address: Market Food Court
Manchester M4 3AQ

#396
Rice
Cuisines: Asian Fusion
Average price: £11-25
Address: Unit 5A The Orient
Manchester M17 8AA
Phone: 0161 755 0577

#397
The Deli on Burton Road
Cuisines: Department Stores, Sandwiches
Average price: £26-45
Area: West Didsbury
Address: BUrton Road
Manchester M20 1LH
Phone: 0161 445 2912

#398
Khan's Kebab House
Cuisines: Halal
Average price: £11-25
Address: 426 Wilmslow Road
Manchester M20 3BW
Phone: 0161 448 2700

#399
Coriander
Cuisines: Indian
Average price: Under £10
Address: 432 Wilmslow Road
Manchester M20 3BW
Phone: 0161 438 2984

#400
Ashoka Restaurant
Cuisines: Indian
Average price: £11-25
Area: Oxford Road Corridor
Address: 105-107 Portland Street
Manchester M1 6DF
Phone: 0161 228 7550

#401
La Tasca
Cuisines: Spanish
Average price: £11-25
Address: 132 The Orient
Manchester M17 8EG
Phone: 0161 749 9966

#402
TGI Fridays
Cuisines: American, Wine Bar
Average price: £11-25
Address: Valley Park Road
Manchester M25 3AJ
Phone: 0161 798 7125

#403
Leo's Fish Bar
Cuisines: Fast Food, Takeaway,
Fish & Chips
Average price: Under £10
Area: Northern Quarter
Address: 12 Oldham Street
Manchester M1 1JQ
Phone: 0161 237 3999

#404
The Great Central
Cuisines: British, Pub
Average price: Under £10
Area: Fallowfield
Address: 343 Wilmslow Road
Manchester M14 6NS
Phone: 0161 248 1740

#405
Pret A Manger
Cuisines: Coffee & Tea, Sandwiches
Average price: £26-45
Area: City Centre
Address: 27 Cross Street
Manchester M2 1WL
Phone: 020 7932 5278

#406
Cafe Rouge
Cuisines: French
Average price: £11-25
Area: City Centre
Address: Unit 1 The Printworks
Manchester M4 2BS
Phone: 0161 839 8897

#407
Beef & Pudding
Cuisines: British
Average price: £26-45
Area: City Centre
Address: 37 Booth Street
Manchester M2 4AA
Phone: 0161 237 3733

#408
Sansou
Cuisines: Cafe, Juice Bar
Average price: Under £10
Area: West Didsbury
Address: 108 Barlow Moor Road
Manchester M20 2PN
Phone: 0161 445 3192

#409
Costa Coffee
Cuisines: Cafe
Average price: Under £10
Area: Spinningfields
Address: 18-20 Bridge Street
Manchester M3 3BZ
Phone: 0161 839 7281

#410
Al Bacio
Cuisines: Italian
Average price: £26-45
Area: City Centre
Address: 10-14 S King Street
Manchester M2 6DW
Phone: 0161 832 7669

#411
24 Bar and Grill
Cuisines: Bar, British
Average price: £26-45
Area: Chinatown
Address: 24 Princess Street
Manchester M1 4LY
Phone: 0161 238 4348

#412
Portland Street Restaurant & Bar
Cuisines: Bar, British
Average price: £11-25
Area: Gay Village
Address: Portland Street
Manchester M1
Phone: 0161 246 3435

#413
Bridgewater Bistro
Cuisines: Bistro
Average price: Under £10
Address: 120 Princess Road
Manchester M15 5AT

#414
Alvinos Caribbean Takeaway and Bakery
Cuisines: Takeaway, Caribbean, Bakery
Average price: Under £10
Area: Rusholme
Address: 180 Great Western Street
Manchester M14 4LH
Phone: 0161 226 6407

#415
Chicken Run
Cuisines: Fast Food, Takeaway
Average price: Under £10
Address: 6 Yarburgh Street
Manchester M16 7FJ
Phone: 0161 226 6714

#416
Pizza Hut
Cuisines: Pizza, Italian
Average price: £11-25
Address: White City Way
Manchester M16 0RP

#417
Charcoal Chicken
Cuisines: Steakhouse
Average price: Under £10
Area: Rusholme
Address: 141-143 Wilmslow Road
Manchester M14 5AW
Phone: 0161 225 8800

#418
Shaygan Halal Take Away
Cuisines: Fast Food, Takeaway
Average price: Under £10
Area: Rusholme
Address: 159 Dickenson Road
Manchester M14 5HZ
Phone: 0161 248 5815

#419
Kebab King
Cuisines: Fast Food, Takeaway
Average price: Under £10
Address: 787 Rochdale Rd
Manchester M9 5XD
Phone: 0161 205 7991

#420
Mia's Sandwich Shop
Cuisines: Sandwiches
Average price: Under £10
Address: 1 Taylors Road
Manchester M32 0JJ
Phone: 0161 865 2188

#421
Sayuri Noodle Bar
Cuisines: Chinese, Fast Food, Takeaway
Average price: £11-25
Area: Fallowfield
Address: 351-353 Wilmslow Road
Manchester M14 6XS
Phone: 0800 061 2528

#422
Kyotoya
Cuisines: Japanese
Average price: £11-25
Address: 28 Copson Street
Manchester M20 3HB
Phone: 0161 445 2555

#423
Pizza Express
Cuisines: Pizza, Italian
Average price: £11-25
Address: 130 Bury New Road
Manchester M25 0AA
Phone: 0161 798 4794

#424
The Little Chippy
Cuisines: Fast Food, Takeaway
Average price: Under £10
Area: Levenshulme
Address: 929 Stockport Road
Manchester M19
Phone: 0161 225 9595

#425
Carluccios
Cuisines: Italian
Average price: £11-25
Address: The Great Hall
Manchester M17 8AA
Phone: 0161 747 4973

#426
Happy Garden Takeaway
Cuisines: Chinese
Average price: Under £10
Address: 304 Parrs Wood Road
Manchester M20 6JY
Phone: 0161 434 3663

#427
Bob's Fish & Chips
Cuisines: Fish & Chips
Average price: Under £10
Area: Didsbury Village
Address: 1 School Lane
Manchester M20 6SA

#428
Club Phoenix
Cuisines: Pub, Burgers
Average price: Under £10
Area: Oxford Road Corridor
Address: 1 University Precinct
Manchester M13 9RN
Phone: 0161 272 5921

#429
Windmill Carving Room
Cuisines: British
Average price: Under £10
Address: 81 Hulme Rd
Manchester M34 2WZ
Phone: 0161 320 6144

#430
La Olla Restaurant
Cuisines: Spanish
Average price: £11-25
Area: Sale
Address: 15 Northenden Road
Manchester M33 2DH
Phone: 0161 973 3000

#431
Chop Chop
Cuisines: Chinese, Fast Food,
Takeaway, Fish & Chips
Average price: £11-25
Area: Northern Quarter
Address: 50 Great Ancoats Street
Manchester M4 5AB
Phone: 0161 228 2228

#432
Label
Cuisines: Restaurants, Lounge, Club
Average price: £26-45
Area: City Centre
Address: 78 Deansgate
Manchester M3 2FW
Phone: 0161 833 1878

#433
Bistro 1847: Manchester
Cuisines: Vegetarian
Average price: £26-45
Area: City Centre
Address: 58 Mosley St
Manchester M2 3HZ
Phone: 0161 236 1811

#434
Wings Dai Pai Dong
Cuisines: Dim Sum, Fast Food, Takeaway
Average price: Under £10
Area: City Centre
Address: 44 Cross St
Manchester M2 4
Phone: 0161 833 3388

#435
Browns
Cuisines: Bar, British
Average price: £11-25
Area: City Centre
Address: 1 York Street
Manchester M2 2AW
Phone: 0161 819 1055

#436
Axm Club
Cuisines: British, Gay Bar
Average price: £11-25
Area: Gay Village
Address: 100 Bloom Street
Manchester M1 3LY
Phone: 0845 834 0297

#437
Istanbul Express
Cuisines: Fast Food, Takeaway
Average price: Under £10
Area: Gay Village
Address: 29-31 Sackville Street
Manchester M1 3LZ
Phone: 0161 237 5555

#438
Cygnet Sandwich Bar
Cuisines: Sandwiches
Average price: Under £10
Area: Ancoats, Petersfield
Address: 18 Swan Street
Manchester M4 5JN
Phone: 0161 835 2827

#439
Florida Fried Chicken
Cuisines: Chicken Wings, Fast Food,
Takeaway, Burgers
Average price: Under £10
Area: Oxford Road Corridor
Address: 263 Upper Brook Street
Manchester M13 0HR
Phone: 0161 273 4327

#440
Tandoori Nights
Cuisines: Indian, Lounge
Average price: £26-45
Address: 252 Middleton Road
Manchester M8 4WA
Phone: 0161 740 3100

#441
Miramar Chinese Restaurant
Cuisines: Chinese, Fast Food, Takeaway
Average price: £11-25
Area: Levenshulme
Address: 1018 Stockport Road
Manchester M19 3WN
Phone: 0161 224 4986

#442
Five Guys Burgers and Fries
Cuisines: Burgers
Average price: £26-45
Address: Great Hall
Manchester M17 8AA

#443
Bella Italia
Cuisines: Italian
Average price: £11-25
Area: Northern Quarter
Address: 11-13 Piccadilly
Manchester M1 1LY
Phone: 0161 236 2342

#444
Lotus Restaurant
Cuisines: Malaysian
Average price: £11-25
Address: 289 Palatine Road
Manchester M22 4ET
Phone: 0161 945 9711

#445
Battered Cod
Cuisines: Fast Food, Takeaway,
Fish & Chips
Average price: Under £10
Address: 444 Wilmslow Road
Manchester M20 3BW
Phone: 0161 448 7520

#446
Gurkha Grill
Cuisines: Indian
Average price: £26-45
Area: West Didsbury
Address: 198 Burton Road
Manchester M20 1LH
Phone: 0161 445 3461

#447
Chorlton Eatery
Cuisines: Breakfast & Brunch,
Coffee & Tea, British
Average price: £11-25
Area: Chorlton
Address: 565 Barlow Moor Road
Manchester M21 8AE
Phone: 0161 860 0200

#448
Evuna
Cuisines: Spanish, Tapas Bar
Average price: £11-25
Area: Northern Quarter
Address: 79 Thomas Street
Manchester M4 1LW
Phone: 0161 833 1130

#449
Antonio's
Cuisines: Fast Food, Takeaway
Average price: Under £10
Area: Piccadilly
Address: 14-15 Station Approach
Manchester M1 2GH

#450
Krunchy Fried Chicken
Cuisines: Fast Food, Takeaway
Average price: Under £10
Area: Rusholme
Address: 50-52 Wilmslow Road
Manchester M14 5TQ
Phone: 0161 256 3694

#451
Purity
Cuisines: Bar, Club, Steakhouse
Average price: £26-45
Address: 36 Peter Street
Manchester M2 5GP
Phone: 0161 819 7777

#452
Pizza Hut
Cuisines: Pizza
Average price: Under £10
Area: Didsbury Village
Address: 766 Wilmslow Road
Manchester M20 2DR
Phone: 0161 434 9920

#453
Hell Fire Club
Cuisines: Soul Food
Average price: £11-25
Address: Queens Road
Manchester M9 5FF
Phone: 0161 277 9346

#454
Dixie Chickens
Cuisines: Fast Food, Takeaway
Average price: Above £46
Area: Chorlton
Address: 450 Wilbraham Road
Manchester M21 0AG
Phone: 0161 881 7910

#455
Olivien Pizza House
Cuisines: Fast Food, Takeaway
Average price: £11-25
Area: West Didsbury
Address: 126 Burton Road
Manchester M20 1JQ
Phone: 0161 434 5444

#456
New Emperor
Cuisines: Chinese
Average price: £11-25
Area: Chinatown
Address: 52-56 George Street
Manchester M1 4HF
Phone: 0161 228 2883

#457
Avalanche Bar & Restaurant
Cuisines: Italian
Average price: £11-25
Area: City Centre
Address: Booth Street
Manchester M2

#458
Café YumYum
Cuisines: Milkshake Bar,
Coffee & Tea, Sandwiches
Average price: Under £10
Area: City Centre
Address: 18 Cross Street
Manchester M2 7AE
Phone: 0161 839 1336

#459
Pret A Manger
Cuisines: Bakery, Sandwiches,
Coffee & Tea
Average price: Under £10
Address: 34 Oxford Street
Manchester M1 5EL
Phone: 0161 228 7965

#460
Rajas Pizza Bar
Cuisines: Pizza
Average price: Under £10
Area: Chinatown
Address: 84 Portland Street
Manchester M1 4GX
Phone: 0161 237 1122

#461
Louis Vuitton
Cuisines: Cafe
Average price: £11-25
Area: City Centre
Address: Exchange Sq
Manchester M3 1BD
Phone: 0161 828 0400

#462
Go Falafel
Cuisines: Falafel
Average price: Under £10
Area: Rusholme
Address: 10 Mayfair Court
Manchester M22

#463
King Kabana
Cuisines: Fast Food, Takeaway
Average price: Under £10
Area: Rusholme
Address: Unit 1 Walmer St East
Manchester M14 5SS
Phone: 0161 256 4767

#464
De Nada
Cuisines: Portuguese
Average price: £11-25
Area: Chorlton
Address: 127 Manchester Road
Manchester M21 9PG
Phone: 0161 881 6618

#465
New Ashy's
Cuisines: Restaurants
Average price: Under £10
Address: 66 Crumpsall Ln
Manchester M8 5SG
Phone: 0161 740 4447

#466
Bento King
Cuisines: British, Food Delivery Services, Asian Fusion
Average price: £11-25
Area: Chorlton
Address: 467 Princess Road
Manchester M20 1BH
Phone: 0161 448 1710

#467
Lusitano
Cuisines: Tapas, Wine Bar
Average price: £11-25
Area: Chorlton
Address: 613 Wilbraham Road
Manchester M21 9AN
Phone: 0161 861 8880

#468
Burger King
Cuisines: American
Average price: Under £10
Address: Birchfields Road
Manchester M14 6FS
Phone: 0161 225 7925

#469
Gold Medal Chip Shop
Cuisines: Fish & Chips
Average price: Under £10
Address: 2 Agnew Road
Manchester M18 7AR
Phone: 0161 223 0426

#470
Zal Takeaway
Cuisines: Fast Food, Takeaway
Average price: £11-25
Area: West Didsbury
Address: 123 Burton Road
Manchester M20 1JP
Phone: 0161 438 2000

#471
The Drum
Cuisines: Pub, Restaurants
Average price: £11-25
Address: Chester Road
Manchester M32 8NB
Phone: 0161 866 8876

#472
The Metropolitan
Cuisines: British, Gastropub, Bar
Average price: £11-25
Area: West Didsbury
Address: 2 Lapwing Lane
Manchester M20 2WS
Phone: 0161 438 2332

#473
Arndale Food Court
Cuisines: Bakery, American
Average price: Under £10
Area: City Centre
Address: Manchester Arndale
Manchester M4 3AQ

#474
Evuna
Cuisines: Tapas Bar, Bar
Average price: £26-45
Address: 277-279 Deansgate
Manchester M3 4EW
Phone: 0161 819 2752

#475
Shere Khan
Cuisines: Indian, Pakistani
Average price: £11-25
Address: The Trafford Centre
Manchester M17 8AA
Phone: 0161 749 9900

#476
Passage To India
Cuisines: Indian, Pakistani
Average price: £26-45
Address: 168 Monton Road
Manchester M30 9GA
Phone: 0161 787 9375

#477
Didsbury Fish Bar
Cuisines: Fish & Chips
Average price: Under £10
Area: Didsbury Village
Address: 1 School Lane
Manchester M20 6SA
Phone: 0161 445 4207

#478
Pond Quay
Cuisines: Chinese
Average price: Under £10
Address: 15 Crofts Bank Road
Manchester M41 0TZ
Phone: 0161 748 0890

#479
Fuel
Cuisines: Coffee & Tea, Vegetarian
Average price: Under £10
Address: 448 Wilmslow Road
Manchester M20 3BW
Phone: 0161 448 9702

#480
Rice
Cuisines: Asian Fusion
Average price: £11-25
Area: City Centre
Address: 79 Deansgate
Manchester M3 2BW
Phone: 0161 833 0113

#481
Pizza Hut
Cuisines: Pizza
Average price: £11-25
Area: City Centre
Address: Arndale Ctr
Manchester M2 1NP
Phone: 0161 839 8307

#482
Annies Restaurant
Cuisines: British
Average price: Above £46
Area: City Centre
Address: 5 Old Bank Street
Manchester M2 7PE
Phone: 0161 839 4423

#483
Jigsaw Sandwich Bar
Cuisines: Coffee & Tea, Sandwiches
Average price: £26-45
Address: 121 Market Street
Manchester M46 0DF
Phone: 0161 1942 887333

#484
New Samsi
Cuisines: Japanese, Supermarket
Average price: £26-45
Area: Gay Village
Address: 36 Whitworth Street
Manchester M1 3NR
Phone: 0161 279 0022

#485
Martins
Cuisines: Bakery, Sandwiches
Average price: Under £10
Area: Ladybarn
Address: 104 Mauldeth Road
Manchester M14 6SQ
Phone: 0161 445 1994

#486
Panicos Kebab House
Cuisines: Fast Food, Takeaway,
Greek, Sandwiches
Average price: Under £10
Area: Chorlton
Address: 418 Barlow Moor Rd
Manchester M21 8AD
Phone: 0161 861 0613

#487
Starbucks
Cuisines: Coffee & Tea, Sandwiches
Average price: £11-25
Area: Castlefield, Spinningfields
Address: Quay St
Manchester M3 3HN
Phone: 0161 834 0836

#488
Fresh Bites
Cuisines: Fast Food, Takeaway
Average price: Under £10
Area: Northern Quarter
Address: 71 Oldham Street
Manchester M4 1LW
Phone: 0161 839 7444

#489
Nando's
Cuisines: Portuguese, Chicken Wings
Average price: £11-25
Area: City Centre
Address: Manchester Arndale
Manchester M4 3AQ
Phone: 0161 834 3073

#490
Giraffe
Cuisines: Desserts, Breakfast & Brunch
Average price: £11-25
Area: Spinningfields
Address: 3 Hardman Square
Manchester M3 3AB
Phone: 0161 839 0009

#491
Archie's
Cuisines: Fast Food, Takeaway
Average price: Under £10
Area: Oxford Road Corridor
Address: 72 Oxford Road
Manchester M1 5NH
Phone: 0161 237 1736

#492
Eastern Pearl Take Away
Cuisines: Fast Food, Takeaway
Average price: £11-25
Area: Didsbury Village
Address: 434 Wilmslow Road
Manchester M20 3BW
Phone: 0161 434 1869

#493
Koreana
Cuisines: Korean
Average price: £11-25
Area: City Centre
Address: 40a King Street West
Manchester M3 2WY
Phone: 0161 832 4330

#494
Design A Sandwich
Cuisines: Fast Food, Takeaway,
Coffee & Tea, Sandwiches
Average price: Under £10
Area: City Centre
Address: 13d Barton Arcade
Manchester M3 2BB
Phone: 0161 839 1900

#495
Dexter's Grill & Bar
Cuisines: American,
Steakhouse, Burgers
Average price: Above £46
Address: 11 The Orient
Manchester M17 8EH
Phone: 0161 1942 887333

#496
Cadishead Charcoal Grill
Cuisines: Fast Food, Takeaway
Average price: Under £10
Address: 192c Liverpool Road
Manchester M44 6FE
Phone: 0161 776 9889

#497
All Bar One
Cuisines: Lounge, European
Average price: £11-25
Area: City Centre
Address: 73 King Street
Manchester M2 4NG
Phone: 0161 830 1811

#498
Wasabi
Cuisines: Japanese, Sushi Bar, Bar
Average price: £11-25
Area: Chinatown
Address: 63 Faulkner Street
Manchester M1 4FF
Phone: 0161 228 7288

#499
Pret A Manger
Cuisines: Coffee & Tea,
Sandwiches, Desserts
Average price: £11-25
Address: 63 Brazennose Street
Manchester M2 5EA
Phone: 0161 228 228 7965

#500
Maxwells Chippy
Cuisines: Fish & Chips
Average price: Under £10
Area: Gay Village
Address: 31 Bloom Street
Manchester M1 3JE
Phone: 0161 236 9038

TOP 500
ARTS & ENTERTAINMENT
The Most Recommended by Locals & Trevelers
(From #1 to #500)

#1
Museum of Science & Industry
Category: Museum, Art Gallery
Address: Liverpool Road
Manchester M3 4FP
Phone: 0161 832 2244

#2
Band on the Wall
Category: Bar, Music Venues,
Jazz & Blues
Address: 25 Swan Street
Manchester M4 5JZ
Phone: 0161 834 1786

#3
Manchester Art Gallery
Category: Art Gallery
Address: Mosley Street
Manchester M2 3JL
Phone: 0161 235 8888

#4
Night & Day
Category: Bar, Music Venues
Address: 26 Oldham Street
Manchester M1 1JN
Phone: 0161 236 4597

#5
Imperial War Museum North
Category: Museum
Address: Trafford Wharf Road
Manchester M17 1TZ
Phone: 0161 836 4000

#6
**Manchester Craft
and Design Centre**
Category: Arts & Crafts, Art Gallery
Address: 17 Oak St
Manchester M4 5JD
Phone: 0161 832 4274

#7
Dulcimer
Category: Bar, Music Venues
Address: 567 Wilbraham Road
Manchester M21 0AE
Phone: 0161 860 6444

#8
The Deaf Institute
Category: Lounge, Music Venues
Address: 135 Grosvenor Street
Manchester M1 7HE
Phone: 0161 276 9350

#9
The Briton's Protection
Category: Pub, Music Venues
Address: 50 Great Bridgewater Street
Manchester M1 5LE
Phone: 0161 236 5895

#10
Old Trafford
Category: Stadium
Address: Sir Matt Busby Way
Manchester M16 0RA
Phone: 0161 868 8000

#11
O2 Apollo Manchester
Category: Music Venues, Theatre,
Comedy Club
Address: Stockport Road
Manchester M12 6AP
Phone: 0844 477 7677

#12
Nexus Art Cafe
Category: Music Venues,
Lounge, Coffee & Tea
Address: 2 Dale Street
Manchester M1 1JW
Phone: 0161 236 0100

#13
Manchester Academy 2
Category: Music Venues, Bar
Address: Oxford Road
Manchester M13 9PR
Phone: 0161 275 2930

#14
St Ann's Church
Category: Music Venues, Church
Address: St Ann's Street
Manchester M2 7LF
Phone: 0161 834 1161

#15
Contact
Category: Theatre, Music Venues
Address: Oxford Road
Manchester M15 6JA
Phone: 0161 274 0600

#16
Manchester Museum
Category: Museum, Art Gallery
Address: Oxford Road
Manchester M13 9PL
Phone: 0161 275 2634

#17
Manchester Academy
Category: Music Venues
Address: Oxford Road
Manchester M13 9PR
Phone: 0161 275 2930

#18
Trafford Centre
Category: Cinema, Shopping Centre
Address: 130 Peel Avenue
Manchester M17 8AA
Phone: 0161 746 7777

#19
Manchester Craft
& Design Centre
Category: Art Gallery
Address: 776 Chester Road
Manchester M32 0QH
Phone: 07024 069543

#20
The Castle Hotel
Category: Pub, Music Venues
Address: 66 Oldham Street
Manchester M4 1LE
Phone: 0161 237 9485

#21
Common
Category: Bar, Music Venues
Address: 39 - 41 Edge Street
Manchester M4 1HW
Phone: 0161 832 9245

#22
Phones 4u Arena
Category: Theatre, Stadium,
Music Venues
Address: Victoria Station
Manchester M3 1AR
Phone: 0161 950 5000

#23
The Star and Garter
Category: Pub, Club, Music Venues
Address: 18-20 Fairfield Street
Manchester M1 2QF
Phone: 0161 273 6726

#24
The Roadhouse
Category: Music Venues
Address: 8 Newton Street
Manchester M1 2AN
Phone: 0161 237 9789

#25
Retro Bar
Category: Music Venues, Dive Bar
Address: 78 Sackville Street
Manchester M1 3NJ
Phone: 0161 274 4892

#26
The Temple
Category: Music Venues, Dive Bar
Address: 100 Great Bridgewater Street
Manchester M1 5JW
Phone: 0161 278 1610

#27
Odeon
Category: Cinema
Address: 27 Withy Grove
Manchester M4 2BS
Phone: 0871 224 4007

#28
Manchester City Football Club
Category: Stadium
Address: Rowsley Street
Manchester M11 3FF
Phone: 0161 438 7650

#29
Manchester Food
and Drink Festival
Category: Festival
Address: Albert Sq
Manchester M2 5DB
Phone: 0161 839 4353

#30
Cornerhouse
Category: Cinema, Bar, Cafe
Address: 70 Oxford Street
Manchester M1 5NH
Phone: 0161 200 1500

#31
Manchester Opera House
Category: Theatre, Opera & Ballet
Address: Quay Street
Manchester M3 3HP
Phone: 0161 823 1700

#32
Hop & Grape Manchester
Academy 3
Category: Music Venues, Bar
Address: Oxford Rd
Manchester M13 9PR
Phone: 0161 275 2930

#33
Richard Goodall Gallery
Category: Art Gallery
Address: 59 Thomas Street
Manchester M4 1NA
Phone: 0161 832 3435

#34
Royal Northern College of Music
Category: Music Venues,
Cultural Center, Theatre
Address: 124 Oxford Road
Manchester M13 9RD
Phone: 0161 907 5200

#35
The Ram
Category: Music Venues, Pub
Address: 393 Wilmslow Road
Manchester M20 4WA
Phone: 0161 283 9296

#36
The Ritz
Category: Club, Music Venues, Bar
Address: Whitworth Street W
Manchester M1 5WW
Phone: 0161 236 3234

#37
Cineworld
Category: Cinema
Address: Wilmslow Road
Manchester M20 5PG
Phone: 0871 200 2000

#38
Grand Central
Category: Music Venues, Pub
Address: 80 Oxford Road
Manchester M1 5NH
Phone: 0161 236 0890

#39
Eastern Bloc Records
Category: Music Venues, Cafe
Address: 5A Stevenson Square
Manchester M1 1DN
Phone: 0161 228 6555

#40
Richard Goodall Gallery
Category: Art Gallery, Museum
Address: 103 High Street
Manchester M4 1HQ
Phone: 0161 834 3330

#41
Dancehouse Theatre
Category: Theatre
Address: 10a Oxford Rd
Manchester M1 5QA
Phone: 0161 237 9753

#42
The Frog and Bucket
Comedy Club
Category: Social Club, Comedy Club
Address: 102 Oldham Street
Manchester M4 1LJ
Phone: 0161 236 9805

#43
The Garratt
Category: Pub, Music Venues
Address: 127 Princess Street
Manchester M1 7AG
Phone: 0161 237 5111

#44
Twenty Twenty Two
Category: Bar, Art Gallery,
Music Venues
Address: 20 Dale Street
Manchester M1 1EZ
Phone: 0161 237 9360

#45
The Printworks
Category: Arcade, Cinema, Bar
Address: 27 Withy Grove
Manchester M4 2BS
Phone: 0161 829 8000

#46
The Ruby Lounge
Category: Club, Music Venues
Address: 28-34 High Street
Manchester M4 1QB
Phone: 0161 834 1392

#47
CUBE
Category: Art Gallery
Address: 113-115 Portland Street
Manchester M1 6DW
Phone: 0161 237 5525

#48
People's History Museum
Category: Museum
Address: Left Bank
Manchester M3 3ER
Phone: 0161 838 9190

#49
Z-Arts
Category: Theatre, Art Gallery,
Music Venues
Address: 335 Stretford Road
Manchester M15 5ZA
Phone: 0161 226 1912

#50
Victoria Baths
Category: Museum,
Venues & Event Space
Address: Hathersage Road
Manchester M13 0FE
Phone: 0161 224 2020

#51
Manchester 235
Category: Gambling, Chinese, Bar
Address: 2 Watson Street
Manchester M3 4LP
Phone: 0161 828 0300

#52
Manchester Metropolitan Students Union
Category: Social Club, Lounge
Address: Grosvenor Square
Manchester M15 6BH
Phone: 0161 247 1162

#53
Chetham's School of Music
Category: Specialty School,
Music Venues, Recording Studio
Address: Long Millgate
Manchester M3 1SB
Phone: 0161 834 9644

#54
Whitworth Art Gallery
Category: Art Gallery
Address: Oxford Road
Manchester M15 6ER
Phone: 0161 275 7450

#55
Sunshine Studio
Category: Dance School,
Theatre, Sports Club
Address: 52 Newton Street
Manchester M1 1ED
Phone: 0161 228 6814

#56
Charlies Karaoke Bar
Category: Karaoke, Venues & Event Space,
Music Venues
Address: 1 Harter Street
Manchester M1 6
Phone: 0161 237 9898

#57
The Three Minute Theatre
Category: Theatre
Address: 35-39 Oldham Street
Manchester M1 1JG
Phone: 0161 834 4517

#58
Manchester United Museum and Tour Centre
Category: Museum
Address: Sir Matt Busby Way
Manchester M16 0RA
Phone: 0870 442 1994

#59
John Rylands Library
Category: Library, Museum
Address: 150 Deansgate
Manchester M3 3EH
Phone: 0161 306 0555

#60
Club Academy
Category: Music Venues
Address: Oxford Road
Manchester M13 9PR
Phone: 0161 275 2930

#61
National Squash Centre
Category: Stadium
Address: Rowsley Street
Manchester M11 3FF
Phone: 0161 220 3800

#62
Nicolas
Category: Winerie
Address: 8 Barton Arcade
Manchester M3 2BB
Phone: 0161 834 7328

#63
The Whim Wham Cafe
Category: Jazz & Blues, Bar, British
Address: Arch 64 Whitworth Street West
Manchester M1 5WQ
Phone: 0161 236 0930

#64
Pitcher & Piano
Category: Pub, Music Venues
Address: Arch 9 and 10
Manchester M1 5LH
Phone: 0161 839 6117

#65
Belle Vue Greyhound Stadium
Category: Stadium
Address: Kirkmanshulme Lane
Manchester M18 7BA
Phone: 0870 840 7557

#66
FAC 251: The Factory
Category: Club, Music Venues
Address: 112-118 Princess St
Manchester M1 7EN
Phone: 0161 272 7251

#67
Sound Control
Category: Club, Music Venues
Address: 1 New Wakefield Street
Manchester M1 5NP
Phone: 0161 236 0340

#68
Dry Bar
Category: Bar, Music Venues
Address: 29-30 Oldham St
Manchester M1 1JN
Phone: 0161 236 9840

#69
Manchester Jewish Museum
Category: Museum, Art Gallery
Address: 190 Cheetham Hill Road
Manchester M8 8LW
Phone: 0161 834 9879

#70
Showcase Cinema
Category: Cinema
Address: Hyde Road
Manchester M12 5AL
Phone: 0871 220 1000

#71
Venus
Category: Club, Music Venues
Address: 42 Maybrook House
Manchester M3 2EQ
Phone: 0161 834 7288

#72
**Alliance Française
de Manchester**
Category: Social Club
Address: 55 Portland Street
Manchester M1 3HP
Phone: 0161 236 7117

#73
Incognito Gallery
Category: Art Gallery
Address: 5 Stevenson Square
Manchester M1 1DN
Phone: 0161 228 7999

#74
Genting Club
Category: Gambling, Lounge
Address: 110 Portland Street
Manchester M1 4RL
Phone: 0161 228 0077

#75
Castlefield Events Arena
Category: Music Venues, Local Flavour
Address: 101 Liverpool Road
Manchester M3 4JN
Phone: 0161 834 4026

#76
The Gallery Café
Category: Coffee & Tea, Art Gallery
Address: Mosley Street
Manchester M2 3JL
Phone: 0161 235 8888

#77
Lowry Art Gallery
Category: Art Gallery
Address: Pier 8
Manchester M50 3AZ
Phone: 0161 876 2121

#78
Gallery Of Costume
Category: Museum
Address: Wilmslow Road
Manchester M14 5LL
Phone: 0161 224 5217

#79
Matt and Phreds
Category: Club, Music Venues
Address: 64 Tib Street
Manchester M4 1LW
Phone: 0161 839 7187

#80
Waterside Arts Centre
Category: Art Gallery, Theatre
Address: 1 Waterside Plaza
Manchester M33 7ZF
Phone: 0161 912 5616

#81
Bouzouki Restaurant
Category: Greek, Music Venues
Address: 88 Princess Street
Manchester M1 6NG
Phone: 0161 236 9282

#82
Museum Of The Greater
Manchester Police
Category: Museum
Address: Newton Street
Manchester M1 1LN
Phone: 0161 856 3287

#83
The Venue
Category: Club, Music Venues
Address: 29 Jacksons Row
Manchester M2 5WD
Phone: 0161 834 3793

#84
Pitcher & Piano
Category: Pub, Music Venues
Address: Lower Mosley Street
Manchester M1 5LH
Phone: 0161 839 6117

#85
Manchester Irish Festival
Category: Festival
Address: Albert Square
Manchester M2 5RT
Phone: 0161 228 0662

#86
Generation Pop
Category: Art Gallery
Address: E3 New York Street
Manchester M1 4BD
Phone: 0161 848 0880

#87
National Winter Ales Festival
Category: Festival
Address: 371 Oldham Road
Manchester M40 8RR
Phone: 01727 867201

#88
Platt Chapel
Category: Music Venues, Venues & Event
Space, Party & Event Planning
Address: 186 Wilmslow Road
Manchester M14 5LL
Phone: 0161 478 4203

#89
Espionage Manchester
Category: Theatre, Florist
Address: Quay Street Manchester M3
Phone: 07502 000072

#90
The Kurdish Creative
Film Centre
Category: Festival, Cinema
Address: 46-50 Oldham Street
Manchester M1 1
Phone: 0161 234 2781

#91
Museum of Transport
Greater Manchester
Category: Museum
Address: Boyle Street
Manchester M8 8UW
Phone: 0161 205 2122

#92
Bridgewater Hall
Category: Music Venues, Bar,
Opera & Ballet
Address: Lower Mosley Street
Manchester M2 3WS
Phone: 0844 907 9000

#93
Castlefield Gallery
Category: Art Gallery
Address: 2 Hewitt St
Manchester M15 4GB
Phone: 0161 832 8034

#94
Kraak
Category: Art Gallery, Music Venues
Address: 11 Stevenson Square
Manchester M1 1DB
Phone: 07855 939129

#95
Colin Jellicoe
Category: Art Gallery
Address: 82 Portland Street
Manchester M1 4QX
Phone: 0161 236 2716

#96
Gamerbase
Category: Arcade
Address: 90 Market Street
Manchester M1 1PB
Phone: 0161 834 2312

#97
Picturehouse
Category: Bar, Music Venues
Address: 25 Swan St
Manchester M4 5JZ
Phone: 0161 834 1786

#98
Odeon Trafford Centre
Category: Cinema
Address: 201 The Dome
Manchester M17 8DF
Phone: 0871 224 4007

#99
Lounge 31
Category: Bar, Music Venues
Address: 31 Withy Grove
Manchester M4 2BJ
Phone: 0161 819 4710

#100
Electric Circus
Category: Gambling
Address: 110 Portland Street
Manchester M1 4RL
Phone: 0161 228 0077

#101
Goethe-Institut
Category: Social Club, Library
Address: 56 Oxford Street
Manchester M1 6EU
Phone: 0161 237 1077

#102
Mint Casino
Category: Gambling, Lounge
Address: 40-44 Princess Street
Manchester M1 6DE
Phone: 0161 236 3034

#103
Masako Art & Flowers
Category: Art Gallery, Florist
Address: 17 Ellesmere St
Manchester M15 5
Phone: 0161 839 5175

#104
KinoFilm European
Short Film
Category: Festival
Address: Unit 7 St Wilfred's Enterprise
Centre Manchester M15 5BJ
Phone: 07954 360989

#105
The Lenagan Library
Category: Library, Universities, Cinema
Address: University of Manchester Oxford
Road Manchester M13 9QS
Phone: 0161 275 4985

#106
Creative Recycling
Category: Art Gallery
Address: 40 Beech Road
Manchester M21 9EL
Phone: 0161 881 4422

#107
Pados House
Category: Theatre
Address: St Marys Rd
Manchester M25
Phone: 0161 773 7729

#108
Wendy J Levy Contemporary Art
Category: Art Gallery
Address: 17 Warburton Street
Manchester M20 6WA
Phone: 0161 446 4880

#109
The International 3
Category: Art Gallery
Address: 8 Fairfield St
Manchester M1 2
Phone: 0161 237 3336

#110
Phoenix Gallery
Category: Art Gallery
Address: 17 Ellesmere Street
Manchester M15 4JY
Phone: 0161 839 2232

#111
Powerleague Trafford
Category: Football, Stadium
Address: Trafford Way
Manchester M17 8DD
Phone: 0161 755 9720

#112
The Press Club
Category: Social Club
Address: 2 Queens Street
Manchester M2 5JB
Phone: 0161 834 8562

#113
Novus Contemporary Art
Category: Art Gallery
Address: Burton Road
Manchester M20 2LW
Phone: 0161 438 3888

#114
Ladbrokes
Category: Gambling
Address: 44 Portland Street
Manchester M1 4GS
Phone: 0800 022 3454

#115
Odeon Cinema
Category: Cinema
Address: 90 Great Bridgewater Street
Manchester M1 5JW
Phone: 0871 224 4007

#116
Bigshots
Category: Arcade
Address: Piccadilly Station
Manchester M1 2BN
Phone: 0161 237 3484

#117
**Prestwich Church
Institute & Mens Club**
Category: Social Club,
Venues & Event Space
Address: Bury New Road
Manchester M25 1AR
Phone: 0161 773 6057

#118
Castle Gallery
Category: Art Gallery
Address: Trafford Centre
Manchester M17 8AA
Phone: 0161 748 7237

#119
Sandbar
Category: Pub, Music Venues
Address: 120 Grosvenor Street
Manchester M1 7HL
Phone: 0161 273 1552

#120
Central Methodist Hall
Category: Music Venues,
Venues & Event Space
Address: Oldham Street
Manchester M1 1JQ
Phone: 0161 236 5194

#121
Stretford Ex Servicemens Club
Category: Social Club
Address: 30 Talbot Road
Manchester M16 0PF
Phone: 0161 872 2732

#122
Altrincham Rehearsal Studio
Category: Dance Studio, Music Venues
Address: Southmoor Road
Manchester M23 9DS
Phone: 0161 946 0008

#123
Contemporary Six, The Gallery
Category: Art Gallery, Arts & Crafts
Address: The Royal Exchange Arcade
Manchester M2 7EA
Phone: 0161 835 2666

#124
Spice UK
Category: Social Club, Sports & Leisure
Address: 13 Thorpe St
Manchester M16 9PR
Phone: 0161 873 8788

#125
Antwerp Mansion
Category: Music Venues
Address: Wilmslow Rd
Manchester M14 5BT
Phone: 07429 578193

#126
Phifer Network
Category: Social Club
Address: 2 Ladybarn Crescent
Manchester M14 6UU
Phone: 07741 606128

#127
The Firework Shop
Category: Wedding Planning
Address: Lowerwhittle farm
Manchester OL10 2QF
Phone: 01706 629926

#128
AMBA Lifestyle
Category: Art Gallery
Address: 15 Market Place
Manchester M24 6AE
Phone: 0161 222 3633

#129
Club V
Category: Music Venues
Address: 111 Deansgate
Manchester M3 2BQ
Phone: 0161 834 9975

#130
Happystorm Theatre
Category: Theatre
Address: 47 Chorlton St
Manchester M1 3FY
Phone: 07547 711839

#131
Dry Live
Category: Club, Music Venues
Address: 28-30 Oldham Street
Manchester M1 1JN
Phone: 0161 236 1444

#132
**Manchester
Photographic Gallery**
Category: Art Gallery
Address: 45 Dale Street
Manchester M1 2HF
Phone: 0161 236 7224

#133
Philharmonic String Quartet
Category: Music Venues, Theatre,
Wedding Planning
Address: 307 Vicus 73 Liverpool Road
Manchester M3 4AQ
Phone: 07545 991621

#134
Hit and Run
Category: Club, Music Venues
Address: Area 51 Eclipse House
Manchester M1 5WZ
Phone: 0161 236 1316

#135
The Edge Theatre & Arts Centre
Category: Theatre
Address: The Edge Theatre & Arts Centre
Manchester Road Manchester M21 9JG
Phone: 0161 282 9776

#136
The Magic of Alex D Fisher
Category: Music Venues, Theatre
Address: 77 Wilton road
Manchester M8 4PD
Phone: 07961 050230

#137
Fitzroy Social Club
Category: Social Club
Address: Durham Street
Manchester M43 6DT
Phone: 0161 370 2400

#138
A1 Ostrich Feathers Manchester
Category: Wedding Planning
Address: Failsworth Antique Mill
Manchester M35
Phone: 0161 219 1082

#139
Ladbrokes
Category: Gambling
Address: 2 Station Approach
Manchester M60 7
Phone: 0800 022 3454

#140
UK Talent Searcher
Category: Theatre
Address: 682 bolton road
Manchester M27 8FH
Phone: 07986 013049

#141
Grosvenor Casino
Category: Casino
Address: Parrswood Entertainment Centre
Manchester M20 5PG
Phone: 0161 669 7165

#142
Social Circle
Category: Social Club
Address: 515 Parrs Wood Road
Manchester M20 5
Phone: 07767 686177

#143
Yvonne Dixon Events
Category: Wedding Planning
Address: 403 Moorside Road
Manchester M41 5SD
Phone: 0161 202 9084

#144
Starlite Productions
Category: Venues & Event Space,
Wedding Planning
Address: 6 Lodge Road
Manchester M26 1AL
Phone: 0161 959 6250

#145
Sand Lime and Soda
Category: Art Gallery
Address: 26g vernon mill
Manchester SK1
Phone: 07951 356328

#146
Cats Drama
Category: Theatre
Address: 54 Colshaw Road
Manchester M23 2QQ
Phone: 0161 945 1051

#147
The Firework Shop
Category: Wedding Planning
Address: Lower Whittle Farm
Manchester OL10 2QF
Phone: 07805 837854

#148
Grosvenor Casino
Category: Casino
Address: 35 George Street
Manchester M1 4HQ
Phone: 0161 236 7121

#149
Actors Centre North
Category: Specialty School, Theatre
Address: 21-31 Oldham St
Manchester M1 1JG
Phone: 0161 819 2513

#150
Tracey Cartledge Mosaic Studio
Category: Art Gallery
Address: 44 Ellesmere Street
Manchester M15 4JY
Phone: 0161 860 0387

#151
Premier Musicians
Category: Venues & Event Space, Wedding
Planning, Music Venues
Address: 307 Vicus 73 Liverpool Road
Manchester M3 4AQ
Phone: 07545 991621

#152
Castlefield Quartet
Category: Venues & Event Space, Wedding
Planning, Theatre
Address: 307 Vicus 73 Liverpool Road
Manchester M3 4AQ
Phone: 07545 991621

#153
Manchester Pride
Category: Arcade
Address: Ducie Street
Manchester M1 2JW
Phone: 0161 236 7474

#154
Desipride Entertainment
Category: Music Venues
Address: 10 Thorncombe Road
Manchester M16 7YB
Phone: 07814 005501

#155
ukshadicom
Category: Social Club
Address: 13 flat4 rectory road crumpsel
Manchester M8 5EA
Phone: 07405 660941

#156
Honest Policy
Category: Social Club
Address: 29 cawdor road
Manchester M14 6LS
Phone: 07709 840065

#157
Medium May
Category: Psychics & Astrologers
Address: 14 Ringwood Avenue
Manchester M12 5TP
Phone: 0161 248 5338

#158
**Levenshulme Bowling
& Social Club**
Category: Social Club
Address: 1 Burnage Range
Manchester M19 2HQ
Phone: 0161 224 4122

#159
Royal British Legion
Category: Social Club, Music Venues
Address: 225 Bury Old Road
Manchester M25 1JE
Phone: 0161 773 5736

#160
Capitol Theatre
Category: Theatre
Address: Cavendish Street
Manchester M15 6BH
Phone: 0161 247 1305

#161
Koolkarts
Category: Kids Activities
Address: 127 Chorley Road
Manchester M27 4AA
Phone: 0161 950 9829

#162
Mariyka's Dance Studio
Category: Dance School
Address: 25-27 Rutland Street
Manchester M27 6AU
Phone: 0161 728 3142

#163
Aukesson Art
Category: Art Gallery
Address: 43 Bucklow Drive
Manchester M22 4WA
Phone: 07533 765999

#164
The Yard Theatre
Category: Theatre
Address: Old Birley Street
Manchester M15 5RF
Phone: 0161 226 7696

#165
Hough End Hall
Category: Castle
Address: 95 Nell Lane
Manchester M21 7RL
Phone: 0161 861 9986

#166
Walkden Labour Club
Category: Social Club
Address: 1 Cecil Street
Manchester M28 3BR
Phone: 0161 790 2915

#167
St. Josephs Players
Category: Theatre
Address: High Legh Old Hall Mill Lane
Manchester M46 0RG
Phone: 01942 674784

#168
Olivers's Personal Portraits
Category: Art Gallery
Address: 21 Farleigh close
Manchester BL5 3ES
Phone: 07850 662758

#169
The Lowry
Category: Art Gallery, Theatre
Address: Pier 8 Salford M50 3AZ
Phone: 0161 876 2121

#170
Heaven
Category: Bar, Club, Music Venues
Address: 36 Peter Street
Manchester M2 5GP
Phone: 0161 819 7798

#171
**Manchester
Geographical Society**
Category: Social Club
Address: 6 Mount Street
Manchester M2 5NS
Phone: 0161 834 2965

#172
Tib Lane Gallery
Category: Art Gallery
Address: 14a Tib Lane
Manchester M2 4JA
Phone: 0161 834 6928

#173
Urban Talent
Category: Theatre
Address: 1 Oxford Court
Manchester M2 3WQ
Phone: 0161 228 6866

#174
St. James Club
Category: Social Club
Address: 45 Spring Garden
Manchester M2 2BG
Phone: 0161 829 3000

#175
Canyon Associates
Category: Arcade
Address: 6 Hewitt Street
Manchester M15 4GB
Phone: 0161 245 4600

#176
Actors Direct
Category: Theatre
Address: 109 Portland Street
Manchester M1 6DN
Phone: 0161 237 1904

#177
Silent Way
Category: Theatre
Address: 384 Deansgate
Manchester M3 4LA
Phone: 0161 832 2111

#178
Nigel Martin Smith
Category: Theatre
Address: 28 Queen Street
Manchester M2 5LF
Phone: 0161 834 4500

#179
Art Lounge
Category: Art Gallery
Address: 8 The Triangle
Manchester M4 3TR
Phone: 0161 832 8228

#180
Guide Bridge Theatre
Category: Theatre
Address: Audenshaw Road
Manchester M34 5HJ
Phone: 0161 330 8078

#181
Pitcher & Piano
Category: Pub, Music Venues
Address: Great Bridgwater Square
Manchester M2 3WS
Phone: 0161 228 7888

#182
Lime Management
Category: Theatre
Address: 1 Oxford Court
Manchester M2 3WQ
Phone: 0161 236 0827

#183
Nidges Casting Agency
Category: Theatre
Address: Half Moon Chambers
Manchester M2 1HN
Phone: 0161 832 8259

#184
Blyth Gallery
Category: Art Gallery
Address: 3 Brazil Street
Manchester M1 3PJ
Phone: 0161 236 1004

#185
Actors Group
Category: Theatre
Address: 21-31 Oldham Street
Manchester M1 1JG
Phone: 0161 834 4466

#186
Breaking Cycles
Category: Theatre
Address: 8 Lower Ormond Street
Manchester M1 5QF
Phone: 0161 237 1655

#187
Alexander Forbes
Category: Insurance, Art Gallery
Address: 30-32 Charlotte Street
Manchester M1 4FD
Phone: 0161 228 0721

#188
Intercity Casting
Category: Theatre
Address: Portland Street
Manchester M1 3LF
Phone: 0161 238 4950

#189
NQ Live
Category: Club, Music Venues
Address: Tib Street
Manchester M4 1LN
Phone: 0161 834 8188

#190
Leaf Street
Category: Theatre
Address: 75 Rockdove Avenue
Manchester M15 5EH
Phone: 0161 232 7326

#191
The Engine House
Category: Theatre, Music Venues
Address: 3 Cambridge St
Manchester M1 5BY
Phone: 07874 152338

#192
Musicans Ltd String Quartet
Category: Theatre
Address: 38 City Road East
Manchester M15 4QL
Phone: 07957 994889

#193
Electriks
Category: Theatre
Address: 24 Lever Street 3rd Floor
Manchester M1 1DZ
Phone: 0161 278 5650

#194
J B Associates
Category: Theatre
Address: 1-3 Stevenson Square
Manchester M1 1DN
Phone: 0161 237 1808

#195
Ear To The Ground (North)
Category: Arcade
Address: 11-13 Spear Street
Manchester M1 1JU
Phone: 0161 237 9786

#196
Hyper Media
Category: Arcade
Address: 59 Piccadilly
Manchester M1 2AQ
Phone: 0161 660 7055

#197
Orpheus String Quartet
Category: Venues & Event Space,
Wedding Planning, Theatre
Address: 307 Vicus 73 Liverpool Road
Manchester M3 4AQ
Phone: 07545 991621

#198
Amber
Category: Theatre
Address: 5 Newton Street
Manchester M1 1HL
Phone: 0161 228 0236

#199
Natural Eye Gallery
Category: Art Gallery
Address: 17 Oak Street
Manchester M4 5JD
Phone: 0161 834 3883

#200
**Ivc Social Sporting
& Cultural Activities**
Category: Social Club
Address: 94-96 Grosvenor Street
Manchester M1 7HL
Phone: 0161 273 2316

#201
KMC
Category: Theatre
Address: 48 Great Ancoats Street
Manchester M4 5AB
Phone: 0161 237 3009

#202
T R C Management
Category: Theatre
Address: 23 New Mount Street
Manchester M4 4DE
Phone: 0161 953 4091

#203
Sparklestreet HQ
Category: Theatre
Address: 18 Sparkle Street
Manchester M1 2NA
Phone: 0161 273 3435

#204
Charabanc Music Management
Category: Theatre
Address: 18 Sparkle Street
Manchester M1 2NA
Phone: 0161 273 5554

#205
T1 Telecoms
Category: Theatre
Address: 2 Jersey Street
Manchester M4 6JB
Phone: 0161 237 1411

#206
Artzu Gallery
Category: Art Gallery
Address: Great Ancoats Street
Manchester M4 5AD
Phone: 0161 228 3001

#207
Proper Job Theatre Company
Category: Theatre
Address: 41 Old Birley Street
Manchester M15 5RF
Phone: 0161 227 9787

#208
Manchester Jazz Festival
Category: Theatre
Address: 37 Ducie Street
Manchester M1 2JW
Phone: 0161 228 0662

#209
The Acting Studio
Category: Theatre
Address: 121 Princess Street
Manchester M1 7AD
Phone: 0161 228 0445

#210
S K Sports & Leisure
Category: Stadium
Address: 10a Lockett Street
Manchester M8 8EE
Phone: 0161 834 0351

#211
Direct 2 U
Category: Arcade
Address: 57a Derby Street
Manchester M8 8HW
Phone: 0161 832 7452

#212
Bullet Management
Category: Theatre
Address: Charlton Place
Manchester M12 6HS
Phone: 0161 274 3000

#213
Dance Initiative Greater Manchester
Category: Theatre
Address: Zion Arts Centretretford Road
Manchester M15 5ZA
Phone: 0161 232 7179

#214
Grosvenor Casino
Category: Casino
Address: 2 Ramsgate Street
Manchester M8 9SG
Phone: 0161 831 6370

#215
Icon Actors Management
Category: Theatre
Address: Tanzaro House
Manchester M12 6FZ
Phone: 0161 273 3344

#216
Temperance World Media
Category: Theatre
Address: 12 Hyde Road
Manchester M12 6BQ
Phone: 0161 275 9000

#217
The Manchester
Young People's Theatre
Category: Theatre
Address: Devas Street
Manchester M15 6JA
Phone: 01604 704900

#218
Polish Parish Club
Category: Social Club
Address: 196 Lloyd Street North
Manchester M14 4QB
Phone: 0161 226 2544

#219
Creative Recycling Handcrafted
Category: Art Gallery
Address: 42 ST. Hildas Road
Manchester M16 9PQ
Phone: 0161 848 0488

#220
One21 Designs
Category: Theatre
Address: Suite 10 4th Floor
Manchester M12 6JH
Phone: 0161 273 3121

#221
West Indian Sports & Social Club
Category: Social Club
Address: Westwood Street
Manchester M14 4SW
Phone: 0161 226 7236

#222
Grand Central Square
Category: Pub, Cinema
Address: Wellington Road
South Stockport SK1 3TA
Phone: 0161 477 6080

#223
Feelgood Theatre Productions
Category: Theatre
Address: 21 Lindum Avenue
Manchester M16 9NQ
Phone: 0161 862 9212

#224
English Martyrs Parish Centre
Category: Social Club
Address: Alexandra Road South
Manchester M16 8GF
Phone: 0161 226 1107

#225
Old Trafford Conservative Club
Category: Social Club
Address: 124 Seymour Grove
Manchester M16 0FF
Phone: 0161 881 1339

#226
Cambos
Category: Social Club
Address: 17 Albert Street
Manchester M1 3HZ
Phone: 0161 237 1723

#227
IndyManBeerCon - Independent Manchester Beer Convention
Category: Festival
Address: Hathersage Road
Manchester M13 0FE
Phone: 0161 224 2020

#228
Polish Circle Club
Category: Social Club
Address: 433 Cheetham Hill Road
Manchester M8 0PF
Phone: 0161 740 9432

#229
Darley Lawn Tennis & Social Club
Category: Social Club
Address: Wood Road North
Manchester M16 9QG
Phone: 0161 881 3203

#230
Gorton Villa Social
Category: Social Club
Address: 34 Gortonvilla Walk
Manchester M12 5ES
Phone: 0161 223 2879

#231
Rusholme Conservative Club
Category: Social Club
Address: Antwerp House
Manchester M14 5RF
Phone: 0161 224 1897

#232
Whizzkiddzz
Category: Arcade
Address: 5 Grosvenor Road
Manchester M16 8JP
Phone: 0161 226 1071

#233
Greater Manchester Bangladesh Association
Category: Social Club
Address: 19a Birch Lane
Manchester M13 0NW
Phone: 0161 225 4012

#234
Pantoworld
Category: Theatre
Address: 29 Milverton Road Victoria Park
Manchester M14 5PJ
Phone: 0161 225 9339

#235
Bunny Lewis Enterprises
Category: Theatre
Address: 41 Alexandra Road South
Manchester M16 8GH
Phone: 0161 227 9879

#236
St Kentigerns Social Club
Category: Social Club
Address: Hart Road
Manchester M14 7BB
Phone: 0161 224 2033

#237
Abraham Moss Centre Theatre
Category: Theatre
Address: 140 Crescent Road
Manchester M8 5UF
Phone: 0161 908 8327

#238
Longsight & District Sports & Social Club
Category: Social Club
Address: Kirkmanshulme Lane
Manchester M12 4WB
Phone: 0161 224 3213

#239
Railway Club
Category: Social Club
Address: 837-839 Chester Road
Manchester M32 0RN
Phone: 0161 865 6755

#240
Royal British Legion
Category: Social Club
Address: 86 Belle Vue Street
Manchester M12 5PP
Phone: 0161 223 0688

#241
Crumpsall Constitutional Club
Category: Social Club
Address: 2 Lansdowne Road
Manchester M8 5SH
Phone: 0161 740 1252

#242
Movin Music
Category: Theatre
Address: 33 Albany Road
Manchester M21 0BH
Phone: 0161 881 9227

#243
Artys
Category: Art Gallery
Address: 412 Wilbraham Road
Manchester M21 0SD
Phone: 0161 861 7177

#244
Trafford Park Heritage Shop
Category: Museum
Address: Eleventh St
Manchester M17 1JF
Phone: 0161 848 9173

#245
Edward Cervenka
Category: Theatre
Address: 30 Wyverne Road
Manchester M21 0ZN
Phone: 0161 881 4314

#246
Lip Service
Category: Theatre
Address: 116 Longford Road
Manchester M21 9NP
Phone: 0161 881 2638

#247
Bar Baroque
Category: Music Venues
Address: 478 Wilbraham Rd
Manchester M21 9AS
Phone: 0161 881 9130

#248
**Barnes Green Catholic
Social Club**
Category: Social Club
Address: 6 Factory Lane
Manchester M9 8AB
Phone: 0161 205 1053

#249
Conservative & Unionist Club
Category: Social Club
Address: 746 Rochdale Road
Manchester M9 4BP
Phone: 0161 205 5252

#250
Lithuanian Social Club
Category: Social Club
Address: 121 Middleton Road
Manchester M8 4JY
Phone: 0161 740 5039

#251
Rhythm & Rhyme
Category: Arcade
Address: 58 Corkland Road
Manchester M21 8XH
Phone: 0161 860 0911

#252
Trafford Athletic Club
Category: Stadium
Address: Ryebank Road
Manchester M21 9TA
Phone: 0161 881 4488

#253
**The Clayton Conservative
Club Company**
Category: Social Club
Address: 625 Ashton New Road
Manchester M11 4RX
Phone: 0161 223 1128

#254
The Buzz
Category: Arcade
Address: Mauldeth Road West
Manchester M21 7SP
Phone: 0870 240 1170

#255
Lauriston Club
Category: Social Club
Address: 12 Manchester Road
Manchester M21 9JG
Phone: 0161 881 3096

#256
Crumpsall Labour Club
Category: Social Club
Address: 98 Wilton Road
Manchester M8 4PX
Phone: 0161 740 3373

#257
**Simpson Memorial
Community Association**
Category: Social Club
Address: Moston Lane
Manchester M9 4HF
Phone: 0161 205 1575

#258
Devil Child Promotions
Category: Arcade
Address: 27 Lichfield Drive
Manchester M25 0HX
Phone: 0161 798 4236

#259
The Voiceover Gallery
Category: Theatre
Address: 34 Stockton Road
Manchester M21 9ED
Phone: 0161 881 8844

#260
**Troydale Tenants
& Residents Association**
Category: Social Club
Address: 5 Dolwen Walk
Manchester M40 2FR
Phone: 0161 682 9846

#261
G M B Whitehouse Club
Category: Social Club
Address: 193 Middleton Road
Manchester M8 4JZ
Phone: 0161 740 1732

#262
Stretford Bridge Club
Category: Social Club
Address: 66 Derbyshire Lane
Manchester M32 8BF
Phone: 0161 865 2846

#263
St Richards Social Club
Category: Social Club
Address: 10-12 Sutcliffe Avenue
Manchester M12 5TN
Phone: 0161 224 1405

#264
Club & Institute Union
Category: Social Club
Address: 534 Hyde Road
Manchester M18 7AA
Phone: 0161 223 1686

#265
Avanti Display
Category: Theatre
Address: 46 Nell Lane
Manchester M21 7SN
Phone: 0161 860 7267

#266
Withington Conservative Club
Category: Social Club
Address: 16 Mauldeth Road
Manchester M20 4ND
Phone: 0161 434 2879

#267
Music Hall
Category: Social Club
Address: 29 Old Church Street
Manchester M40 2JN
Phone: 0161 681 7665

#268
HM Music Promotions
Category: Arcade
Address: 55 Bluestone Road
Manchester M40 9JB
Phone: 0161 688 6738

#269
Royal British Legion
Category: Social Club
Address: Slade Lane
Manchester M19 2EX
Phone: 0161 248 6010

#270
Withington Public Hall Institute
Category: Social Club
Address: 2 Burton Road
Manchester M20 3ED
Phone: 0161 445 2672

#271
**Newton Heath Catholic
Mens Club**
Category: Social Club
Address: 137 Culcheth Lane
Manchester M40 1LY
Phone: 0161 681 7003

#272
Royal British Legion
Category: Social Club
Address: Ross Avenue
Manchester M19 2HW
Phone: 0161 224 4716

#273
St James Conservative Club
Category: Social Club
Address: 572 Gorton Lane
Manchester M18 8EH
Phone: 0161 223 0455

#274
Plush UK
Category: Arcade
Address: 64 Victoria Road
Manchester M32 0AB
Phone: 0161 864 4746

#275
Amber Club
Category: Social Club
Address: 1143 Oldham Road
Manchester M40 2FU
Phone: 0161 681 3892

#276
**Deus Ex Machina
Theatre Company**
Category: Theatre
Address: 18 Elder Mount Road
Manchester M9 8BT
Phone: 0161 795 4709

#277
Royal British Legion
Category: Social Club
Address: Beverly Road
Manchester M14 6TZ
Phone: 0161 224 6210

#278
**The Manchester Song
& Dance Company**
Category: Theatre
Address: 12 Barnhill Road
Manchester M25 9NH
Phone: 0161 798 4365

#279
Young Gifted & Green
Category: Arcade
Address: 6 Wald Avenue
Manchester M14 6TE
Phone: 0161 225 0706

#280
Stretford Conservative Club
Category: Social Club
Address: 20 King Street
Manchester M32 8AE
Phone: 0161 865 1292

#281
The Manchester Bridge Club
Category: Social Club
Address: 30 Palatine Road
Manchester M20 3JJ
Phone: 0161 445 3712

#282
Pupfish
Category: Theatre
Address: 9 Brixton Avenue
Manchester M20 1JF
Phone: 0161 610 7529

#283
Royal British Legion Ladybarn
Category: Social Club
Address: & District Club
Manchester M14 6TE
Phone: 0161 225 8105

#284
Mccafferty Illustrations
Category: Theatre
Address: Flat 2 41 Alan Road Withington
Manchester M20 4WG
Phone: 0161 434 2201

#285
Pro Music UK
Category: Theatre
Address: 30 Victoria Avenue
Manchester M19 2PE
Phone: 0161 224 6236

#286
Proper Job Theatre Company
Category: Theatre
Address: 1 Hoscar Drive
Manchester M19 2LS
Phone: 0161 249 0564

#287
Swinton Masonic Hall
Category: Social Club
Address: Hospital Road
Manchester M27 4EY
Phone: 0161 794 5377

#288
**Manchester Maccabi
Community & Sports Club**
Category: Social Club
Address: Bury Old Road
Manchester M25 0EG
Phone: 0161 492 0040

#289
G M Buses Social Club
Category: Social Club
Address: 301 Mount Road
Manchester M19 3ET
Phone: 0161 224 1176

#290
Higher Openshaw Working Men's Club
Category: Social Club
Address: 49 Stanley Street
Manchester M11 1LE
Phone: 0161 370 1048

#291
Sonic Tonic
Category: Arcade
Address: 204 Barlow Road
Manchester M19 3HF
Phone: 0161 224 6587

#292
Eccles Liberal Club
Category: Social Club
Address: 34 Wellington Road
Manchester M30 0NP
Phone: 0161 789 3047

#293
West Didsbury Conservative Club
Category: Social Club
Address: 173 Burton Road
Manchester M20 2LN
Phone: 0161 445 3917

#294
Prestwich Amateur Dramatic & Operatic Society
Category: Theatre
Address: 23 ST. Marys Road
Manchester M25 1AQ
Phone: 0161 773 7729

#295
Failsworth Home Guard Old Comrades
Category: Social Club
Address: Poplar Street
Manchester M35 0HY
Phone: 0161 681 1891

#296
Goldengate Promotions
Category: Arcade
Address: 3 Danesmoor Road
Manchester M20 3JT
Phone: 0161 283 7273

#297
Sale Harriers Manchester
Category: Social Club
Address: 16 Whitethorn Avenue
Manchester M19 1EU
Phone: 0161 432 1831

#298
Animount Systems
Category: Theatre
Address: The Old Town Hall Lapwing Lane
Manchester M20 2WR
Phone: 0161 448 9990

#299
Carlton Club
Category: Social Club
Address: 279 Bury Old Road
Manchester M25 1JA
Phone: 0161 773 2284

#300
Openshaw A E U Club & Institute
Category: Social Club
Address: Toxteth Street
Manchester M11 1EZ
Phone: 0161 370 2069

#301
Heaton Park Sports & Social Bar
Category: Social Club
Address: 315 Bury Old Road
Manchester M25 1JA
Phone: 0161 773 1091

#302
P Snowden
Category: Social Club
Address: Overdale
Manchester M27 5WZ
Phone: 0161 281 5694

#303
Victoria Avenue East Ex Service Mens Club
Category: Social Club
Address: White Moss Road
Manchester M9 6EF
Phone: 0161 740 5832

#304
Gorton Working Mens Club
Category: Social Club
Address: 2 Thornwood Avenue
Manchester M18 7HW
Phone: 0161 223 3509

#305
Cricket Club
Category: Social Club
Address: Wilmslow Road
Manchester M20 2ZY
Phone: 0161 445 5347

#306
Heaton Hall
Category: Art Gallery
Address: Heaton Park
Manchester M25 2SW
Phone: 0161 773 1231

#307
Royal British Legion
Category: Social Club
Address: Manchester Road
Manchester M43 6SF
Phone: 0161 370 1367

#308
Joku Entertainment
Category: Arcade
Address: Barton Dock Road
Manchester M41 7BQ
Phone: 0161 747 7779

#309
Royal British Legion
Category: Social Club
Address: Victoria Avenue
Manchester M9 0RA
Phone: 0161 740 6138

#310
Royal British Legion Swinton
Category: Social Club
Address: Cheetham Road
Manchester M27 4UQ
Phone: 0161 794 2422

#311
Swinton Catholic Club
Category: Social Club
Address: 11 Worsley Road
Manchester M27 5WN
Phone: 0161 794 3365

#312
Taylor's
Category: Social Club
Address: Barton Lane
Manchester M30 0FR
Phone: 0161 789 3016

#313
**Middleton & Chadderton
Sea Cadets**
Category: Social Club
Address: 265 Oldham Road
Manchester M35 0AS
Phone: 0161 681 8697

#314
Droylsden Working Men's Club
Category: Social Club
Address: Lloyd Street
Manchester M43 6UB
Phone: 0161 301 4722

#315
Droylsden Catholic Club
Category: Social Club
Address: Sunnyside Road
Manchester M43 7WW
Phone: 0161 370 2046

#316
Prestwich Liberal Club
Category: Social Club
Address: 509 Bury New Road
Manchester M25 3AJ
Phone: 0161 773 3518

#317
Royal British Legion
Category: Social Club
Address: 609 Bolton Road
Manchester M27 4EJ
Phone: 0161 794 3511

#318
Failsworth Liberal Club
Category: Social Club
Address: 339 Oldham Road
Manchester M35 0AN
Phone: 0161 681 1606

#319
Medlock Gymnastics Academy
Category: Social Club, Sports & Leisure
Address: Greenside Trading Centre
Greenside Lane Manchester M43 7AJ
Phone: 0161 371 7666

#320
Audenshaw Masonic Club
Category: Social Club
Address: Manchester Road
Manchester M34 5GB
Phone: 0161 370 2235

#321
Moston Ward Labour Club
Category: Social Club
Address: 841 Moston Lane
Manchester M40 5RT
Phone: 0161 681 4665

#322
Swinton Conservative Club
Category: Social Club
Address: 1 The Parade
Manchester M27 4BH
Phone: 0161 794 1784

#323
Droylsden Little Theatre
Category: Theatre
Address: Market Street
Manchester M43 7AY
Phone: 0161 370 7713

#324
**Swinton & Pendlebury
Labour Club**
Category: Social Club
Address: 10 Station Road
Manchester M27 6AF
Phone: 0161 794 2556

#325
Salisbury Conservative Club
Category: Social Club
Address: Ashton Road
Manchester M43 7BW
Phone: 0161 370 2314

#326
Borough Social Club
Category: Social Club
Address: 167 Station Road
Manchester M27 6BU
Phone: 0161 794 1239

#327
Folly Lane A R L F Club
Category: Social Club
Address: Station Road
Manchester M27 6AH
Phone: 0161 728 2205

#328
Cosmo Bingo & Social Club
Category: Social Club
Address: 241 Liverpool Road
Manchester M30 0QN
Phone: 0161 789 3524

#329
Royal British Legion
Category: Social Club
Address: 109 Moston Lane East
Manchester M40 3GJ
Phone: 0161 681 3703

#330
Patricroft Conservative Club
Category: Social Club
Address: 1 Edison Road
Manchester M30 7AW
Phone: 0161 789 3729

#331
Wanderscan
Category: Theatre
Address: 22 Parkside
Manchester M24 1NL
Phone: 0161 653 1460

#332
Cat's Dance & Fitness
Category: Theatre
Address: 35 St Josephs Avenue
Manchester M45 6NT
Phone: 0161 796 7064

#333
Patricroft Working Mens Club
Category: Social Club
Address: 17 Legh Street
Manchester M30 0UT
Phone: 0161 789 3989

#334
Talbot Catholic Club
Category: Social Club
Address: 12 Eldon Place
Manchester M30 8QE
Phone: 0161 789 1021

#335
Urmston Masonic Hall
Category: Social Club
Address: 15 Westbourne Road
Manchester M41 0XQ
Phone: 0161 748 6533

#336
Urmston Mens' Club & Institute
Category: Social Club
Address: 81 Higher Road
Manchester M41 9AP
Phone: 0161 748 9022

#337
New Moston Club
Category: Social Club
Address: Parkfield Road North
Manchester M40 3RQ
Phone: 0161 681 1632

#338
J M Leisure
Category: Theatre
Address: 580 Manchester Old Road
Manchester M24 4PJ
Phone: 0161 653 2029

#339
Taxplan
Category: Theatre
Address: 234 Manchester New Road
Manchester M24 1NP
Phone: 0161 643 3215

#340
Urmston Social Club
Category: Social Club
Address: 1 & 3 Old Crofts Bank
Manchester M41 7AA
Phone: 0161 748 3666

#341
The Stockport Motor Club
Category: Theatre
Address: 18 Lynwood Road
Manchester M19 1RJ
Phone: 0161 432 9161

#342
G M B Cringlewood Social Club
Category: Social Club
Address: Yew Tree Lane
Manchester M23 0DN
Phone: 0161 998 2561

#343
Moorside Social Club
Category: Social Club
Address: 207 Moorside Road
Manchester M27 9LD
Phone: 0161 794 1934

#344
**Unsworth South Social
Working Mens Club**
Category: Social Club
Address: Derwent Avenue
Manchester M45 8HU
Phone: 0161 766 5915

#345
Flat & Round Records
Category: Arcade
Address: 26 Wilton Street
Manchester M45 7EU
Phone: 0161 766 8781

#346
**Northenden Players
Theatre Club**
Category: Social Club
Address: Boat Lane
Manchester M22 4HR
Phone: 0161 945 4160

#347
Brackley Conservative Club
Category: Social Club
Address: 1 Hazelhurst Fold
Manchester M28 2JU
Phone: 0161 794 1735

#348
Cineworld
Category: Cinema
Address: Wilmslow Road
Manchester M20 5PG
Phone: 0871 200 2000

#349
Faze 2
Category: Arcade
Address: 61 Church Road
Manchester M22 4WD
Phone: 0161 998 9966

#350
Gallery
Category: Art Gallery
Address: 59 Flixton Road
Manchester M41 5AN
Phone: 0161 748 4109

#351
Royal British Legion
Category: Social Club
Address: 10 Royle Green Road
Manchester M22 4NG
Phone: 0161 998 4684

#352
H Donn
Category: Art Gallery
Address: 138-142 Bury New Road
Manchester M45 6AD
Phone: 0161 766 8819

#353
Fresh Management
Category: Theatre
Address: 891 Kingsway
Manchester M20 5PB
Phone: 0161 434 8333

#354
Philip Partridge Entertainment
Category: Arcade
Address: 34 Winwood Road
Manchester M20 5PE
Phone: 0161 448 2672

#355
Royal British Legion
Category: Social Club
Address: Grosvenor Street
Manchester M34 3WN
Phone: 0161 336 4340

#356
Denton West End Social Club
Category: Social Club
Address: Grosvenor Street
Manchester M34 3WN
Phone: 0161 337 9816

#357
Flixton Ex Servicemen's Association
Category: Social Club
Address: Flixton Road
Manchester M41 6QY
Phone: 0161 748 2617

#358
Flixton Conservative Club
Category: Social Club
Address: Flixton Road
Manchester M41 5DF
Phone: 0161 748 2846

#359
Our Lady Parochial Centre
Category: Social Club
Address: Wood Street
Manchester M24 4DH
Phone: 0161 643 6303

#360
Denton Villa Football & Netball Club
Category: Social Club
Address: 32 Jackson Garden
Manchester M34 2EH
Phone: 0161 336 8681

#361
New Millbeck Club
Category: Social Club
Address: Millbeck Road
Manchester M24 4HR
Phone: 0161 653 5448

#362
Woodside Working Mens Social Club
Category: Social Club
Address: Higher Wood Street
Manchester M24 5SW
Phone: 0161 643 3212

#363
Colour Of Sport
Category: Theatre
Address: 36 Radcliffe New Road
Manchester M45 7GY
Phone: 0161 796 6842

#364
Brooklands Trade & Labour Club
Category: Social Club
Address: Carrswood Road
Manchester M23 9HQ
Phone: 0161 998 5838

#365
Rome Fine Arts
Category: Art Gallery
Address: 284 Stand Lane
Manchester M26 1JE
Phone: 0161 766 9991

#366
Denton Workingmen's Club & Institute
Category: Social Club
Address: 3 Frederick Street
Manchester M34 3JB
Phone: 0161 336 2227

#367
Conservative Club
Category: Social Club
Address: 45 Manchester Road
Manchester M34 2AF
Phone: 0161 336 2085

#368
Denton Labour Party Holdings
Category: Social Club
Address: Ashton Road
Manchester M34 3JF
Phone: 0161 336 2883

#369
Denton Liberal Club
Category: Social Club
Address: 1 Bowden Street
Manchester M34 2AB
Phone: 0161 336 2307

#370
St Bernadettes Social Centre
Category: Social Club
Address: Selby Avenue
Manchester M45 8UT
Phone: 0161 766 2116

#371
Winston Conservative Club
Category: Social Club
Address: Hall Lane
Manchester M23 1AQ
Phone: 0161 945 1450

#372
Boarshaw Working Mens Club
Category: Social Club
Address: 1 Dixon Street
Manchester M24 6GB
Phone: 0161 643 2820

#373
Cheshire Arts Theatre
Category: Theatre
Address: 20 Birch Grove
Manchester M34 5DN
Phone: 0161 320 4268

#374
Sacred Heart Parish Centre
Category: Social Club
Address: 92 Floatshall Road
Manchester M23 1HP
Phone: 0161 998 4626

#375
Waterfall Theatre Co
Category: Theatre
Address: 39a Porlock Road
Manchester M23 1LZ
Phone: 0161 998 8844

#376
Hebers Working Mens Club & Institute
Category: Social Club
Address: 231 Hollin Lane
Manchester M24 5LU
Phone: 0161 643 3636

#377
PC Rescued
Category: Theatre
Address: 10 Erlesmere Avenue
Manchester M34 3FD
Phone: 0161 320 5518

#378
Stanycliffe Social Centre
Category: Social Club
Address: Stanycliffe Lane
Manchester M24 2PB
Phone: 0161 643 2276

#379
St. Johns Catholic Mens Club
Category: Social Club
Address: Greenwood Road
Manchester M22 8AU
Phone: 0161 998 5807

#380
Cessxpress Intermusic'N'Sports Pleasure Leisure Company
Category: Arcade
Address: 10 Tamar Drive
Manchester M23 2QB
Phone: 0161 087 2968

#381
St. Marys Catholic Social Club
Category: Social Club
Address: Pine Street
Manchester M26 2WQ
Phone: 0161 723 2181

#382
Kearsley & Ringley Conservative Club
Category: Social Club
Address: 52 Ringley Road
Manchester M26 1FS
Phone: 01204 571796

#383
Benchill & District Conservative Club
Category: Social Club
Address: Crossacres Road
Manchester M22 5BS
Phone: 0161 437 4980

#384
D Bradley
Category: Arcade
Address: 50 Ringley Road Stoneclough
Manchester M26 1FS
Phone: 01204 400508

#385
Greenbrow Social Club
Category: Social Club
Address: Greenbrow Road
Manchester M23 2TU
Phone: 0161 437 3329

#386
Radcliffe British Legion Club
Category: Social Club
Address: 50 Water Street
Manchester M26 4DF
Phone: 0161 723 2586

#387
Royal British Legion
Category: Social Club
Address: Wilfred Road
Manchester M28 3AJ
Phone: 0161 790 2434

#388
Longley Road Club
Category: Social Club
Address: 17 Longley Road
Manchester M28 3JA
Phone: 0161 790 2446

#389
Wythenshawe Forum Trust
Category: Stadium
Address: Forum Square
Manchester M22 5RX
Phone: 0161 935 4000

#390
Walkden Science Club
Category: Social Club
Address: Bolton Road
Manchester M28 3AX
Phone: 0161 799 0881

#391
Buckingham Bingo Club
Category: Social Club
Address: 10-12 New Ellesmere Approach
Manchester M28 3EE
Phone: 0161 790 6655

#392
Urmston Conservative Club
Category: Social Club
Address: Moorfield Walk
Manchester M41 0TT
Phone: 0161 748 2108

#393
Bridge For All Teaching Group
Category: Social Club
Address: 425 Bolton Road
Manchester M26 3QG
Phone: 0161 724 5670

#394
The Royal British Legion
Category: Social Club
Address: Victoria Street
Manchester M28 1HQ
Phone: 0161 790 2928

#395
St. Anthony's Parish Centre
Category: Social Club
Address: Portway Road
Manchester M22 0NT
Phone: 0161 437 6588

#396
Higher Irlam Social Club
Category: Social Club
Address: Cutnook Lane
Manchester M44 6JS
Phone: 0161 775 2868

#397
Pictor Framing Studio
Category: Art Gallery
Address: 29 Chaddock Lane
Manchester M28 1DE
Phone: 0161 790 8008

#398
Pentdale
Category: Theatre
Address: 32 Windmill Road
Manchester M28 3RP
Phone: 0161 790 8346

#399
Irlam Steel Recreation Club
Category: Social Club
Address: Liverpool Road
Manchester M44 6AJ
Phone: 0161 775 2346

#400
Holy Family
Category: Social Club
Address: Chaddock Lane
Manchester M28 1DN
Phone: 0161 790 1898

#401
Armitage Social Club
Category: Social Club
Address: Madams Wood Road
Manchester M28 0JU
Phone: 0161 790 5293

#402
Entertainment Trade Management
Category: Theatre
Address: 122 Mosley Common Rd
Manchester M28 1AN
Phone: 0161 799 9513

#403
Irlam Catholic Men's Social Club
Category: Social Club
Address: 617 Liverpool Road
Manchester M44 5BE
Phone: 0161 777 9512

#404
Royal British Legion
Category: Social Club
Address: Woodhouse Lane
Manchester M22 9TF
Phone: 0161 437 2952

#405
The Aviation Shop
Category: Social Club
Address: LVL 13 Term 1 Multi Storey Car P
Manchester M90 1QX
Phone: 0161 489 2444

#406
Irlam Conservative Club
Category: Social Club
Address: Astley Road
Manchester M44 6AB
Phone: 0161 775 2499

#407
Astley Conservative Club
Category: Social Club
Address: 90-94 Higher Green Lane
Manchester M29 7HZ
Phone: 01942 882009

#408
Astley Labour Club
Category: Social Club
Address: Manchester Road
Manchester M29 7DY
Phone: 01942 882977

#409
Top Club
Category: Social Club
Address: Manchester Road West
Manchester M38 9EG
Phone: 0161 790 5241

#410
Partington Social Club
Category: Social Club
Address: 2 Warburton Lane
Manchester M31 4NR
Phone: 0161 776 1318

#411
Cadishead Labour Club
Category: Social Club
Address: Fir Street
Manchester M44 5AG
Phone: 0161 775 2045

#412
Conservative Club
Category: Social Club
Address: 5 Stanley Street
Manchester M29 8AE
Phone: 01942 882713

#413
R A O B Club
Category: Social Club
Address: Castle Street
Manchester M29 8EG
Phone: 01942 884707

#414
**Sacred Heart Parochial
Club & Centre**
Category: Social Club
Address: Lodge Road
Manchester M46 9BN
Phone: 01942 882464

#415
Atherton Liberal Club
Category: Social Club
Address: 30 Flapper Fold Lane
Manchester M46 0FA
Phone: 01942 882240

#416
Atherton Sports & Social Club
Category: Social Club
Address: Formby Avenue
Manchester M46 9PZ
Phone: 01942 888811

#417
Atherton Laburnam Rovers F C
Category: Stadium
Address: Spa Road
Manchester M46 9NQ
Phone: 01942 883950

#418
Atherton Village Club
Category: Social Club
Address: Leigh Road
Manchester M46 0PA
Phone: 07979 633453

#419
Lyme Park
Category: Botanical Garden
Address: Disley Disley SK12 2NR
Phone: 01633 762023

#420
**National Trust: Quarry Bank Mill
and Styal Estate**
Category: Cultural Center
Address: Styal Wilmslow SK9 4LA
Phone: 01625 527468

#421
Plaza Theatre
Category: Music Venues, Theatre
Address: Mersey Square
Stockport SK1 1SP
Phone: 0161 477 7779

#422
Salford Museum & Art Gallery
Category: Museum, Art Gallery
Address: The Crescent Salford M5 4WU
Phone: 0161 778 0800

#423
Red Cinema
Category: Cinema
Address: The Lowry Designer Outlet
Salford M50 3AG
Phone: 0870 998 1878

#424
**Bolton Museum, Art Gallery
and Aquarium**
Category: Art Gallery, Aquarium
Address: Le Mans Crescent Bolton BL1
1SE Phone: 01204 332211

#425
Knutsford Wine Bar
Category: Wine Bar, Music Venues
Address: 41a King Street
Knutsford WA16 6DW
Phone: 01565 750459

#426
Palace Theatre
Category: Theatre, Music Venues
Address: Oxford Street
Manchester M1 6FT
Phone: 0161 245 6600

#427
The Quays Theatre
Category: Theatre, Bar
Address: 140 The Quays
Salford M50 3AG
Phone: 0870 787 5780

#428
Witchwood Public House
Category: Pub, Music Venues
Address: 152 Old St
Ashton Under Lyne OL6 7SF
Phone: 0161 344 0321

#429
Lancashire County Cricket Club
Category: Sports Club, Stadium
Address: Talbot Road
Manchester M16 0PX
Phone: 0161 282 4000

#430
Cineworld Bolton
Category: Cinema
Address: 15 The Valley
Bolton BL1 8TS
Phone: 0870 777 2775

#431
Chorley Little Theatre
Category: Theatre, Cinema
Address: Dole Lane
Chorley PR7 2RL
Phone: 01257 275123

#432
Eureka
Category: Museum
Address: Discovery Road
Halifax HX1 2NE
Phone: 01422 330069

#433
Chads Theatre Co
Category: Theatre
Address: Mellor Road
Cheadle SK8 5AU
Phone: 0161 486 1788

#434
Justicia Craft Centre
Category: Arts & Crafts
Address: 81 Knowsley Street
Bolton BL1 2BJ
Phone: 01204 363308

#435
The Birdcage Manchester
Category: Club, Music Venues
Address: Withy Grove
Manchester M4 3AQ
Phone: 0161 832 1700

#436
Jodrell Bank Centre for Astrophysics
Category: Museum, Landmark
Address: Jodrell Bank
Manchester SK11 9DL
Phone: 01477 571339

#437
County Gallery
Category: Framing, Art Gallery
Address: 32-34 Railway Street
Altrincham WA14 2RE
Phone: 0161 928 9942

#438
Lyme Hall
Category: Museum
Address: Disley Stockport SK12 2NR
Phone: 01663 766492

#439
Ordsall Hall Museum
Category: Museum
Address: Ordsall Lane
Salford M5 3AN
Phone: 0161 872 0251

#440
Air Raid Shelters Tour
Category: Local Flavour, Art Gallery
Address: 61 Great Underbank
Stockport SK1 1NE
Phone: 0161 474 1940

#441
Hat Works
Category: Museum
Address: Wellington Mill
Stockport SK3 0EU
Phone: 0845 833 0975

#442
Bury Art Gallery & Museum
Category: Art Gallery
Address: Moss Street
Bury BL9 0DF
Phone: 0161 253 5878

#443
The Cinnamon Club
Category: Jazz & Blues, European
Address: The Bowdon Room
Trafford WA14 2TQ
Phone: 0161 926 8992

#444
Cadishead Conservative Club
Category: Social Club
Address: Grange Place
Manchester M44 5UN
Phone: 0161 775 2433

#445
Quarry Bank Mill
Category: Museum
Address: Styal
Manchester SK9 4LA
Phone: 01625 527468

#446
Pavillion Garden
Category: Venues & Event Space, Swimming Pool, Festival, Park
Address: St John's Road
Buxton SK17 6XN
Phone: 01298 23114

#447
Bolton Albert Hall
Category: Venues & Event Space, Music Venues, Theatre
Address: Victoria Square
Bolton BL1 1RJ
Phone: 01204 334433

#448
Games Workshop
Category: Sports & Leisure, Hobby Shop, Social Club
Address: 31 St Mary Street
Cardiff CF10 1PU
Phone: 029 2064 4917

#449
Carlton Club
Category: Social Club
Address: 113 Carlton Road
Manchester M16 8BE
Phone: 0161 881 3042

#450
Filmworks
Category: Cinema
Address: Withy Grove
Manchester M4 2BS
Phone: 0870 010 2030

#451
Un-Convention Festival
Category: Festival
Address: 20 Huddart Close
Salford M5 3RS
Phone: 0161 872 3767

#452
Savoy Cinema
Category: Cinema
Address: Heaton Moor Road
Stockport SK4 4HY
Phone: 0161 432 2114

#453
Powerleague
Category: Social Club, Football
Address: Stadium Way
Wigan WN5 0UN
Phone: 01942 210080

#454
**Museum Of The
Manchester Regiment**
Category: Museum
Address: Wellington Road
Ashton-under-Lyne OL6 6DL
Phone: 0161 342 3078

#455
Thackeray Music
Category: Theatre, Music & DVDs
Address: 7 Woodlands Road
Stockport SK4 3AF
Phone: 0161 432 3351

#456
**Woodhouses Working
Mens Club**
Category: Social Club
Address: 62-64 Medlock Road
Manchester M35 9WN
Phone: 0161 681 3562

#457
Portland Basin Museum
Category: Museum
Address: Portland Place
Ashton-under-Lyne OL7 0QA
Phone: 0161 343 2878

#458
ConservativeClub
Category: Social Club
Address: Mellor Street
Stockport SK8 5AT
Phone: 0161 485 1087

#459
Stalybridge Labour Club
Category: Social Club,
Venues & Event Space
Address: Acres Lane
Stalybridge SK15 2JR
Phone: 0161 338 4796

#460
Busy Bee Networking Group
Category: Social Club
Address: 5 Cedar Rd
Altrincham WA15 9
Phone: 07870 601168

#461
The Heywood
Category: Social Club, Pub
Address: 1 Tower Street
Heywood OL10 3AA
Phone: 01706 369710

#462
Astley Green Colliery Museum
Category: Museum
Address: Higher Green Lane
Astley Green
Manchester M29 7JB
Phone: 01772 431937

#463
George Lawton Hall
Category: Theatre
Address: Stamford St
Mossley OL5 0HR
Phone: 01457 832223

#464
**Warrington Museum
& Art Gallery**
Category: Museum, Art Gallery
Address: Museum Street / Bold Street
Warrington WA1 1JB
Phone: 01925 442399

#465
Micklehurst Cricket Club
Category: Social Club, Sports Club
Address: Castle Lane Ashton
Under Lyne SK15 3QG
Phone: 01457 832163

#466
Harlequin Theatre
Category: Theatre
Address: Queen Street
Northwich CW9 5JN
Phone: 01606 44235

#467
JB's
Category: Music Venues
Address: Grains Road
Shaw OL2 8JB
Phone: 01706 841460

#468
Morley Green Club
Category: Social Club
Address: Mobberley Road
Wilmslow SK9 5NT
Phone: 01625 525224

#469
Vue Entertainment
Category: Cinema
Address: The Linkway
Bolton BL6 6JA
Phone: 01204 668809

#470
Bradshaw Conservative Club
Category: Social Club
Address: Lee Gate
Bolton BL2 3ET
Phone: 01204 416947

#471
Uppermill Conservative Club
Category: Social Club
Address: 74 High Street
Oldham OL3 6AP
Phone: 01457 873077

#472
Astley Bridge Cricket Club
Category: Social Club, Sports & Leisure
Address: Moss Bank Way
Bolton BL1 6PZ
Phone: 01204 415515

#473
Astley Bridge Conservative Club
Category: Social Club
Address: Moss Bank Way
Bolton BL1 8NP
Phone: 01204 301233

#474
**Astley Hall Museum
and Art Gallery**
Category: Museum, Art Gallery
Address: Astley Park
Chorley PR7 1NP
Phone: 01257 515555

#475
Lowton Civic Hall
Category: Venues & Event Space,
Recreation Center, Cultural Center
Address: Hesketh Meadow Lane
Warrington WA3 2AH
Phone: 01942 672971

#476
Parr Hall Concert Hall
Category: Theatre
Address: Palmyra Square
South Warrington WA1 1BL
Phone: 01925 442345

#477
Stockport Story
Category: Museum
Address: 30-31 Market Place
Stockport SK1 1ES
Phone: 0161 480 1460

#478
The Halliwell Jones Stadium
Category: Stadium
Address: Winwick Road
Warrington WA2 7NE
Phone: 01925 248880

#479
Cubecure
Category: Art Gallery
Address: 16 Peel Street
Huddersfield HD7 6BW
Phone: 01484 842305

#480
**Powerleague
Manchester South**
Category: Stadium
Address: The Range Stadium Whalley
Range High School Wilbraham Road
Manchester M16 8GW
Phone: 0161 881 8442

#481
John Bull Chop House
Category: Pub, Music Venues
Address: 2 Coopers Row
Wigan WN1 1PQ
Phone: 01942 242862

#482
Irish Democratic League
Category: Social Club
Address: George Street
Rossendale BB4 5RX
Phone: 01706 214787

#483
Legoland Discovery Centre
Category: Toy Shop, Arcade
Address: Barton Square
Trafford M17 8AS
Phone: 0871 222 2662

#484
The Boulevard
Category: Pub, Music Venues
Address: 17A Wallgate
Wigan WN1 1LD
Phone: 01942 497165

#485
Halifax Playhouse
Category: Theatre
Address: King Cross Street
Halifax HX1 2SH
Phone: 01422 365998

#486
Cineworld Stockport
Category: Cinema
Address: 4 Grand Central Square
Stockport SK1 3TA
Phone: 0870 777 2775

#487
Antrobus Village Hall
Category: Venues & Event Space
Address: Knutsford Road
Northwich CW9 6LB
Phone: 07544 567708

#488
Bury Met Theatre
Category: Theatre
Address: Market Street
Bury BL9 0BW
Phone: 0161 761 2216

#489
Cosmo Bingo Club
Category: Arcade
Address: 62 Market Street
Stalybridge SK15 2AB
Phone: 0161 338 5277

#490
Castle Gallery
Category: Art Gallery
Address: 75 Deansgate
Manchester M2 7
Phone: 0161 839 3800

#491
Vue Bury
Category: Cinema
Address: Park 66 Bury BL9 8RS
Phone: 0871 224 0240

#492
Cineworld Cinema
Category: Cinema
Address: Fold Way
Ashton-under-Lyne OL7 0PG
Phone: 0871 200 2000

#493
Bolton Museum & Art Gallery
Category: Museum
Address: Victoria Square
Bolton BL1 1RJ
Phone: 01204 332211

#494
The Lowry Gift Shop
Category: Cinema, Gift Shop
Address: Pier 8 Salford Quays
Manchester M50 3AZ
Phone: 0870 787 5780

#495
Salt Museum
Category: Museum
Address: 162 London Road
Northwich CW9 8AB
Phone: 01606 41331

#496
Odeon Cinema
Address: 100 Westbrook Centre
Warrington WA5 8UD
Phone: 0871 224 4007

#497
The Original Art Shop
Category: Art Gallery
Address: Market Street
Manchester M4 3AT
Phone: 0161 834 3370

#498
The Art Surgery
Category: Art Gallery, Photographers
Address: 33-35 Tib Street
Manchester M4 1LX
Phone: 0161 819 2888

#499
Odeon Rochdale
Category: Cinema
Address: Sandbrook Park
Rochdale OL11 1RY
Phone: 0871 224 4007

#500
New Century Hall
Category: Venues & Event Space
Address: Corporation Street
Manchester M60 4ES
Phone: 0161 827 5198

TOP 500 NIGHTLIFE

The Most Recommended by Locals & Trevelers

(From #1 to #500)

#1
Band on the Wall
Category: Bar, Music Venues,
Jazz & Blues
Average price: Modest
Area: Northern Quarter
Address: 25 Swan Street
Manchester M4 5JZ
Phone: 0161 834 1786

#2
The Marble Arch
Category: Pub, Gastropub
Average price: Modest
Area: Ancoats, Petersfield
Address: 73 Rochdale Road
Manchester M4 4HY
Phone: 0161 832 5914

#3
Cornerhouse
Category: Cinemas, Bar, Cafe
Average price: Modest
Area: Oxford Road Corridor
Address: 70 Oxford Street
Manchester M1 5NH
Phone: 0161 200 1500

#4
Sandbar
Category: Pub, Music Venues
Average price: Modest
Area: Oxford Road Corridor
Address: 120 Grosvenor Street
Manchester M1 7HL
Phone: 0161 273 1552

#5
Matt and Phreds
Category: Club, Jazz & Blues,
Music Venues
Average price: Modest
Area: Northern Quarter
Address: 64 Tib Street
Manchester M4 1LW
Phone: 0161 839 7187

#6
Sinclair's Oyster Bar
Category: Pub, British
Average price: Inexpensive
Area: City Centre
Address: 2 Cathedral Gates
Manchester M3 1SW
Phone: 0161 834 0430

#7
Pi
Category: British, Pub
Average price: Modest
Area: Chorlton
Address: 99 Manchester Road
Manchester M21 9GA
Phone: 0161 882 0000

#8
FAB Café
Category: Lounge, Club, Dive Bar
Average price: Modest
Area: Chinatown
Address: 109 Portland Street
Manchester M1 6DN
Phone: 0161 212 2997

#9
The Deaf Institute
Category: Lounge, Music Venues
Average price: Modest
Area: Oxford Road Corridor
Address: 135 Grosvenor Street
Manchester M1 7HE
Phone: 0161 276 9350

#10
Chaophraya
Category: Thai, Bar
Average price: Expensive
Area: City Centre
Address: Chapel Walks Manchester
Manchester M2 1HN
Phone: 0161 832 8342

#11
Big Hands
Category: Pub, Lounge, Dive Bar
Average price: Modest
Area: Oxford Road Corridor
Address: 296 Oxford Road
Manchester M13 9NS
Phone: 0161 272 7309

#12
Trof
Category: Bar, British
Average price: Modest
Area: City Centre
Address: 6-8 Thomas Street
Manchester M4 1EU
Phone: 0161 833 3197

#13
Nexus Art Cafe
Category: Music Venues, Lounge
Average price: Inexpensive
Area: Northern Quarter
Address: 2 Dale Street
Manchester M1 1JW
Phone: 0161 236 0100

#14
Manchester Academy 2
Category: Music Venues, Bar
Average price: Modest
Area: Oxford Road Corridor
Address: Oxford Road
Manchester M13 9PR
Phone: 0161 275 2930

#15
Sam's Chop House
Category: British, Pub
Average price: Modest
Area: City Centre
Address: Blackpool Hold
Manchester M2 1HN
Phone: 0161 834 3210

#16
St Ann's Church
Category: Music Venues
Area: City Centre
Address: St Ann's Street
Manchester M2 7LF
Phone: 0161 834 1161

#17
Soup Kitchen
Category: Bar, Cafe
Average price: Modest
Area: Northern Quarter
Address: 31-33 Spear Street
Manchester M1 1DF
Phone: 0161 236 5100

#18
The Font
Category: Pub, Lounge
Average price: Inexpensive
Area: Oxford Road Corridor
Address: 7-9 New Wakefield Street
Manchester M1 5NP
Phone: 0161 236 0944

#19
Manchester Academy
Category: Music Venues
Average price: Modest
Area: Oxford Road Corridor
Address: Oxford Road
Manchester M13 9PR
Phone: 0161 275 2930

#20
The Ox
Category: Hotel, Gastropub, Bar
Average price: Expensive
Area: Castlefield
Address: Liverpool Road
Manchester M3 4NQ
Phone: 0161 839 7740

#21
The Old Wellington
Category: Gastropub, Pub, British
Average price: Modest
Area: City Centre
Address: 4 Cathedral Gates
Manchester M3 1SW
Phone: 0161 839 5179

#22
Sankeys
Category: Club
Average price: Expensive
Area: Ancoats, Petersfield
Address: Radium Street
Manchester M4 6AY
Phone: 0161 236 5444

#23
Kro Bar
Category: Pub, European
Average price: Modest
Area: Oxford Road Corridor
Address: 325 Oxford Road
Manchester M13 9PG
Phone: 0161 274 3100

#24
Dukes 92
Category: Pub, British
Average price: Modest
Area: Castlefield
Address: 18 Castle Street
Manchester M3 4LZ
Phone: 0161 839 3522

#25
Room
Category: Bar, European
Average price: Expensive
Area: City Centre
Address: 81 King Street
Manchester M2 4AH
Phone: 0161 839 2005

#26
The Metropolitan
Category: British, Gastropub, Bar
Average price: Modest
Area: West Didsbury
Address: 2 Lapwing Lane
Manchester M20 2WS
Phone: 0161 438 2332

#27
Michael Caines Restaurant
Category: British, Champagne Bar
Average price: Expensive
Area: Piccadilly
Address: 107 Piccadilly
Manchester M1 2DB
Phone: 0161 200 5678

#28
The Bay Horse
Category: Pub
Average price: Modest
Area: Northern Quarter
Address: 35-37 Thomas Street
Manchester M4 1NA
Phone: 0161 661 1041

#29
The Ruby Lounge
Category: Club, Music Venues
Average price: Modest
Area: Northern Quarter
Address: 28-34 High Street
Manchester M4 1QB
Phone: 0161 834 1392

#30
The Art of Tea
Category: Tea Room, Bar
Average price: Modest
Area: Didsbury Village
Address: 47 Barlow Moor Road
Manchester M20 6TW
Phone: 0161 448 9323

#31
English Lounge
Category: Pub, British, Burgers
Average price: Modest
Area: Northern Quarter
Address: 64-66 High Street
Manchester M4 1EA
Phone: 0161 832 4824

#32
The Castle Hotel
Category: Pub, Music Venues
Average price: Modest
Area: Northern Quarter
Address: 66 Oldham Street
Manchester M4 1LE
Phone: 0161 237 9485

#33
Common
Category: Bar, Music Venues
Average price: Modest
Area: Northern Quarter
Address: 39 - 41 Edge Street
Manchester M4 1HW
Phone: 0161 832 9245

#34
Phones 4u Arena
Category: Theatre, Music Venues
Average price: Expensive
Area: City Centre
Address: Victoria Station
Manchester M3 1AR
Phone: 0161 950 5000

#35
Corbieres
Category: Wine Bar, Pizza, Dive Bar
Average price: Inexpensive
Area: City Centre
Address: 2 Half Moon Street
Manchester M2 7PB
Phone: 0161 834 3381

#36
The Alchemist
Category: European, Cocktail Bar
Average price: Expensive
Area: Spinningfields
Address: 3 Hardman Street
Manchester M3 3HF
Phone: 0161 817 2950

#37
Marble Beerhouse
Category: Pub, Brewerie
Average price: Modest
Area: Chorlton
Address: 57 Manchester Road
Manchester M21 9PW
Phone: 0161 881 9206

#38
Bar Fringe
Category: Pub
Average price: Modest
Area: Ancoats, Petersfield
Address: 8 Swan Street
Manchester M4 5JN
Phone: 0872 107 7077

#39
The Star and Garter
Category: Pub, Club, Music Venues
Average price: Inexpensive
Area: Piccadilly
Address: 18-20 Fairfield Street
Manchester M1 2QF
Phone: 0161 273 6726

#40
The Roadhouse
Category: Music Venues
Average price: Modest
Area: Northern Quarter
Address: 8 Newton Street
Manchester M1 2AN
Phone: 0161 237 9789

#41
The Woodstock
Category: Pub, Gastropub
Average price: Modest
Area: Didsbury Village
Address: 139 Barlow Moor Road
Manchester M20 2DY
Phone: 0161 448 7951

#42
Cord Bar
Category: Cocktail Bar
Average price: Modest
Area: Northern Quarter
Address: 8 Dorsey Street
Manchester M4 1LU
Phone: 0161 832 9494

#43
The Crown and Kettle
Category: Pub
Average price: Modest
Area: Ancoats, Petersfield
Address: 2 Oldham Road
Manchester M4 5FE
Phone: 0161 236 2923

#44
Retro Bar
Category: Music Venues, Dive Bar
Average price: Inexpensive
Area: Gay Village
Address: 78 Sackville Street
Manchester M1 3NJ
Phone: 0161 274 4892

#45
The Railway
Category: Pub
Average price: Inexpensive
Area: West Didsbury
Address: 3 Lapwing Lane
Manchester M20 2WS
Phone: 0161 445 9839

#46
The City Arms
Category: Pub
Average price: Modest
Area: City Centre
Address: 48 Kennedy Street
Manchester M2 4BQ
Phone: 0161 236 4610

#47
Java Bar Espresso
Category: Coffee & Tea, Bar
Average price: Inexpensive
Area: Oxford Road Corridor
Address: 1 - 3 Station Approach Oxford
Road Manchester M1 6FU
Phone: 0161 236 3656

#48
Thirsty Scholar
Category: Pub
Average price: Modest
Area: Oxford Road Corridor
Address: 50 New Wakefield Street
Manchester M1 5NP
Phone: 0161 236 6071

#49
Canal Street
Category: Bar, Club, Local Flavour
Average price: Inexpensive
Area: Gay Village
Address: Canal Street
Manchester M1 3

#50
O'Sheas Irish Bar
Category: Pub
Average price: Modest
Area: Oxford Road Corridor
Address: 80 Princess Street
Manchester M1 6NF
Phone: 0161 236 3906

#51
Horse & Jockey
Category: Pub
Average price: Expensive
Area: Chorlton
Address: 9 Chorlton Green
Manchester M21 9HS
Phone: 0161 860 7794

#52
The Spoon Inn
Category: Wine Bar
Average price: Modest
Area: Chorlton
Address: 364 Barlow Moor Road
Manchester M21 8AZ
Phone: 0161 881 2400

#53
Hardy's Well
Category: Pub
Average price: Inexpensive
Area: Rusholme
Address: 257 Wilmslow Road
Manchester M14 5LN
Phone: 0161 224 8034

#54
The Oast House
Category: Pub
Average price: Modest
Area: Spinningfields
Address: Crown Square
Manchester M3 3AY
Phone: 0161 829 3830

#55
Folk Café Bar
Category: Bar, Cafe
Average price: Modest
Area: West Didsbury
Address: 169-171 Burton Road
Manchester M20 2LN
Phone: 0161 445 2912

#56
Efes Taverna
Category: Turkish, Bar
Average price: Inexpensive
Area: Oxford Road Corridor
Address: 46 Princess Street
Manchester M1 6HR
Phone: 0161 236 1824

#57
**Hop & Grape Manchester
Academy 3**
Category: Music Venues, Bar
Average price: Modest
Area: Oxford Road Corridor
Address: Oxford Rd
Manchester M13 9PR
Phone: 0161 275 2930

#58
The Drawing Room
Category: Lounge, Wine Bar
Average price: Modest
Area: West Didsbury
Address: Burton Road
Manchester M20 2LW
Phone: 0161 283 6244

#59
Royal Northern College of Music
Category: Music Venues, Theatre
Average price: Modest
Area: Oxford Road Corridor
Address: 124 Oxford Road
Manchester M13 9RD
Phone: 0161 907 5200

#60
South
Category: Club
Average price: Expensive
Address: 4a S King St
Manchester M2 6DQ
Phone: 0161 831 7756

#61
Odd
Category: Pub
Average price: Modest
Area: Northern Quarter
Address: 30-32 Thomas Street
Manchester M4 1ER
Phone: 0161 833 0070

#62
Kro Piccadilly
Category: Bar, European, British
Average price: Modest
Area: Piccadilly
Address: 1 Piccadilly Gardens
Manchester M1 1RG
Phone: 0161 244 5765

#63
Ape & Apple
Category: Pub
Average price: Modest
Area: City Centre
Address: 28 John Dalton Street
Manchester M2 6HQ
Phone: 0161 839 9624

#64
Taurus
Category: Wine Bar, Gay Bar
Average price: Modest
Area: Gay Village
Address: 1 Canal Street
Manchester M1 3HE
Phone: 0161 236 4593

#65
Reserve
Category: Off Licence, Wine Bar
Average price: Modest
Area: West Didsbury
Address: 176 Burton Road
Manchester M20 1LH
Phone: 0161 438 0101

#66
The Blue Pig
Category: Bar, Persian/Iranian
Average price: Modest
Area: Northern Quarter
Address: 69 High St Manchester
Manchester M4 1FS
Phone: 0161 832 0630

#67
Wasabi
Category: Japanese, Sushi Bar, Bar
Average price: Modest
Area: Chinatown
Address: 63 Faulkner Street
Manchester M1 4FF
Phone: 0161 228 7288

#68
The Northern
Category: Pub
Average price: Modest
Area: Northern Quarter
Address: 56 Tib Street
Manchester M4 1LW
Phone: 0161 835 2548

#69
Walrus
Category: Lounge, Tapas
Average price: Modest
Area: Northern Quarter
Address: 78-88 High Street
Manchester M4 1ES
Phone: 0161 828 8700

#70
Seven Oaks
Category: Pub, Sports Bar
Average price: Inexpensive
Area: Chinatown
Address: 5 Nicholas Street
Manchester M1 4HL
Phone: 0161 237 1233

#71
The Molly House
Category: Pub, Specialty Food,
Coffee & Tea
Average price: Modest
Area: Gay Village
Address: 26/28 Richmond Street
Manchester M1 3NB
Phone: 0161 237 9329

#72
The Fat Loaf
Category: Pub
Average price: Expensive
Area: Didsbury Village
Address: 846 Wilmslow Road
Manchester M20 2RN
Phone: 0161 438 0319

#73
Apotheca Lounge
Average price: Modest
Area: Northern Quarter
Address: 17 Thomas Street
Manchester M4 1FS
Phone: 0161 834 9411

#74
Dusk til Pawn
Category: Cocktail Bar, Pub
Average price: Modest
Area: Northern Quarter
Address: Stevenson Square
Manchester M1 1FB
Phone: 0161 236 5355

#75
Squirrels Bar
Category: Bar
Average price: Inexpensive
Area: Fallowfield
Address: 1 Moseley Road
Manchester M14 6HX
Phone: 0161 248 3050

#76
Hula
Category: Bar
Average price: Modest
Area: Northern Quarter
Address: 11 Stevenson Square
Manchester M1 1DB
Phone: 0161 228 7421

#77
Hangingditch Wine Merchants
Category: Wine Bar, Off Licence
Average price: Modest
Area: City Centre
Address: 42-44 Victoria Street
Manchester M3 1ST
Phone: 0161 832 8222

#78
Copacabana
Category: Mexican, Club, Bar
Area: Northern Quarter
Address: Dale Street
Manchester M1 2HF
Phone: 0161 237 3441

#79
Kosmonaut
Category: Bar, Food
Average price: Modest
Area: Northern Quarter
Address: 10 Tariff Street
Manchester M1 2FF

#80
Boggart microbar
Category: Bar
Average price: Inexpensive
Area: Northern Quarter
Address: High Street
Manchester M4 3AJ
Phone: 0161 277 9666

#81
Zinc Bar and Grill
Category: British, Bar, American
Average price: Expensive
Area: City Centre
Address: The Triangle
Manchester M4 3TR
Phone: 0161 827 4200

#82
Dog & Partridge
Category: Pub
Average price: Modest
Area: Didsbury Village
Address: 665-667 Wilmslow Road
Manchester M20 6RA
Phone: 0161 445 5322

#83
Via Fossa
Category: Gay Bar
Average price: Modest
Area: Gay Village
Address: 28 Canal Street
Manchester M1 3EZ
Phone: 0161 236 6523

#84
Eastern Bloc Records
Category: Music Venues, Cafe
Average price: Modest
Area: Northern Quarter
Address: 5A Stevenson Square
Manchester M1 1DN
Phone: 0161 228 6555

#85
Hard Rock Cafe
Category: American, Bar
Average price: Modest
Area: City Centre
Address: 27 Withy Grove
Manchester M4 2BS
Phone: 0161 831 6700

#86
Terrace
Category: Bar
Average price: Modest
Area: Northern Quarter
Address: 43 Thomas Street
Manchester M4 1NA
Phone: 0161 819 2345

#87
Velvet Bar & Restaurant
Category: British, Lounge, Hotel
Average price: Modest
Area: Gay Village
Address: 2 Canal Street
Manchester M1 3HE
Phone: 0161 236 9003

#88
Mr Thomas's Chop House
Category: British, Pub
Average price: Expensive
Area: City Centre
Address: 52 Cross Street
Manchester M2 7AR
Phone: 0161 832 2245

#89
Mint Lounge
Category: Lounge, Club
Average price: Modest
Area: Northern Quarter
Address: 46-50 Oldham Street
Manchester M4 1LE
Phone: 0161 228 1495

#90
Bluu
Category: Lounge, British
Average price: Modest
Area: Northern Quarter
Address: 85 High Street
Manchester M4 1BD
Phone: 0161 839 7195

#91
Black Dog Ballroom
Category: Lounge, Snooker & Pool Hall,
American
Average price: Modest
Area: Northern Quarter
Address: 43 Oldham Street
Manchester M1 1JG
Phone: 0161 839 0664

#92
The Liar's Club
Category: Pub, Club, Cocktail Bar
Average price: Modest
Address: 19A Back Bridge Street
Manchester M2 3PB
Phone: 0161 834 5111

#93
Proof
Category: Lounge
Average price: Modest
Area: Chorlton
Address: 30a Manchester Road
Manchester M21 9PH
Phone: 0161 8629 3333

#94
One Lounge Bar
Category: Cocktail Bar
Average price: Exclusive
Area: West Didsbury
Address: 1 Lapwing Lane
Manchester M20 2NT
Phone: 0161 448 0101

#95
Las Iguanas
Category: Lounge, Latin American
Average price: Modest
Area: City Centre
Address: 84 Deansgate
Manchester M3 2ER
Phone: 0161 819 2606

#96
The Bank
Category: Pub, British
Average price: Modest
Area: Chinatown, City Centre
Address: 57 Mosley Street
Manchester M2 3FF
Phone: 0872 107 7077

#97
Bem Brasil
Category: Brazilian, Wine Bar
Average price: Expensive
Area: Northern Quarter
Address: 58 Lever Street
Manchester M1 1FJ
Phone: 0161 923 6888

#98
The Mark Addy
Category: Pub
Average price: Modest
Area: City Centre
Address: Stanley Street
Manchester M3 5EJ
Phone: 0161 832 4080

#99
Joshua Brooks
Category: Club, Pub
Average price: Modest
Area: Oxford Road Corridor
Address: 106 Princess Street
Manchester M1 6NG
Phone: 0161 273 7336

#100
Lammars
Category: Lounge, Tapas Bar
Average price: Modest
Area: Northern Quarter
Address: 57 Hilton Street
Manchester M1 2EJ
Phone: 0161 237 9058

#101
The Frog and Bucket Comedy Club
Category: Comedy Club, Bar
Average price: Modest
Area: Northern Quarter
Address: 102 Oldham Street
Manchester M4 1LJ
Phone: 0161 236 9805

#102
BarMC
Category: Lounge, Hotel
Average price: Modest
Address: 107 Piccadilly
Manchester M1 2DB
Phone: 0161 200 5665

#103
The Footage
Category: Pub, Burgers, Club
Average price: Inexpensive
Area: Oxford Road Corridor
Address: 137 Grosvenor Street
Manchester M1 7DZ
Phone: 0161 275 9164

#104
Black Dog Ballroom NWS
Category: Barbeque, Snooker & Pool Hall
Average price: Modest
Area: Oxford Road Corridor
Address: 11-13 New Wakefield Street
Manchester M1 5NP
Phone: 0161 236 4899

#105
Crown & Anchor
Category: Pub
Average price: Modest
Area: Northern Quarter
Address: 41 Hilton Street
Manchester M1 2EE
Phone: 0161 228 1142

#106
Twenty Twenty Two
Category: Bar, Art Gallery, Music Venues
Average price: Modest
Area: Northern Quarter
Address: 20 Dale Street
Manchester M1 1EZ
Phone: 0161 237 9360

#107
Grinch
Category: Wine Bar, Pizza
Average price: Modest
Area: City Centre
Address: 5-7 Chapel Walks
Manchester M2 1HN
Phone: 0161 907 3210

#108
All Bar One
Category: Lounge, European
Average price: Modest
Area: City Centre
Address: 73 King Street
Manchester M2 4NG
Phone: 0161 830 1811

#109
The Waterhouse
Category: Pub, British
Average price: Inexpensive
Area: City Centre
Address: 67-71 Princess Street
Manchester M2 4EG
Phone: 0161 200 5380

#110
The Printworks
Category: Arcade, Cinemas, Bar
Average price: Expensive
Area: City Centre
Address: 27 Withy Grove
Manchester M4 2BS
Phone: 0161 829 8000

#111
Tribeca
Category: Pub, Lounge, Cocktail Bar
Average price: Modest
Area: Gay Village
Address: 50 Sackville Street
Manchester M1 3WF
Phone: 0161 236 8300

#112
The Salutation
Category: Pub
Average price: Inexpensive
Area: Oxford Road Corridor
Address: 12 Higher Chatham Street
Manchester M15 6ED
Phone: 0161 272 7832

#113
Volta Eaterie & Bar
Category: Gastropub, Pub
Average price: Expensive
Area: West Didsbury
Address: 167 Burton Rd
Manchester M20 2LN
Phone: 0161 448 8887

#114
The Fitzgerald
Category: Club
Average price: Modest
Area: Northern Quarter
Address: 11 Stevenson Square
Manchester M1 1DB

#115
Cruz 101
Category: Club, Gay Bar
Average price: Modest
Area: Gay Village
Address: 101 Princess Street
Manchester M1 6DD
Phone: 0161 950 0101

#116
Marble
Category: Pub
Average price: Modest
Area: Northern Quarter
Address: 57 Thomas Street
Manchester M4 1NA
Phone: 0161 832 0521

#117
Noho Bar
Category: Lounge, Cocktail Bar
Average price: Modest
Area: Northern Quarter
Address: Spear Street
Manchester M1 1FB
Phone: 0161 236 5381

#118
New Union Hotel
Category: Bar, Hotel
Average price: Modest
Area: Oxford Road Corridor
Address: 111 Princess St
Manchester M1 6JB
Phone: 0161 228 1492

#119
Satan's Hollow
Category: Club, Bar
Average price: Inexpensive
Area: Oxford Road Corridor
Address: 101 Princess St
Manchester M1 6DD
Phone: 0161 236 0666

#120
The Bulls Head
Category: Pub
Average price: Modest
Area: Piccadilly
Address: 84 London Road
Manchester M1 2PN
Phone: 0161 236 1724

#121
Great John Street Hotel
Category: Hotel, Bar
Average price: Modest
Area: Castlefield
Address: Great John Street
Manchester M3 4FD
Phone: 0161 831 3211

#122
The Old Monkey
Category: Pub
Average price: Modest
Area: Chinatown
Address: 90-92 Portland Street
Manchester M1 4GX
Phone: 0161 228 6262

#123
Bakerie
Category: Wine Bar, Bakery
Average price: Modest
Area: Northern Quarter
Address: 43-45 Lever Street
Manchester M1 1FN
Phone: 0161 236 9014

#124
**Manchester Metropolitan
Students Union**
Category: Social Club, Lounge
Area: Oxford Road Corridor
Address: Grosvenor Square
Manchester M15 6BH
Phone: 0161 247 1162

#125
Chetham's School of Music
Category: Music Venues
Area: City Centre
Address: Long Millgate
Manchester M3 1SB
Phone: 0161 834 9644

#126
5th Avenue
Category: Club
Average price: Inexpensive
Area: Gay Village
Address: 121 Princess St
Manchester M1 7AG
Phone: 0161 236 2754

#127
Fletcher Moss
Category: Pub
Average price: Modest
Area: Didsbury Village
Address: 1 William St
Manchester M20 6RQ
Phone: 0161 438 0073

#128
The Angel
Category: Pub
Average price: Expensive
Area: Ancoats, Petersfield
Address: 6 Angel Street
Manchester M4 3BQ
Phone: 0161 833 4786

#129
Revolution
Category: Bar, British
Average price: Modest
Area: Oxford Road Corridor
Address: 88-94 Oxford Street
Manchester M1 5WH
Phone: 0161 237 5377

#130
Rosso Restaurant
Category: Italian, Cocktail Bar
Average price: Expensive
Area: City Centre
Address: 43 Spring Gardens
Manchester M2 2BG
Phone: 0161 832 1400

#131
Club Alterego
Category: Club
Average price: Modest
Area: Oxford Road Corridor
Address: 105-107 Princess Street
Manchester M1 6DD
Phone: 0161 236 9266

#132
The Green
Category: Bar, Golf
Average price: Modest
Area: Piccadilly
Address: 26 Ducie Street
Manchester M1 2DQ
Phone: 0161 228 0681

#133
The Salisbury
Category: Pub
Average price: Modest
Area: Oxford Road Corridor
Address: 2 Wakefield Street
Manchester M1 5NE
Phone: 0161 236 5590

#134
The Crescent
Category: Pub
Average price: Exclusive
Area: Salford University Campus
Address: 20 The Crescent
Manchester M5 4PF
Phone: 0161 736 5600

#135
The Warehouse Project
Category: Club
Average price: Expensive
Area: Salford Quays
Address: Trafford Wharf Road
Manchester M17 1AB

#136
Charlies Karaoke Bar
Category: Karaoke, Venues & Event
Spaces, Music Venues
Average price: Exclusive
Area: Oxford Road Corridor
Address: 1 Harter Street
Manchester M1 6
Phone: 0161 237 9898

#137
Baa Bar
Category: Lounge, Club
Average price: Modest
Area: Fallowfield
Address: 258 Wilmslow Rd
Manchester M14 6JR
Phone: 0161 224 9559

#138
Night & Day
Category: Bar, Music Venues
Average price: Modest
Area: Northern Quarter
Address: 26 Oldham Street
Manchester M1 1JN
Phone: 0161 236 4597

#139
Revolution
Category: Lounge, Club
Average price: Modest
Area: City Centre
Address: Arkwright House Parsonage
Gardens Manchester M3 2LF
Phone: 0161 839 9675

#140
The Pub/Zoo
Category: Pub, Club
Average price: Inexpensive
Area: Oxford Road Corridor
Address: 126 Grosvenor Street
Manchester M1 7HL
Phone: 0161 273 1471

#141
Churchills Public House
Category: Pub, Karaoke
Average price: Modest
Area: Gay Village
Address: 37 Chorlton Street
Manchester M1 3HN
Phone: 0161 236 5529

#142
Moon Under Water
Category: Pub, British
Average price: Inexpensive
Area: City Centre
Address: 68-74 Deansgate
Manchester M3 2FN
Phone: 0161 834 5882

#143
Slug & Lettuce
Category: Pub, British
Area: Didsbury Village
Address: 651 Wilmslow Road
Manchester M20 6QZ
Phone: 0161 434 1011

#144
The Font
Category: Lounge, Burgers
Average price: Inexpensive
Area: Fallowfield
Address: 236 Wilmslow Road
Manchester M14 6LE
Phone: 0161 248 4820

#145
Lime
Category: Bar
Average price: Expensive
Area: City Centre
Address: 2 Booth Street
Manchester M2 4AT
Phone: 0161 233 2929

#146
The Whiskey Jar
Category: Bar
Average price: Modest
Area: Northern Quarter
Address: 14 Tariff Street
Manchester M1 2FF
Phone: 0161 237 5686

#147
Ford Madox Brown
Category: Pub
Average price: Inexpensive
Area: Oxford Road Corridor
Address: Oxford Road
Manchester M13 9NG
Phone: 0161 256 6660

#148
Sandinista
Category: Tapas Bar, Lounge
Average price: Modest
Area: City Centre
Address: 2 Old Bank Street
Manchester M2 7PF
Phone: 0161 832 9955

#149
Ducie Bridge
Category: Pub
Average price: Modest
Area: City Centre
Address: 152 Corporation Street
Manchester M4 4DU
Phone: 0161 831 9725

#150
Club Academy
Category: Music Venues
Area: Oxford Road Corridor
Address: Oxford Road
Manchester M13 9PR
Phone: 0161 275 2930

#151
Chez Gerard
Category: Wine Bar, French
Average price: Expensive
Area: City Centre
Address: 2 -8 Commerical Union House
Manchester M2 6LP
Phone: 0161 834 7633

#152
Wahlbar
Category: Bar
Average price: Modest
Area: Fallowfield
Address: 310 Wilmslow Road
Manchester M14 6XQ
Phone: 0161 637 3736

#153
Electrik
Category: Bar
Average price: Modest
Area: Chorlton
Address: 559 Wilbraham Rd
Manchester M20 0AE
Phone: 0161 881 3315

#154
Liquorice
Category: Cocktail Bar
Average price: Modest
Area: City Centre
Address: 50 Pall Mall
Manchester M2 1AQ
Phone: 0161 832 4600

#155
Mother Mac's
Category: Pub
Average price: Expensive
Area: Northern Quarter
Address: 33 Back Piccadilly
Manchester M1 1HP
Phone: 0161 236 1507

#156
Gusto
Category: Italian, Bar
Average price: Modest
Area: Didsbury Village
Address: 756 Wilmslow Road
Manchester M20 2DW
Phone: 0161 445 8209

#157
The Font
Category: Lounge
Average price: Modest
Area: Chorlton
Address: 115-117 Manchester Road
Manchester M21 9PG
Phone: 0161 871 2022

#158
Tib Street Tavern
Category: Pub, Sports Bar
Average price: Modest
Area: Northern Quarter
Address: 74 Tib St
Manchester M4 1LG
Phone: 0161 834 1600

#159
Panacea
Category: Lounge, Champagne Bar
Average price: Exclusive
Area: City Centre
Address: 14 John Dalton St
Manchester M2 6JP
Phone: 0161 833 1111

#160
Scubar
Category: Club, Lounge
Average price: Inexpensive
Area: Oxford Road Corridor
Address: 136 York St
Manchester M1 7XN
Phone: 0161 274 3189

#161
The Living Room
Category: Wine Bar, British, Club
Average price: Expensive
Area: City Centre
Address: 80 Deansgate
Manchester M3 2ER
Phone: 0161 832 0083

#162
Grand Pacific
Category: Asian Fusion, Bar
Average price: Exclusive
Area: Oldham
Address: 1 The Avenue
Manchester M3 3AP
Phone: 0161 831 0288

#163
Harvey Nichols
Category: British, Bar
Average price: Exclusive
Area: City Centre
Address: 21 New Cathedral Street
Manchester M1 1AD
Phone: 0161 828 8898

#164
FAC 251: The Factory
Category: Club, Music Venues
Average price: Inexpensive
Area: Oxford Road Corridor
Address: 112-118 Princess St
Manchester M1 7EN
Phone: 0161 272 7251

#165
O'Neills
Category: Pub
Average price: Inexpensive
Area: Didsbury Village
Address: 655-657 Wilmslow Road
Manchester M20 6RA
Phone: 0161 448 7941

#166
Prohibition
Category: Lounge
Average price: Modest
Area: City Centre
Address: 2-10 St Mary's St
Manchester M3 2LB
Phone: 0161 831 9326

#167
Rampant Lion
Category: Pub
Average price: Modest
Area: Longsight
Address: 17 Anson Road
Manchester M14 5BZ

#168
Islington Mill
Category: Music Venues
Average price: Modest
Area: Salford University Campus
Address: James St
Manchester M3 5HW
Phone: 07947 649896

#169
Sound Control
Category: Club, Music Venues
Average price: Modest
Area: Oxford Road Corridor
Address: 1 New Wakefield Street
Manchester M1 5NP
Phone: 0161 236 0340

#170
Vine Inn
Category: Pub, British
Average price: Modest
Area: City Centre
Address: 42-46 Kennedy Street
Manchester M2 4BQ
Phone: 0161 237 9740

#171
Corridor
Category: Lounge
Average price: Modest
Area: City Centre
Address: 6-8 Barlows Croft
Manchester M3 5DY
Phone: 0161 832 6699

#172
Siam Orchid
Category: Thai, Karaoke
Average price: Modest
Area: Chinatown
Address: 54 Portland Street
Manchester M1 4QU
Phone: 0161 236 1388

#173
Dry Bar
Category: Bar, Music Venues
Average price: Modest
Area: Northern Quarter
Address: 29-30 Oldham St
Manchester M1 1JN
Phone: 0161 236 9840

#174
The Shakespeare
Category: Pub, Food
Average price: Inexpensive
Area: City Centre
Address: 16 Fountain Street
Manchester M2 2AA
Phone: 0161 834 5515

#175
Wetherspoons
Category: Pub, British
Average price: Modest
Area: Northern Quarter
Address: 49 Piccadilly
Manchester M1 2AP
Phone: 0161 236 9206

#176
The Lloyd's Hotel
Category: Pub
Average price: Modest
Area: Chorlton
Address: 617 Wilbraham Road
Manchester M21 9AN
Phone: 0161 862 6990

#177
The Piccadilly
Category: British, Pub
Average price: Modest
Area: Northern Quarter
Address: 60 - 75 Piccadilly
Manchester M1 2BS
Phone: 0872 107 7077

#178
G-A-Y Manchester
Category: Gay Bar
Average price: Inexpensive
Area: Piccadilly
Address: Canal Street
Manchester M1 3

#179
The Grove
Category: Pub, Snooker & Pool Hall
Average price: Inexpensive
Area: Oxford Road Corridor
Address: 316 Oxford Road
Manchester M13 9WJ
Phone: 0161 273 1702

#180
Pure
Category: Club
Average price: Expensive
Area: City Centre
Address: The Printworks
Manchester M4 2BS
Phone: 0161 819 7770

#181
The Union Bar
Category: Bar
Average price: Modest
Area: Oxford Road Corridor
Address: Steve Biko Bldg Oxford Rd
Manchester M13 9PR
Phone: 0161 275 2930

#182
Coyotes Bar
Category: Gay Bar
Average price: Modest
Area: Gay Village
Address: 14 Chorlton Street
Manchester M1 3HW
Phone: 0161 236 4007

#183
Royal Oak
Category: Pub
Average price: Expensive
Area: Didsbury Village
Address: 729 Wilmslow Road
Manchester M20 6WF
Phone: 0161 434 4788

#184
Walkabout
Category: Pub, Club
Average price: Modest
Area: Castlefield, Spinningfields
Address: 13 Quay Street
Manchester M3 3
Phone: 0870 850 4508

#185
Baa Bar
Category: Dive Bar, Club
Average price: Modest
Area: Piccadilly
Address: Arch 11 Deansgate Locks
Manchester M1 5LH
Phone: 0161 832 4446

#186
The Oxford
Category: Pub, Lounge
Average price: Inexpensive
Area: Oxford Road Corridor
Address: 423 Oxford Road
Manchester M13 9WG
Phone: 0161 273 1490

#187
Manto Cafe
Category: Bar
Average price: Modest
Area: Gay Village
Address: 46 Canal Street
Manchester M1 3WD
Phone: 0161 236 2667

#188
Arabesque
Category: Hookah Bar
Area: Northern Quarter
Address: 68 Newton Street
Manchester M1 1EE
Phone: 0161 228 0336

#189
Bowling Green
Category: Pub
Average price: Inexpensive
Area: Chorlton
Address: Brookburn Road
Manchester M21 9ES
Phone: 0161 860 2800

#190
Tiger Tiger
Category: Club, Lounge
Average price: Expensive
Area: City Centre
Address: Units 5-6 The Printworks
Manchester M4 2BS
Phone: 0161 385 8080

#191
Venus
Category: Club, Music Venues
Area: City Centre
Address: 42 Maybrook House
Manchester M3 2EQ
Phone: 0161 834 7288

#192
Cubacafe Bar
Category: Bar
Average price: Modest
Area: Northern Quarter
Address: 43 Port St
Manchester M1 2EQ
Phone: 0161 236 3630

#193
The Queen Of Hearts
Category: Dive Bar
Average price: Inexpensive
Area: Fallowfield
Address: 256 Wilmslow Road
Manchester M14 6LB
Phone: 0161 249 0271

#194
Genting Club
Category: Gambling, Lounge
Average price: Expensive
Area: Oxford Road Corridor
Address: 110 Portland Street
Manchester M1 4RL
Phone: 0161 228 0077

#195
Castlefield Events Arena
Category: Music Venues
Area: Castlefield
Address: 101 Liverpool Road
Manchester M3 4JN
Phone: 0161 834 4026

#196
University of Manchester Student's Union
Category: University, Pub
Average price: Inexpensive
Address: Oxford Road
Manchester M13 9PR
Phone: 0161 275 2930

#197
Revolution
Category: Club, Lounge
Average price: Expensive
Area: Fallowfield
Address: 311-313 Wilmslow Road
Manchester M14 6NW
Phone: 0161 256 4754

#198
The Bar
Category: Bar, British
Average price: Modest
Area: Chorlton
Address: 533 Wilbraham Rd
Manchester M21 0UE
Phone: 0161 861 7576

#199
Tandle Hill Tavern
Category: Pub, British
Average price: Inexpensive
Area: Oldham
Address: 14 Thornham Lane
Manchester M24 2SD
Phone: 01706 345297

#200
Bouzouki Restaurant
Category: Greek, Music Venues
Average price: Modest
Area: Oxford Road Corridor
Address: 88 Princess Street
Manchester M1 6NG
Phone: 0161 236 9282

#201
The Beagle
Category: Street Vendor, Pub
Average price: Modest
Area: Chorlton
Address: 456-458 Barlow Moor Road
Manchester M21 0BQ
Phone: 0161 881 8596

#202
M20 Bar
Category: Lounge
Average price: Expensive
Area: West Didsbury
Address: 158 Burton Rd
Manchester M20 1LH
Phone: 0161 445 6800

#203
Waxy O'Connors
Category: Bar
Average price: Expensive
Area: City Centre
Address: 27 Withy Grove
Manchester M4 2BS
Phone: 0161 831 0885

#204
Old Monkey
Category: Bar
Average price: Modest
Area: Chinatown
Address: 90 Portland Street
Manchester M1
Phone: 0161 228 6262

#205
Opus
Category: Club
Average price: Expensive
Area: City Centre
Address: 27 Withy Grove
Manchester M4 2BS
Phone: 0161 834 2414

#206
Zombie Shack
Category: Cocktail Bar
Average price: Modest
Area: Oxford Road Corridor
Address: 50 New Wakefield Street
Manchester M1 5NP
Phone: 0161 236 6071

#207
The Paramount
Category: Pub, Burgers
Average price: Inexpensive
Area: Oxford Road Corridor
Address: 33-35 Oxford Street
Manchester M1 4BH
Phone: 0161 233 1820

#208
The B Lounge
Category: Pub, European
Average price: Modest
Area: Piccadilly
Address: 97 Piccadilly
Manchester M1 2DB
Phone: 0161 236 4161

#209
The Sedge Lynn
Category: Pub
Average price: Expensive
Area: Chorlton
Address: 21a Manchester Road
Manchester M21 9PN
Phone: 0161 860 0141

#210
The Famous Trevor Arms
Category: Pub
Area: Chorlton
Address: 135 Beech Road
Manchester M21 9EQ
Phone: 0161 636 0250

#211
The Famous Crown
Category: Pub
Average price: Exclusive
Area: Didsbury Village
Address: 770 Wilmslow Rd
Manchester M20 2DR
Phone: 0161 434 7085

#212
Label
Category: Lounge, Club
Average price: Expensive
Area: City Centre
Address: 78 Deansgate
Manchester M3 2FW
Phone: 0161 833 1878

#213
The Liquor Store
Category: Bar
Average price: Modest
Area: City Centre
Address: 40 Blackfriars Street
Manchester M3 2EG
Phone: 0161 834 6239

#214
The Hare and Hounds
Category: Pub
Average price: Inexpensive
Area: Northern Quarter
Address: 46 Shudehill
Manchester M4 1
Phone: 0161 832 4737

#215
Monrose Hotel
Category: Hotel, Bar
Area: Piccadilly
Address: 38 London Road
Manchester M1 2PF
Phone: 0161 236 0564

#216
Lava Cafe Bar
Category: Sports Bar
Area: Castlefield
Address: Castle Quay
Manchester M15 4NJ
Phone: 0161 833 2444

#217
The Station
Category: Pub
Average price: Expensive
Area: Didsbury Village
Address: 682 Wilmslow Road
Manchester M20 2DN
Phone: 0161 445 9761

#218
Legends Manchester
Category: Pub
Average price: Inexpensive
Area: Oxford Road Corridor
Address: 6 Whitworth Street
Manchester M1 3QW
Phone: 0161 236 5400

#219
Café North
Category: Coffee & Tea, Bar
Average price: Modest
Area: Northern Quarter
Address: 66 Shudehill
Manchester M4 4AA
Phone: 0161 839 4916

#220
Room
Category: Bar, British
Area: City Centre
Address: 81 King Street
Manchester M2 4ST
Phone: 0161 839 2005

#221
Burton Arms Hotel
Category: Pub, Bed & Breakfast
Area: Northern Quarter
Address: 31 Swan Street
Manchester M4 5JZ
Phone: 0161 834 3455

#222
Vina Karaoke Bar
Category: Karaoke, Club, Dive Bar
Area: Chinatown
Address: 34 Charlotte Street
Manchester M1 4FD
Phone: 0161 237 9838

#223
Platt Chapel
Category: Music Venues
Area: Rusholme
Address: 186 Wilmslow Road
Manchester M14 5LL
Phone: 0161 478 4203

#224
The Ducie Arms
Category: Pub
Average price: Modest
Area: Oxford Road Corridor
Address: 52 Devas Street
Manchester M15 6HS
Phone: 0161 273 2279

#225
Morley Cheeks
Category: Pub
Average price: Modest
Area: Chorlton
Address: 575 Barlow Moor Road
Manchester M21 8AE
Phone: 0161 860 7878

#226
Beggar's Bush
Category: Bar, British
Area: Chorlton
Address: 48 Beech Road
Manchester M21 9EQ
Phone: 0161 861 7393

#227
Long Legs Table Dancing
Category: Adult Entertainment
Area: Chinatown
Address: 46 George Street
Manchester M1 4HF
Phone: 0161 237 3977

#228
The Bijou Club, Manchester
Category: Club
Area: City Centre
Address: 1-7 Chapel Street
Manchester M3 7NJ
Phone: 0161 834 6377

#229
Kahlua Coffee House
Category: Mexican, Cocktail Bar
Area: Northern Quarter
Address: 104 High Street
Manchester M4 1HQ
Phone: 0161 833 0035

#230
Kyoto Lounge
Category: Lounge
Area: Oxford Road Corridor
Address: 131 Grosevenor Street
Manchester M1 7HE
Phone: 07771 744909

#231
Parrswood Hotel
Category: Pub
Average price: Inexpensive
Area: East Didsbury
Address: 356 Parrswood Road
Manchester M20 6JD
Phone: 0161 445 1783

#232
New York-New York
Category: Bar
Average price: Modest
Area: Gay Village
Address: 94-98 Bloom Street
Manchester M1 3LY
Phone: 0161 236 6556

#233
The Courtyard Bar
Category: Pub
Average price: Inexpensive
Area: Oxford Road Corridor
Address: Chester Streer
Manchester M1 5SH

#234
Shotz Cafe
Category: Hookah Bar
Average price: Inexpensive
Area: Rusholme
Address: 114-116 Wilmslow Road
Manchester M14 5AJ
Phone: 0161 879 2694

#235
Rotana Cafe
Category: Hookah Bar
Average price: Inexpensive
Area: Rusholme
Address: 122 Wilmslow Rd
Manchester M14 5AH
Phone: 0161 249 0930

#236
Norwegian Blue
Category: Bar, Club
Average price: Modest
Area: City Centre
Address: 27 Withy Grove
Manchester M4 2BS
Phone: 0161 839 1451

#237
MTwenty
Category: Lounge
Area: West Didsbury
Address: 158 Burton Rd
Manchester M20 1LH
Phone: 07773 016539

#238
The Green Finch
Category: Pub
Average price: Inexpensive
Area: West Didsbury
Address: 108 Palatine Road
Manchester M20 3ZA
Phone: 0161 448 9397

#239
Henry J Beans
Category: American, Bar
Area: City Centre
Address: Unit 18 Dantzic Street
Manchester M4 2AD
Phone: 0161 827 7820

#240
The Burlington Room
Category: Lounge
Area: Oxford Road Corridor
Address: The University of Manchester
Manchester M13 9PL
Phone: 0161 275 2392

#241
Sachas Hotel
Category: Hotel, Bar
Average price: Inexpensive
Area: Northern Quarter
Address: 12 Tib St
Manchester M4 1SH
Phone: 0161 228 1234

#242
Circle Club
Category: Wine Bar, Champagne Bar
Average price: Expensive
Area: City Centre
Address: 13 Barton Arcade
Manchester M3 2BB
Phone: 0161 288 8118

#243
Lloyds Bar
Category: Pub
Average price: Modest
Area: City Centre
Address: 27 Withy Grove
Manchester M4 2BS
Phone: 0161 817 2980

#244
Lawn Club
Category: Club
Average price: Modest
Area: Spinningfields
Address: Hardman Square
Manchester M3 3EB
Phone: 07857 964334

#245
Waldorf Hotel
Category: Pub
Average price: Modest
Area: Piccadilly
Address: 12 Gore Street
Manchester M1 3AQ
Phone: 0161 228 3269

#246
Kraak
Category: Music Venues
Average price: Modest
Area: Northern Quarter
Address: 11 Stevenson Square
Manchester M1 1DB
Phone: 07855 939129

#247
TGI Fridays
Category: American, Bar
Average price: Modest
Area: City Centre
Address: Cross Street
Manchester M2 7DH
Phone: 0844 692 8903

#248
Jolly Angler
Category: Pub
Area: Piccadilly
Address: 47 Ducie Street
Manchester M1 2JW
Phone: 0161 236 5307

#249
Albaghdady Cafe
Category: Hookah Bar
Area: Rusholme
Address: 118 Wilmslow Rd
Manchester M14 5AJ
Phone: 0161 248 8868

#250
The Beech Inn
Category: Pub
Average price: Modest
Area: Chorlton
Address: 72 Beech Road
Manchester M21 9EG
Phone: 0161 881 1180

#251
Albert Inn
Category: Pub
Area: Didsbury Village
Address: 454 Wilmslow Road
Manchester M20 3BG
Phone: 0161 445 5747

#252
BarCa
Category: Bar
Average price: Modest
Area: Castlefield
Address: 8 & 9 Catalan Square
Manchester M3 4RU
Phone: 0161 839 7099

#253
The Orange Grove
Category: Pub
Average price: Inexpensive
Area: Rusholme
Address: 304 Wilmslow Road
Manchester M14 6NL
Phone: 0161 224 1148

#254
Gullivers
Category: Pub
Average price: Inexpensive
Area: Northern Quarter
Address: 109 Oldham Street
Manchester M4 1LW
Phone: 07807 884399

#255
Mulligans
Category: Pub
Average price: Modest
Area: City Centre
Address: 12 Southgate
Manchester M3 2RB
Phone: 0161 832 9233

#256
Thistle Manchester Hotel
Category: Hotel, Bar
Area: Piccadilly
Address: 3-5 Portland Street
Manchester M1 6DP
Phone: 0870 333 9139

#257
The Milton Club
Category: Bar, Club
Average price: Expensive
Area: Castlefield
Address: 244 Milton Hall
Manchester M3 4BQ
Phone: 0161 850 2353

#258
Cast
Category: Bar
Area: Oxford Road Corridor
Address: 97 Oxford Street
Manchester M1 6ET
Phone: 0161 237 9407

#259
Lass O'Gowrie
Category: British, Pub
Average price: Inexpensive
Area: Gay Village
Address: 36 Charles Street
Manchester M1 7DB
Phone: 0161 273 6932

#260
Wood Wine & Deli
Category: Wine Bar
Average price: Modest
Area: Northern Quarter
Address: 44 Tib Street
Manchester M4 1LA
Phone: 0161 478 7100

#261
Picturehouse
Category: Bar, Music Venues
Area: Northern Quarter
Address: 25 Swan St
Manchester M4 5JZ
Phone: 0161 834 1786

#262
**The Martin Harris Centre
for Music and Drama**
Category: Theatre, Music Venues
Area: Oxford Road Corridor
Address: Bridgeford St
Manchester M13 9PL
Phone: 0161 275 2930

#263
Blue Bell Inn
Category: Pub
Average price: Inexpensive
Area: Levenshulme
Address: 170 Barlow Road
Manchester M19 3HF
Phone: 0161 224 1723

#264
Odder Bar
Category: Bar
Average price: Modest
Area: Oxford Road Corridor
Address: 14 Oxford Road
Manchester M1 5QA
Phone: 0161 238 9132

#265
Edwards
Category: Lounge
Average price: Modest
Area: Piccadilly
Address: 11 Portland St
Manchester M1 3HU
Phone: 0161 237 0631

#266
All Bar One
Category: Wine Bar
Area: City Centre
Address: 73-79 King Street
Manchester M2 4NG
Phone: 0161 830 1811

#267
Arora Hotel Manchester
Category: Hotel, Bar
Average price: Expensive
Area: Chinatown
Address: 18-24 Princess St
Manchester M1 4LG
Phone: 0161 236 8999

#268
Lounge 31
Category: Bar, Music Venues
Average price: Modest
Area: City Centre
Address: 31 Withy Grove
Manchester M4 2BJ
Phone: 0161 819 4710

#269
Overdraught
Category: Club, Dive Bar
Average price: Inexpensive
Area: Gay Village
Address: 121 Princess St
Manchester M1 7AG
Phone: 0161 237 0811

#270
Gardens Hotel
Category: Hotel, Bar
Average price: Inexpensive
Area: Northern Quarter
Address: 55 Piccadilly
Manchester M1 2AP
Phone: 0161 236 5155

#271
Harry's Bar
Category: Lounge
Area: Gay Village
Address: Sackville Street
Manchester M1 3QJ
Phone: 0872 107 7077

#272
Sanctuary
Category: Pub
Area: Didsbury Village
Address: 653 Wilmslow Road
Manchester M20 6QZ
Phone: 0161 445 9130

#273
Cheshire Cat
Category: Pub, Food
Average price: Modest
Area: Fallowfield
Address: 256 Wilmslow Road
Manchester M14 6LB
Phone: 0161 249 0271

#274
Bloom Bar
Category: Bar
Average price: Modest
Area: Spinningfields
Address: Spinningfields Estate
Manchester M3 3AP

#275
Old Granada Studios
Category: Festival, Music Venues
Average price: Inexpensive
Area: Spinningfields
Address: Quay Street
Manchester M3 3JE

#276
MOJO
Category: Pub, Lounge
Area: Spinningfields
Address: 59A Bridge Street
Manchester M3 3BQ
Phone: 0845 611 8643

#277
24 Bar and Grill
Category: Bar, British
Average price: Expensive
Area: Chinatown
Address: 24 Princess Street
Manchester M1 4LY
Phone: 0161 238 4348

#278
Electric Circus
Category: Gambling
Average price: Expensive
Area: Oxford Road Corridor
Address: 110 Portland Street
Manchester M1 4RL
Phone: 0161 228 0077

#279
Mint Casino
Category: Casino, Lounge
Area: Oxford Road Corridor
Address: 40-44 Princess Street
Manchester M1 6DE
Phone: 0161 236 3034

#280
El Capo
Category: Cocktail Bar
Average price: Modest
Area: Northern Quarter
Address: 12 Tariff Street
Manchester M1 2FF
Phone: 0161 237 3154

#281
Portland Street Restaurant & Bar
Category: Bar, British
Average price: Modest
Area: Gay Village
Address: Portland Street
Manchester M1
Phone: 0161 246 3435

#282
Spektrum
Category: Club
Area: Ancoats, Petersfield
Address: Radium St
Manchester M4 6AY
Phone: 0161 236 5444

#283
256 Wilmslow Road
Category: Pub
Average price: Modest
Area: Fallowfield
Address: 256 Wilmslow Road
Manchester M14 6LB
Phone: 0161 249 0271

#284
Lansdowne Hotel
Category: Hotel, Bar
Area: Fallowfield
Address: 346-348 Wilmslow Road
Manchester M14 6AB
Phone: 0161 224 6244

#285
Rileys Sports Bar
Chorlton Cum Hardy
Category: Snooker & Pool Hall,
Sports Bar
Area: Chorlton
Address: 302B Barlow Moor Road
Manchester M21 8AY
Phone: 0161 860 4960

#286
Union Inn
Category: Pub
Area: Levenshulme
Address: Stockport Road
Manchester M19 3AD
Phone: 0161 224 1271

#287
The Violet Hour
Category: Cocktail Bar
Average price: Expensive
Area: West Didsbury
Address: 236 Burton Road
Manchester M20 2LW

#288
Mitre Hotel
Category: Hotel, Bar
Average price: Modest
Area: City Centre
Address: Cathedral Gates
Manchester M3 1SW
Phone: 0161 834 4128

#289
Club Phoenix
Category: Pub
Average price: Inexpensive
Area: Oxford Road Corridor
Address: 1 University Precinct
Manchester M13 9RN
Phone: 0161 272 5921

#290
Ramada
Manchester Piccadilly Hotel
Category: Hotel, Bar
Area: Northern Quarter
Address: Piccadilly Plz
Manchester M60 1QR
Phone: 0844 815 9024

#291
Bar 4 Eighty
Category: Pub
Area: Chorlton
Address: 480 Wilbraham Road
Manchester M21 9AS
Phone: 0161 861 9558

#292
The Spread Eagle
Category: Pub
Average price: Modest
Area: Chorlton
Address: 526 Wilbraham Road
Manchester M21 9LD
Phone: 0161 861 0385

#293
Orchid Lounge
Category: Karaoke, Bar
Area: Chinatown
Address: 54 Portland St
Manchester M1 4QU
Phone: 0161 236 1388

#294
The Rembrandt Bar and Hotel
Category: Hotel, Bar
Average price: Modest
Area: Gay Village
Address: 33 Sackville St
Manchester M1 3LZ
Phone: 0161 236 1311

#295
Browns
Category: Bar, British
Average price: Modest
Area: City Centre
Address: 1 York Street
Manchester M2 2AW
Phone: 0161 819 1055

#296
Axm Club
Category: British, Gay Bar
Average price: Modest
Area: Gay Village
Address: 100 Bloom Street
Manchester M1 3LY
Phone: 0845 834 0297

#297
Expo Lounge
Category: Lounge
Average price: Modest
Area: Didsbury Village
Address: 766 Wilmslow Road
Manchester M20 2DR

#298
Cafe Casablanca
Category: Hookah Bar
Area: Rusholme
Address: 100 Wilmslow Road
Manchester M14 5AJ
Phone: 0161 256 2555

#299
Fiddlers Green
Category: Pub
Average price: Inexpensive
Area: Levenshulme
Address: 881 Stockport Road
Manchester M19 3PG
Phone: 0161 224 2254

#300
Yates's
Category: Bar
Average price: Inexpensive
Area: Gay Village
Address: 49 Portland Street
Manchester M1 3HG
Phone: 0161 228 0162

#301
The Royal Oak
Category: Pub
Average price: Inexpensive
Area: Chorlton
Address: 440 Barlow Moor Road
Manchester M21 0AE
Phone: 0161 860 7438

#302
Grey Horse Inn
Category: Pub
Average price: Inexpensive
Area: Chinatown
Address: 80 Portland Street
Manchester M1 4QX
Phone: 0161 236 1874

#303
Mansion Club
Category: Club
Area: Castlefield
Address: Longworth St
Manchester M3 4BQ
Phone: 0161 832 3038

#304
Entourage
Category: Club, Champagne Bar
Average price: Expensive
Area: City Centre
Address: The Printworks
Manchester M4 2
Phone: 0161 839 1344

#305
The Eagle Bar
Category: Gay Bar
Average price: Modest
Area: Gay Village
Address: Bloom St
Manchester M1 3

#306
Napoleons Night Club
Category: Club
Average price: Inexpensive
Area: Gay Village
Address: 35 Bloom Street
Manchester M1 3LY
Phone: 0161 236 8800

#307
BED
Category: Lounge
Area: Gay Village
Address: 50 Sackville Street
Manchester M1 3WF
Phone: 0161 236 8300

#308
Piccadilly Lounge
Category: Lounge, British
Area: Piccadilly
Address: 1 Auburn St
Manchester M1 3DG
Phone: 0161 242 1030

#309
The Wheatsheaf
Category: Pub
Area: Northern Quarter
Address: 30 Oak Street
Manchester M4 5JE
Phone: 0871 230 5513

#310
The Cavendish Bar
Category: Pub
Area: Oxford Road Corridor
Address: 44 Cavendish Street
Manchester M15 6BQ
Phone: 0161 226 7600

#311
Kro Bar
Category: Pub
Average price: Inexpensive
Area: Oxford Road Corridor
Address: 60 Pencroft Way
Manchester M15 6SZ
Phone: 0161 232 9796

#312
Lusitano
Category: Tapas, Wine Bar
Average price: Modest
Area: Chorlton
Address: 613 Wilbraham Road
Manchester M21 9AN
Phone: 0161 861 8880

#313
The Laundrette
Category: Cocktail Bar
Average price: Modest
Area: Chorlton
Address: 32 Beech Road
Manchester M21 9EL
Phone: 0161 881 5777

#314
Verso
Category: Lounge
Average price: Inexpensive
Area: West Didsbury
Address: 110 Burton Rd
Manchester M20 1LP
Phone: 0161 438 6633

#315
Old House At Home
Category: Pub
Area: West Didsbury
Address: 61-63 Burton Road
Manchester M20 1HB
Phone: 0161 446 2315

#316
The Thompsons Arms
Category: Club, Pub
Average price: Inexpensive
Area: Gay Village
Address: 23 Sackville Street
Manchester M1 3LZ
Phone: 0161 228 3012

#317
Blue Parrot Bar and Grille
Category: Bar
Average price: Modest
Area: Piccadilly
Address: 11 Westminster House
Manchester M1 3DY
Phone: 0161 236 8359

#318
Contact
Category: Theatre, Music Venues
Average price: Modest
Area: Oxford Road Corridor
Address: Oxford Road
Manchester M15 6JA
Phone: 0161 274 0600

#319
Paddys Goose
Category: Pub
Area: Gay Village
Address: 29 Bloom Street
Manchester M1 3JE
Phone: 0161 236 1246

#320
Wetherspoons
Category: British, Pub
Area: Oxford Road Corridor
Address: 33-36 Oxford Street
Manchester M1 4BH
Phone: 0161 233 1820

#321
Area 51 Club
Category: Club
Average price: Modest
Area: Piccadilly
Address: Whitworth St West
Manchester M1 5WZ
Phone: 0161 236 1316

#322
Port Street Beer House
Category: Pub
Average price: Modest
Area: Northern Quarter
Address: 39-41 Port Street
Manchester M1 2EQ
Phone: 0161 237 9949

#323
The Great Central
Category: British, Pub
Average price: Inexpensive
Area: Fallowfield
Address: 343 Wilmslow Road
Manchester M14 6NS
Phone: 0161 248 1740

#324
K2 Karaoke Nightclub
Category: Karaoke, Club, Bar
Area: Chinatown
Address: 52 George Street
Manchester M1 4HF
Phone: 0871 230 4226

#325
View
Category: Club, Gay Bar
Area: Gay Village
Address: 40 Chorlton Street
Manchester M1 3HW
Phone: 0161 236 9033

#326
Victorias Gentlemens Club
Category: Adult Entertainment
Average price: Expensive
Area: City Centre
Address: Dantzic Street
Manchester M4 2AD
Phone: 0161 832 4444

#327
Central Methodist Hall
Category: Music Venues,
Venues & Event Spaces
Area: Northern Quarter
Address: Oldham Street
Manchester M1 1JQ
Phone: 0161 236 5194

#328
Bar21
Category: Bar, Italian, American
Area: Northern Quarter
Address: 10 Thomas Street
Manchester M4 1DH
Phone: 0161 832 2769

#329
W A K Films
Category: Pub
Average price: Exclusive
Area: Ancoats, Petersfield
Address: Jersey Street
Manchester M4 6JG
Phone: 0161 279 0546

#330
Royal Oak Hotel
Category: Pub
Area: Chorlton
Address: 440 Barlow Moor Road
Manchester M21 0BQ
Phone: 0161 860 7438

#331
Dulcimer
Category: Bar, Music Venues
Average price: Modest
Area: Chorlton
Address: 567 Wilbraham Road
Manchester M21 0AE
Phone: 0161 860 6444

#332
Bar Rogue & Bar Wave
Category: Bar, Club
Area: Gay Village
Address: Portland Street
Manchester M1 3LA
Phone: 0161 228 7007

#333
Palace Theatre
Category: Theatre, Music Venues
Average price: Expensive
Area: Oxford Road Corridor
Address: Oxford Street
Manchester M1 6FT
Phone: 0161 245 6600

#334
Richmond Park Bar
Category: Pub
Average price: Inexpensive
Area: Fallowfield
Address: Whitworth Lane
Manchester M14 6YY

#335
JD Wetherspoons
Category: Pub, British
Area: Northern Quarter
Address: 49 Piccadilly
Manchester M1 1
Phone: 0161 236 9206

#336
Fridays
Category: Bar
Area: Northern Quarter
Address: Tib Street
Manchester M4 1SH
Phone: 0161 228 1234

#337
The Shack
Category: Bar
Average price: Modest
Area: Northern Quarter
Address: 26-28 Hilton House
Manchester M1 2EH
Phone: 0161 236 6009

#338
Merchant Hotel
Category: Hotel, Bar
Area: Northern Quarter
Address: Back Piccadilly
Manchester M1 1HP
Phone: 0161 236 2939

#339
The Brewer's Arms
Category: Pub
Area: Ladybarn
Address: 151 Ladybarn Lane
Manchester M14 6RQ
Phone: 0161 224 5576

#340
Chalk Bar and Grill
Category: Bar
Average price: Expensive
Area: Didsbury Village
Address: 784-788 Wilmslow Road
Manchester M20 2DR
Phone: 0161 445 1042

#341
Sackville Lounge
Category: Gay Bar
Average price: Modest
Area: Gay Village
Address: Sackville Street
Manchester M1

#342
The Lower Turks Head
Category: Pub
Average price: Modest
Area: Northern Quarter
Address: Short Street
Manchester M1 1JG

#343
Knott Bar
Category: Pub, British,
Average price: Modest
Area: Castlefield
Address: 374 Deansgate
Manchester M3 4LY
Phone: 0161 839 9229

#344
Bar Pop
Category: Gay Bar, Club
Average price: Inexpensive
Area: Gay Village
Address: 10 Canal Street
Manchester M1 3EZ

#345
Sanctuary On Sackville
Category: British, Wine Bar, Lounge
Area: Gay Village
Address: 46 Sackville Street
Manchester M1
Phone: 0161 237 5551

#346
Bakerie
Category: Wine Bar
Average price: Modest
Area: Northern Quarter
Address: 51 Lever Street
Manchester M1 1FN

#347
Shamrock Inn
Category: Pub
Area: Ancoats, Petersfield
Address: 17 Bengal Street
Manchester M4 6AQ
Phone: 0161 238 8578

#348
Woolton Hall Bar
Category: Pub
Average price: Inexpensive
Area: Fallowfield
Address: Whitworth Lane
Manchester M14 6WS

#349
Antwerp Mansion
Category: Music Venues
Area: Rusholme
Address: Wilmslow Rd
Manchester M14 5BT
Phone: 07429 578193

#350
The Long Bar
Category: Wine Bar, Lounge,
Champagne Bar
Average price: Modest
Area: Spinningfields
Address: Spinningfield Estate
Manchester M3 3JE
Phone: 07917 058924

#351
The Lost Dene
Category: Pub
Area: Spinningfields
Address: 144 Deansgate
Manchester M3 3EE
Phone: 0161 839 9035

#352
Club V
Category: Music Venues
Area: City Centre
Address: 111 Deansgate
Manchester M3 2BQ
Phone: 0161 834 9975

#353
Mud Crab
Category: Burgers, Bar
Area: City Centre
Address: 5-7 Chapel Walks
Manchester M2 1HN
Phone: 0161 907 3210

#354
Red Hot Karaoke!!
Category: Karaoke
Area: City Centre
Address: 48 Deansgate
Manchester M3 2EG
Phone: 07984 627576

#355
Montpellier
Category: Bar, Cafe
Area: Northern Quarter
Address: 36 Back Turner Street
Manchester M4
Phone: 0161 832 3146

#356
Dry Live
Category: Club, Music Venues
Average price: Modest
Area: Northern Quarter
Address: 28-30 Oldham Street
Manchester M1 1JN
Phone: 0161 236 1444

#357
Philharmonic String Quartet
Category: Music Venues, Theatre
Area: Castlefield
Address: 307 Vicus 73 Liverpool Road
Manchester M3 4AQ
Phone: 07545 991621

#358
Hit and Run
Category: Club, Music Venues
Area: Piccadilly
Address: Area 51 Eclipse House
Manchester M1 5WZ
Phone: 0161 236 1316

#359
Dubai Cafe
Category: Coffee & Tea, Hookah Bar
Area: Rusholme
Address: 86 Wilmslow Road
Manchester M14 5AL
Phone: 0161 224 9040

#360
Booze Manchester
Category: Off Licence, Pub
Average price: Exclusive
Area: Longsight
Address: Cariocca Business Park
Manchester M12 4AH
Phone: 07799 338875

#361
Fallow Cafe
Category: British, Pub
Area: Fallowfield
Address: 2a Landcross Road
Manchester M14 6NA
Phone: 0161 224 0467

#362
MantraSound Disco
Category: DJs, Karaoke
Average price: Modest
Area: Fallowfield
Address: Fallowfield
Manchester M14
Phone: 01691 649044

#363
The Stoker's Arms
Category: Pub
Area: Didsbury Village
Address: 657 Wilmslow Road
Manchester M20 6RA
Phone: 0161 448 7941

#364
Parrswood Hotel
Category: British, Pub
Area: East Didsbury
Address: 356 Parrswood Road
Manchester M20
Phone: 0161 445 1783

#365
Bar Six 2
Category: Bar
Area: Stockport
Address: 62 Middle Hillgate
Manchester SK1 3EH
Phone: 07531 730304

#366
Red House Pub
Category: Pub
Area: Ashton Under Lyne
Address: lees road
Manchester OL6
Phone: 0161 343 5594

#367
Sparking Clog
Category: Pub
Average price: Inexpensive
Area: Bolton
Address: Radcliffe Moor Road
Manchester M26 3WY
Phone: 0161 723 5690

#368
Regent Inns
Category: Hotel, Pub
Average price: Inexpensive
Area: Castlefield, Spinningfields
Address: 13 Quay Street
Manchester M3 3HN
Phone: 0870 765 1221

#369
The Lost Dene
Category: Pub
Area: City Centre
Address: 19-23 King Street
Manchester M2 6AN
Phone: 0161 839 9035

#370
White Lion Hotel
Category: Pub
Area: Castlefield
Address: 43 Liverpool Road
Manchester M3 4NQ
Phone: 0161 832 7373

#371
Grosvenor Casino
Category: Casino
Area: Chinatown
Address: 35 George Street
Manchester M1 4HQ
Phone: 0161 236 7121

#372
Long Legs Table Dancing
Category: Adult Entertainment
Area: Chinatown
Address: 46 George Street
Manchester M1 4HF
Phone: 0161 237 3977

#373
Uber Lounge
Category: Cocktail Bar
Area: Castlefield
Address: 8-9
Manchester M3 4RU
Phone: 0161 839 7099

#374
Sub61
Category: Bar
Area: Castlefield
Address: Artillery Street
Manchester M3
Phone: 07910 431115

#375
Alibi
Category: Bar
Area: Gay Village
Address: Unit 1 the Circus Development
Cnr Oxford Str & Portland Str
Manchester M1
Phone: 0845 604 9904

#376
Wetherspoons
Category: Pub, British
Area: City Centre
Address: Princess Street
Manchester M2 4EG
Phone: 0161 200 5380

#377
The Old Monkey
Category: Pub
Area: City Centre
Address: 90-92 Portland Street
Manchester M1 4GX
Phone: 0161 228 6262

#378
Holmes Place Health Club
Category: Gym, Pub
Average price: Modest
Area: City Centre
Address: 4 The Printworks
Manchester M4 2BS
Phone: 0161 831 9922

#379
Stockport Garrick Theatre
Category: Theatre, Music Venues
Address: Exchange Street
Stockport, Greater Manchester
Phone: 0161 480 5866

#380
Gallery Oldham
Category: Art Gallery
Address: Oldham Cultural Quater
Oldham OL1 1AL
Phone: 0161 770 4653

#381
Forum Theatre
Category: Theatre
Average price: Modest
Address: The Precinct
Stockport SK6 4EA
Phone: 0161 430 6570

#382
City Shisha Lounge
Category: Hookah Bar
Area: City Centre
Address: 85 Greengate
Manchester M3 7NA
Phone: 0161 637 7764

#383
Bar Rogue & Bar Wave
Category: Bar
Average price: Inexpensive
Area: Gay Village
Address: Portland Street
Manchester M1 3LA
Phone: 0161 228 7007

#384
Lola's
Category: Cocktail Bar
Area: Northern Quarter
Address: 17 Tariff Street
Manchester M1 2EJ
Phone: 0161 228 7813

#385
Premier Musicians
Category: Venues & Event Spaces,
Wedding Planning, Music Venues
Area: Castlefield
Address: 307 Vicus 73 Liverpool Road
Manchester M3 4AQ
Phone: 07545 991621

#386
Companion
Manchester Escorts
Category: Adult Entertainment
Area: Oxford Road Corridor
Address: Oxford Road
Manchester M13 9PL
Phone: 07714 751329

#387
Marrakesh Cafe
Category: Hookah Bar
Area: Rusholme
Address: 119 Wilmslow Road
Manchester M14 5AN
Phone: 0161 224 0700

#388
Marrakesh Shisha Bar
Category: Venues & Event Spaces
Area: Rusholme
Address: 119 Wilmslow Rd
Manchester M14 5AP
Phone: 0161 637 0424

#389
Sher Akbar
Category: Bar, Indian
Area: Chorlton
Address: 72-74 Manchester Road
Manchester M21 9PQ
Phone: 0161 862 0000

#390
The King's Arms
Category: Pub
Area: City Centre
Address: 11 Bloom Street
Salford M3 6AN
Phone: 0161 832 3605

#391
Duffy's Bar
Category: Dive Bar
Area: Chorlton
Address: 398 Barlow Moor Road
Manchester M21 8AD
Phone: 0872 107 7077

#392
The Huntington
Category: Pub
Area: Levenshulme
Address: Northmoor Road
Manchester M12 4HP
Phone: 0161 225 6400

#393
Strange Brew
Category: Pub
Area: Chorlton
Address: 370 Barlow Moor Road
Manchester M21 8AZ
Phone: 0161 862 9911

#394
Nouveau Mancurian
Male Escort Service
Category: Adult Entertainment
Area: Didsbury Village
Address: 792 Wilmslow Rd
Manchester M20 6UG
Phone: 07855 504838

#395
White Lion
Category: Pub, Sports Bar
Average price: Modest
Area: Castlefield
Address: 43 Liverpool Road
Manchester M3 4NQ
Phone: 0161 832 7373

#396
The Bridge
Category: Pub
Average price: Modest
Area: Spinningfields, City Centre
Address: 58 Bridge Street
Manchester M3 3BW
Phone: 0161 834 0242

#397
Cask
Category: Pub
Average price: Modest
Area: Castlefield
Address: 29 Liverpool Road
Manchester M3 4NQ
Phone: 0161 819 2527

#398
The Lowry
Category: Music Venues, Theatre
Average price: Expensive
Area: Salford Quays
Address: Pier 8 Salford M50 3AZ
Phone: 0161 876 2121

#399
Unicorn Hotel
Category: Pub
Area: Northern Quarter
Address: 26 Church Street
Manchester M4 1PW
Phone: 0161 879 9863

#400
Fantasy Bar
Category: Adult Entertainment
Area: Spinningfields
Address: 140 Deansgate
Manchester M3 2RP
Phone: 0161 835 1973

#401
Gainsborough House
Category: Bar
Area: Chinatown
Address: 109 Portland Street
Manchester M1 6DN
Phone: 0161 237 9990

#402
Lowry Hotel
Category: Hotel, Bar
Area: City Centre
Address: 50 Dearmans Place
Salford M3 5LH
Phone: 0161 827 4000

#403
Charlie's Night Club & Restaurant
Category: Club
Area: Oxford Road Corridor
Address: 1 Harter Street
Manchester M1 6HY
Phone: 0161 237 9898

#404
Kimberley Consultancy
Category: Club
Area: City Centre
Address: Back Bridge Street
Manchester M3 2PB
Phone: 0161 832 6975

#405
Mutz Nutz
Category: Club
Area: Oxford Road Corridor
Address: 105-107 Princess Street
Manchester M1 6DD
Phone: 0161 236 9266

#406
Baby Platinum
Category: Adult Entertainment
Area: Gay Village
Address: 109 Princess Street
Manchester M1 6JB
Phone: 0161 236 6126

#407
Cibar
Category: Pub
Area: Northern Quarter
Address: 28-34 High Street
Manchester M4 1QB
Phone: 0161 834 4828

#408
Presha
Category: Bar
Area: Northern Quarter
Address: 28-34 High Street
Manchester M4 1QB
Phone: 0161 834 1392

#409
Carlisle Staffing
Category: Bar
Area: City Centre
Address: 2 Old Bank Street
Manchester M2 7PF
Phone: 0161 835 3588

#410
The Lodge Bar
Category: Gay Bar, Cocktail Bar
Area: Gay Village
Address: Richmond Street The Village
Manchester M1 3HZ
Phone: 0161 237 9667

#411
Oscars
Category: Bar
Area: Gay Village
Address: 34 Canal Street
Manchester M1 3WD
Phone: 0161 237 9201

#412
Tiger Lounge
Category: Italian, Bar
Area: City Centre
Address: 5 Cooper Street
Manchester M2 2FW
Phone: 0161 236 6007

#413
Bar 38 Pub
Area: Gay Village
Address: 10 Canal Street
Manchester M1 3EZ
Phone: 0161 236 6005

#414
Industry
Category: Club
Area: Oxford Road Corridor
Address: 112-116 Princess Street
Manchester M1 7EN
Phone: 0161 273 5422

#415
The Sedgelynn
Category: Gastropub
Area: Chorlton
Address: 21A Manchester Road
Manchester M21 9PN
Phone: 0161 860 0141

#416
Sanctuary
Category: Bar
Area: Gay Village
Address: 46 Sackville Street
Manchester M1
Phone: 0161 237 5551

#417
Illusions Magic Bar
Category: Pub, Wine Bar
Area: City Centre
Address: 27 Withy Grove
Manchester M4 2BS
Phone: 0161 819 7791

#418
Pinnacle Intertional College
Category: University, Club
Area: Gay Village
Address: 10 Minshull Street
Manchester M1 3EF
Phone: 0161 236 5646

#419
The New Oxford
Category: Wine Bar, Pub
Address: 11 Bexley Square
Salford M3 6DB
Phone: 0161 832 7082

#420
Joe's Bar
Category: Wine Bar, Lounge
Area: Northern Quarter
Address: 4 Oldham Street
Manchester M1 1JQ
Phone: 0161 228 0517

#421
Hale Leisure
Category: Pub
Area: Oxford Road Corridor
Address: 106 Princess Street
Manchester M1 6NG
Phone: 0161 273 7543

#422
Goldsmith & Rybka
Category: Pub
Area: Northern Quarter
Address: 35-37 Thomas Street
Manchester M4 1NA
Phone: 0161 834 5650

#423
NQ Live
Category: Club, Music Venues
Area: Northern Quarter
Address: Tib Street
Manchester M4 1LN
Phone: 0161 834 8188

#424
The Engine House
Category: Theatre, Music Venues
Area: Oxford Road Corridor
Address: 3 Cambridge St
Manchester M1 5BY
Phone: 07874 152338

#425
D G P International
Category: Bar
Area: Oxford Road Corridor
Address: 54 Princess Street
Manchester M1 6HS
Phone: 0161 907 3500

#426
Babushka
Category: Bar
Area: City Centre
Address: Withy Grove
Manchester M4 2BS
Phone: 0161 832 1234

#427
Sweet P
Category: Pub
Area: Northern Quarter
Address: 46-50 Oldham Street
Manchester M4 1LE
Phone: 0161 228 1495

#428
North Nightclub
Category: Club
Area: Northern Quarter
Address: 34-43 Oldham Street
Manchester M1 1JG
Phone: 0161 839 1989

#429
Bravo Management
Category: Pub
Area: Northern Quarter
Address: 25 Swan Street
Manchester M4 5JZ
Phone: 0161 834 1786

#430
On Q Pool Club
Category: Snooker & Pool Hall
Area: Northern Quarter
Address: 7 Dale Street
Manchester M1 1JA
Phone: 0161 228 7808

#431
Tango's
Category: Cocktail Bar,
British, Champagne Bar
Area: City Centre
Address: 15 Chapel Walks
Manchester M2 1HN
Phone: 0161 819 1997

#432
Church Inn
Category: Pub
Area: Oxford Road Corridor
Address: 84 Cambridge Street
Manchester M15 6BP
Phone: 0161 227 9503

#433
Arch Wine Bar
Category: Wine Bar
Area: Oxford Road Corridor
Address: 20 Stretford Road
Manchester M15 6HE
Phone: 0161 227 7550

#434
Absolute Strippers Manchester
Category: Adult Entertainment
Area: Oxford Road Corridor
Address: Oxford Road
Manchester M1 6FU
Phone: 07956 22318

#435
Homes For You
Category: Pub
Area: Oxford Road Corridor
Address: Oxford Road
Manchester M1 7ED
Phone: 0161 236 0202

#436
King Inn
Category: Pub
Area: Northern Quarter
Address: 73 Oldham Street
Manchester M4 1LW
Phone: 0161 835 2548

#437
The Star and Garter
Category: Pub
Area: Piccadilly
Address: 18-20 Fairfield Street
Manchester M1 2QF
Phone: 0161 273 6726

#438
The Park Night Club
Category: Pub
Area: Oxford Road Corridor
Address: Grosvenor Street
Manchester M1 7HL
Phone: 0161 274 4442

#439
Barney Mcgrew's Public House
Category: Pub
Area: Oxford Road Corridor
Address: Oxford Road
Manchester M13 9RN
Phone: 0161 272 6806

#440
GX Bar
Category: Wine Bar
Area: Ancoats, Petersfield
Address: Great Ancoats Street
Manchester M60 4BT
Phone: 0161 236 0851

#441
Church Inn
Category: Pub
Area: Oxford Road Corridor
Address: 45-47 Ardwick Green North
Manchester M12 6FZ
Phone: 0161 273 5652

#442
Wheatsheaf Hotel
Category: Pub
Area: Ancoats, Petersfield
Address: 208 Oldham Road
Manchester M4 6BQ
Phone: 0161 205 4821

#443
Kimgary Fabrics
Category: Pub
Area: Ancoats, Petersfield
Address: Pollard Street
Manchester M4 7JB
Phone: 0161 273 7777

#444
Phoenix Karaoke
Category: Karaoke
Area: Oxford Road Corridor
Address: 62 Stockport Road
Manchester M12 6AL
Phone: 0161 273 7006

#445
Grafton Arms
Category: Pub
Area: Oxford Road Corridor
Address: 27 Grafton Street
Manchester M13 9WU
Phone: 0161 273 2303

#446
The Admiral
Category: Pub
Area: Ancoats, Petersfield
Address: Butler Street
Manchester M4 6JY
Phone: 0161 205 5896

#447
Gold Cup
Category: Pub
Area: Longsight
Address: 260 Stockport Road
Manchester M13 0RB
Phone: 0161 273 8887

#448
Clarence Inn
Category: Pub
Area: Rusholme
Address: 97 Wilmslow Road
Manchester M14 5SU
Phone: 0161 248 1911

#449
Maydale
Category: Pub
Area: Salford Quays
Address: Trafford Wharf Road
Manchester M17 1EX
Phone: 0161 872 6836

#450
Welcome Public House
Category: Pub
Area: Rusholme
Address: 26 Rusholme Grove
Manchester M14 5AR
Phone: 0161 224 4685

#451
Mason
Category: Pub
Area: Rusholme
Address: 257 Wilmslow Road
Manchester M14 5LN
Phone: 0161 257 0450

#452
Bay Horse Hotel
Category: Pub
Area: Longsight
Address: 548 Stockport Road
Manchester M12 4JJ
Phone: 0161 248 9855

#453
Springbank Public House
Category: Pub
Area: Levenshulme
Address: 579 Stockport Road
Manchester M13 0RG
Phone: 0161 225 8980

#454
Office
Category: Wine Bar
Area: Chorlton
Address: 537 Wilbraham Road
Manchester M21 0UE
Phone: 0161 860 6660

#455
Revise Cafe Bar
Category: Pub
Area: Chorlton
Address: 559 Wilbraham Road
Manchester M21 0AE
Phone: 0161 861 7626

#456
P Heathcote
Category: Pub
Area: Chorlton
Address: 478 Wilbraham Road
Manchester M21 9AS
Phone: 0161 881 9130

#457
Bar Baroque
Category: Music Venues
Area: Chorlton
Address: 478 Wilbraham Rd
Manchester M21 9AS
Phone: 0161 881 9130

#458
Vanessa's
Category: Adult Entertainment
Area: Chorlton
Address: 430a Barlow Moor Road
Manchester M21 8AD
Phone: 0161 861 7302

#459
Glass Public House
Category: Pub
Area: Fallowfield
Address: 258 Wilmslow Road
Manchester M14 6JR
Phone: 0161 257 0770

#460
Wetherspoon
Category: Pub
Area: Fallowfield
Address: 306 Wilmslow Road
Manchester M14 6NL
Phone: 0161 248 1740

#461
Garratt Hotel
Category: Pub
Area: Levenshulme
Address: Pink Bank Lane
Manchester M12 5RF
Phone: 0161 224 7530

#462
Hookahs Cafe
Category: Hookah Bar, Lounge
Area: Chorlton
Address: 320 Barlow Moor Road
Manchester M21
Phone: 0161 917 2713

#463
Tonic
Category: Pub
Area: Chorlton
Address: 48 Beech Road
Manchester M21 9EG
Phone: 0161 862 9934

#464
Old House At Home
Category: Pub
Area: Fallowfield
Address: 74-76 Braemar Road
Manchester M14 6PG
Phone: 0161 224 5557

#465
Pack Horse
Category: Pub
Area: Levenshulme
Address: 861 Stockport Road
Manchester M19 3PW
Phone: 0161 224 4355

#466
Church Inn
Category: Pub
Area: Levenshulme
Address: 874 Stockport Road
Manchester M19 3BP
Phone: 0161 221 0111

#467
Levenshulme Pub
Category: Pub
Area: Levenshulme
Address: 959 Stockport Road
Manchester M19 3NP
Phone: 0161 256 2255

#468
Clearissue Bar
Category: Wine Bar
Area: West Didsbury
Address: 2 Lapwing Lane
Manchester M20 2WS
Phone: 0161 448 1356

#469
Cotton Inn The Public House
Category: Pub
Area: Didsbury Village
Address: 2 Cotton Lane
Manchester M20 4UX
Phone: 0161 434 8545

#470
Cotton Tree Inn
The Public House
Category: Pub
Area: Didsbury Village
Address: 2-6 Cotton Hill
Manchester M20 4XR
Phone: 0161 448 2360

#471
The Sidings
Category: Pub
Area: Levenshulme
Address: Broom Lane
Manchester M19 2UB
Phone: 0161 257 2084

#472
The Muldeth Hotel
Category: Pub
Area: East Didsbury
Address: Kingsway
Manchester M19 1BB
Phone: 0161 224 6529

#473
The Barleycorn
Category: Pub
Area: Didsbury Village
Address: 120 Barlow Moor Road
Manchester M20 2PU
Phone: 0161 448 9941

#474
Clock Tower
Category: Pub
Area: Didsbury Village
Address: 700 Wilmslow Road
Manchester M20 2DN
Phone: 0161 445 1686

#475
Karma Sutra Girls
Category: Adult Entertainment
Area: Didsbury Village
Address: 743A Wilmslow Road
Manchester M20 2
Phone: 0161 434 0135

#476
Victoria Inn
Category: Pub
Area: Oldham
Address: 252 Grimshaw Lane
Manchester M24 2AL
Phone: 0161 643 3526

#477
Railway & Linnet
Category: Pub
Area: Oldham
Address: 369 Grimshaw Lane
Manchester M24 1GQ
Phone: 0161 655 3889

#478
Hare & Hounds
Category: Pub
Area: Oldham
Address: 228 Oldham Road
Manchester M24 2JZ
Phone: 0161 643 3100

#479
The Kenyon
Category: Pub
Area: Oldham
Address: 71 Kenyon Lane
Manchester M24 2QS
Phone: 0161 654 0898

#480
Royal Oak Hotel
Category: Pub
Area: Oldham
Address: 44 Boarshaw Road
Manchester M24 6AG
Phone: 0161 653 6142

#481
Old Cock Inn
Category: Pub
Area: Oldham
Address: 528 Oldham Road
Manchester M24 2EB
Phone: 0161 654 8333

#482
Gardners Arms
Category: Pub
Area: Oldham
Address: 266 Hollin Lane
Manchester M24 5LE
Phone: 0161 643 4761

#483
Papermakers Arms
Category: Pub
Area: Bury
Address: Church St East
Manchester M26 2PG
Phone: 0161 723 3415

#484
Old Tower Inn
Category: Pub
Area: Bury
Address: 6 Sandford Street
Manchester M26 2PT
Phone: 0161 723 4212

#485
The Masons Arms
Category: Pub
Area: Bolton
Address: 190 Sion Street
Manchester M26 3SB
Phone: 0161 725 9322

#486
Lord Nelson Hotel
Category: Pub
Area: Bolton
Address: Ringley Road
Manchester M26 1GT
Phone: 01204 579302

#487
The Black Bull
Category: Pub
Area: Oldham
Address: Rochdale Road
Manchester M24 2QA
Phone: 0161 643 6684

#488
Central Snooker Club
Category: Snooker & Pool Hall
Area: Bolton
Address: Abden Street
Manchester M26 3AT
Phone: 0161 723 1237

#489
Royal Oak
Category: Pub
Area: Bolton
Address: 28 Water Street
Manchester M26 4TW
Phone: 0161 723 3557

#490
Market Street Tavern
Category: Pub
Area: Bolton
Address: 131 Market Street
Manchester M26 1HF
Phone: 01204 572985

#491
Bridge Inn
Category: Pub
Area: Bury
Address: 409 Dumers Lane
Manchester M26 2QN
Phone: 0161 766 1370

#492
Horse Shoe
Category: Pub
Area: Bolton
Address: 395 Fold Road
Manchester M26 1NW
Phone: 01204 571714

#493
Hare & Hounds
Category: Pub
Area: Bolton
Address: 13 Market Street
Manchester M26 1GF
Phone: 01204 572974

#494
Beer Engine
Category: Pub
Area: Bolton
Address: 351 Bolton Road
Manchester M26 3QQ
Phone: 0161 723 3307

#495
Victoria Hotel
Category: Pub
Area: Bolton
Address: 119 Ainsworth Road
Manchester M26 4FD
Phone: 0161 724 4774

#496
Ship Inn
Category: Pub
Area: Oldham
Address: 693 Rochdale Road
Manchester M24 2RN
Phone: 0161 643 5871

#497
Wilton Arms
Category: Pub
Area: Bolton
Address: Coronation Road
Manchester M26 3LP
Phone: 0161 724 7068

#498
Railway Hotel
Category: Pub
Area: Bolton
Address: 427 Ainsworth Road
Manchester M26 4HN
Phone: 0161 723 1810

#499
Ainsworth Arms
Category: Pub
Area: Bolton
Address: 207 Bury Bolton Road
Manchester M26 4JY
Phone: 0161 764 1405

#500
**La Dolce Vita Restaurant
& Wine Bar**
Category: Italian, Wine Bar
Area: Stockport
Address: 27 Stockport Road
Manchester M12
Phone: 0161 449 0648

Alan Marks · Over the Hills and Far Away · * * *

MARTIN WADDELL · HELEN OXENBURY · FARMER DUCK · CANDLEWICK PRESS

CK and the BEANSTALK ~ · Alan Garner/Julek Heller

URSERY VERSES · H.G.C.Marsh Lambert · WARD LO

CHAEL FOREMAN'S WORLD OF FAIRY TALES

ROALD DAHL · THE MINPINS · Patrick Benson

OWL BABIES · WADDELL · BENSON · WALKER BOOKS

NOTHING · MICK INKPEN

TOM THUMB

YOU'RE A HERO, DALEY B!

S CROCODILE · ROALD DAHL and QUENTIN BLAKE

1. ◆ HARVEY SLUMFENBURGER'S CHRISTMAS PRESENT · ◆ · WALKER

Sheep in Wolves' Clothing · ANDERSEN

HAPPY TALE OF HONEY BEAR

C000077622

HA

ACKNOWLEDGMENTS

For making the conference the joyful day it was, we would like to thank the Fielder Centre for their faultless hospitality and Bookmarks for taking the discussion forward. For the book, special thanks go to Julie Gregory for inspiration, Lloyd Spencer and Peter Hoare for the lively images of the day and the publishers who have allowed reproduction from their books. We are grateful for the dedication and creativity of Tony McDermott, the patience of UH Press and, particularly, for Michael Rosen's idea. Thanks to Jon Berry for getting us started and Lisa Garner for holding it together.

First published in Great Britain in 2007 by
University of Hertfordshire Press
Learning and Information Services
University of Hertfordshire
College Lane
Hatfield
Hertfordshire AL10 9AB

British Library Cataloguing in Publication Data
A catalogue record for this book is available from the British Library

ISBN 978-1-902806-65-5

Printed in Great Britain by 4edge, Hockley, Essex

University of Hertfordshire
School of Education

CHILDREN'S LITERATURE
ANNUAL No.1

Owners of the means of instruction?
Children's Literature
some Marxist perspectives

papers and presentations
from conference 2006

Contents:

Jenny Plastow

What were we thinking of?
a beginning

A CONFERENCE on Children's Literature and Marxism. Mm. Not the first
thing that came to mind when I imagined what I might be doing in this new
post but hey, that's what being a new broom is for and everyone's heard of
Michael Rosen. And by now, everyone knows about the academic
importance of children's literature. They don't? Oh...OK. No, it's not about
people standing about saying aaah, not in this day and age. I can think of
quite a few children's novels that would make you say aaah, but for quite
different reasons - gasping with pain, perhaps. Stunned by the way children's
literature can represent what we believe to be reality in ways adult readers
find astonishing. Frightened by the grittiness of the reality that modern
writers perceive in children's worlds. Shaken by the way that children's books
may represent racism, violence, economic strife, aspiration, spirituality....
Children's literature wins prizes in competitions intended for the highest
level of adult fiction. Thousands of adults read Philip Pullman, J.K.Rowling,
Anne Fine. Not an academic subject? Hmmm.... this is going to take more
than one conference to address. Let's have a series!

And so, in the state-of-the-art de Havilland campus at the University of
Hertfordshire, in a twenty-first century building on the site of the biggest
aircraft manufacturer of the mid-twentieth century, we started planning. I
find all this significant; the engineering and manufacturing origins of our site,
the emphasis on construction, the importance of the worker; and the
overarching metaphor of flight. The University itself has its roots in the
education of the worker. The polytechnic movement of the last century,
with its commitment to providing vocational courses alongside those of pure

academe, was a major contribution to, and acknowledgment of, the importance of education in all its guises, to everyone, and from this movement our University grew. This speaks to me of egalitarianism, solidarity; of Marxism, if you like, though Marxism isn't the word on everyone's lips these days, even when politics is under discussion. So what's the relevance now? And what's the link? Why consider Marxist perspectives on children's literature? Well - read. Dip into our Annual anywhere you like; be entertained, instructed, moved, as we all were, when our first major endeavour came to fruition.

Because of the way children read fiction, focusing on the story and detaching the text from its conditions of production, and because of adults' nostalgia for the way they themselves read as children, Leavisite criticism (if any) of children's texts continued long after critical theory was being applied rigorously to other literary text. However, as childhood itself has become a focus of interest in cultural studies, and modern texts produced for children have come to seem increasingly more complex and less negligible, the study of children's literature has become a serious discipline within literary studies. Application of literary theory to texts written for children has inevitably led to analysis of the purpose and intention of writers for children, and from there it is a short step to full-blown political analysis. The appropriateness of applying Marxist perspectives to readings of children's literature can be seen in the pages that follow. In the years that follow we will be viewing the canon - and all sorts of other works - from psychoanalytical, international and further, varying, perspectives. Jack Zipes, writing in 2001 in 'Walter Benjamin, Children's Literature, and the Children's Public Sphere' describes Benjamin's goal in his consideration of children's literature; 'to discover how one could become productive with one's childhood without becoming nostalgic and trapped by reminiscences and destructive tendencies', recognising the pitfalls within pedagogy of 'eternal repetition and self-destruction'. Perhaps by honouring the significance and uniqueness of texts produced for child readers, we can move a little nearer to empowering them – and ourselves - as the 'directors....re-utilising things according to their taste and imagination' for whom Walter Benjamin so profoundly hoped.

You may not find this 'Annual' very conventional, as a set of conference proceedings. This was our intention. Just as the conference itself was heteroglossic, alive with voices from many different perspectives, those of writers juxtaposed with those of academics and again with those of performers, so our style of presentation, in both the conference and the Annual, has gone against the grain. One of the purposes of children's literature is to entertain - we entertain. Another is to explore deeply - we explore deeply. Yet another is to represent reality in unexpected and sometimes shocking ways - yes, you will find that as well. Overall, we want the Annual to give you the flavour of the event, salty and challenging, engaging and confrontational - and funny!

The papers in the book are not presented in the order in which they were heard on the day. We chose for the benefit of our audience to group the research papers mainly in the morning and to have the later part of the day for readings, discussions and fora involving the writers who brought their work and thought to share. In the Annual, we have arranged these differently, juxtaposing serious and thought provoking research papers with writerly readings or discussion papers, and the odd joke. Nevertheless, Michael Rosen's introductory paper, setting the keynote of the conference and providing a rationale for the whole endeavour, is still in its opening position. Beyond that, you can mix and match to your own enjoyment. Some of the fora were difficult to represent; the searching questions from the audience and the inspirational discussions that arose from them are vanished like swans carved in ice. Instead, we have, for example in the section called 'Writing the Future Red', asked the members of the panel to outline their views and give you ideas for future reading. Others have changed much from their original presentation; notice Beverley Naidoo's explanation of how this occurred for her. One or two, despite my best endeavours, are missing altogether, which makes me feel like Bill Cracker in Brecht's *Bilbao Song*; 'it's just that I've forgotten the words - it was a long time ago. But it was so much fun!' Well, we still have some photos.

Our contributors came from miles away, travelling overnight, arriving trailing their own metaphors of journey which ended in a bus ride from Hatfield station. Others only came from London, but brought with them their extraordinary wealth of experience and the questioning attitudes which characterise the scholars of this discipline. For, make no mistake, this is scholarship, and of the highest calibre – perhaps some of the most forward looking and exploratory you could encounter. And this is only the beginning. Leaf to the end of the book to find out more about our next conference – and maybe start considering your own contribution to *The Story and the Self – Children's Literature, some **psychoanalytic** perspectives.*

And now, read on....

Jenny Plastow *University of Hertfordshire: October 2006.*

Michael Rosen

Introduction to the conference
"General, your tank has one flaw -"

I'D LIKE TO BEGIN with a bit of a negative definition – that is, saying what we're not, or at least what we have never intended this conference to be.

It's not been convened in order to found a political party, group, tendency, fragment, faction, or, as the French would say, 'groupuscule'. No one behind this conference has called it with the intention of putting over what is sometimes called 'a line' that must be adhered to. It has been held with a view to exploring the possibility that children's literature can be investigated fruitfully and interestingly using what we've called 'Some Marxist Perspectives'. If it turns out that there is some running in this, then we have the opportunity to do any or some of the following: publish a book based on today's proceedings, start a journal, carry on having conferences....

That said, I would like to put us on the map in the following way: you are attending what I think is the first ever conference with these terms of reference and this programme on offer.

Let's do a bit of situating. We're a group of what I suspect is a mix of teachers, librarians and writers meeting together in a university in one of the wealthiest countries of the world. It seems to me that we're positioned on a cycle that repeats itself all over the western world. Social democratic governments (such as those headed by Clinton, Blair, Mitterand and Schroeder) alternate with explicitly neo-liberal governments (like those of Reagan, Thatcher, Chirac and now Merkel) in trying to privatise whatever is left of these countries' state-run welfare systems. This is called 'modernisation' and directly affects the standard of living, care and education of the children we write for and teach. Governments of either hue show themselves to be unable or unwilling to do anything about staggering inequalities at home or between the rich and poor anywhere else in the world. In the face of this, for us, to talk about 'the child', as if he or she is one uniform entity with common experience, can not be sustained.

Somewhere here, we also have to factor in the way in which these inequalities alter the cultural make-up of countries. In the west, the old fantasies (some would say 'lies') about a homogenous race or homogenous national culture can't be sustained because of ever-increasing diversity. Again, the question 'Who is the child?' can't be answered simply. Not that it ever could be, but that's another matter.

Meanwhile, we know that a massive geo-political crisis is coming over the horizon in the forms of humanly made climate-change and a humanly made energy shortfall. The semi-permanent state of war that we now find ourselves in seems to be a consequence of how our leaders try to handle this. Again, this is something that has a direct impact on children, schools and parents in particular, in and around the many battlefields across the world and away from the battlefields in the minds and consciousness of all children. Yesterday, my five year old asked me *'Why was the woman's head put on a pole?'* She had overheard a report from the Congo on the 'Today' programme on BBC Radio 4.

If this is our epoch, where are we in it? Economically, some of us are employees in the institutions (schools, colleges, libraries and the like) that the state has asked to deliver to the economy the workforce that the economy says it needs. Others of us are earners of fees and freelance payments in the leisure and entertainment industry [open brackets] 'book section' [close brackets]. These two sides (the institutional and the freelance) have relationships with each other: as expressed by such processes as writers in schools, teachers reading books, or indeed examiners using literary texts. But we also have relationships with the institutions we find ourselves in: on the one hand, education and on the other the publishing business.

Each of these two institutions has been directly affected by the epoch we are in and people like us, working in them, have responded. So, it's not hard to see that the publishing industry in this country has moved from being dominated by small family units to one dominated by massive world units. Meanwhile, education all over the West has come under greater and greater pressure to dispense with humanistic and liberal ideas and adopt instrumental approaches (of which the rush to synthetic phonics is only one) policed by systems of testing, inspection, grading and selection.

The day to day matter of what books are written, get published and indeed read is, as I see it, held within this matrix. Not only that, but also the strands of power - or lack of power - and the environments created by this matrix have an impact on what gets written, what gets read and how it's read. I'm not sure that this area has ever been fully theorised or explored. I hope we can do that. So, for example, it's always been my argument that the way in which literature is examined and tested has an impact on the way it's taught and the way it's read. It is examined and tested in a certain way now because education has been re-structured in order to deliver more accurately the segregated sections of the labour force that industry is asking for, and that, in turn, is a consequence of the increasing desperation of those in charge of the economy in the global environment.

Thus, open a KS2 SATs English paper and you'll find that very nearly all the questions involve the child re-stating the chronology, logic and empirical sense-data-type facts of the story. There is no space for the child to relate aspects of his or her experience and feelings to those that appear to be manifested within the story, no space for the child to speculate about the ebb and flow of feelings that the story appears to engender. The kind of questioning the tests demand has had a knock-on effect on how stories are read in class and indeed, what kind of role children's literature is now seen as having within the curriculum. In essence it is being pushed more and more into the role of being the handmaiden to something called 'literacy' — a manageable, instrumental entity which they think can be measured and thus, in their terms, can be given an economic value. Again, this is an area that could be explored much more.

As 'literacy' has become increasingly regarded as being culture-free (so, for example, the bilingualism of a Bangladeshi child doesn't register anywhere on the evaluations of literacy that the state demands or publishes) so we have moved towards an education strategy that has removed the being of the child from the learning process. The education documents that have landed in teachers' lockers over the last twenty years do not include references to anyone we could identify as this or that child in this or that mode of thinking, or being anything other than a creature who is acted on. It is the final perfect match of the industrial production line that begins with raw material, is acted on by processes and emerges as a car or a biscuit.

If this were the total picture we would be living in a totalitarian state and human beings would have become automata. But we're not. As Bertolt Brecht put it,

General, your tank is a powerful vehicle
It tramples the forest, it crushes a hundred men,
But it has one flaw:
It requires a driver.
General, your bomber is strong.
It flies faster than the storm, it loads more than an elephant.
But it has one flaw:
It requires a mechanic.
General, man is very useful.
He knows how to fly, he knows how to murder.
But he has one flaw:
He knows how to think.

Editors, authors, teachers, librarians, parents and children have resisted many of the processes I've described and I'll be as bold as to suggest that we, here today, are in part evidence of this too. There have been many attempts to assert the humanism in literature for children (think of the interventions of people like Philip Pullman and Michael Morpurgo), to talk subversively (as it now is) about an activity known as 'reading for pleasure' and to resist the regimes of selecting and testing.

But there is also the matter of what is written, pictured, edited and published. How or where precise works fit (or don't fit) in this picture of the epoch that I've given is, I suspect, one of the many matters we'll debate. So, by way of introduction I'd like to ask the question: what can Marxism or 'some Marxist perspectives' offer us by way of explanation, critical power, methodology and even perhaps, some suggestions as to what is worth doing?

I acknowledge that we may never reach some kind of neat agreement as to what constitutes 'a' or 'the' Marxist approach to children's literature. And to tell the truth, I don't think we need to. However, I would like to pick out what I think are amongst the most interesting and useful observations that Marx and Marxists have made.

I think these centre on class, the 'base and superstructure' question and ideology. Following from these my own inclination leads me to value the questions raised by Raymond Williams and his notion of dominant, residual and emergent cultures; Frederic Jameson and Pierre Macherey and the political unconscious; Pierre Bourdieu on reproduction; various writers on race and post-colonialism; and again various writers on how (and indeed why) gender, patriarchy, childhood and sexuality are constructed.

I'll begin with class. Sadly, this is an area full of misunderstandings. The Marxist approach is neither one that relies on what individuals think nor one based on a league table of incomes. People often talk subjectively about what class they think they or others belong to. Again, we are often given what is supposed to be a more objective analysis of class by rating people according to incomes or expenditure. A Marxist approach says that there is a different way of looking at class which is suited to explaining how the great wheels of society grind away. It says that the underlying structure of society is not static; it is a process in which one class, which owns and controls the vast majority of a society's - or indeed the world's - resources and systems of production and distribution, is in perpetual conflict with a class of people who own very little more than their ability to sell their labour power.

The needs and requirements of these two classes of people are not only in conflict with each other, they are in contradiction with each other and create further contradictions. Put simply, it is in the interests of the class that owns to keep what it calls its 'labour costs' at a minimum. Meanwhile it is in the interests of the class that sells its labour to keep those same costs (which it prefers to call 'pay' or 'wages' or 'salary'!) as high as it can. However, this conflict is not always as bald or as plain as this. We can see it at work in the upheavals going on in the UK over pensions (a classic case of what the owning class sees as a 'cost') or in France over youth employment laws. Again, when we look at what are sometimes called communal upheavals, like the ones that have taken place over the years in, say, Brixton or Blackburn, it's clear that the fact that those communities are made up of people trying to survive on what are, in effect, labour costs kept low by the owning class, is the underlying reason for their difficulties. Yet again, when we look closely at our own field, the main indicator of educational success and

failure has been shown over and over again to be income. However, by putting it in this language - by using the word 'income' - we are thrown back on to the conventional causes of what makes people rich and poor (luck, merit, innate idiocy and the rest) and not to considerations of class.

I'll say here that class (in the sense that I'm talking about) delivers a massive differential in income through a process whereby the value of what a workforce produces is greatly in excess of the total value of what they earn. This differential or profit is not, as is sometimes claimed, beautifully and elegantly recycled for the benefit of all, but, as all statistics show, is appropriated by and within the class that owns and which continues to acquire more and more of the world's wealth.

But where in all this is the group of people we think we all know so well and who are of immense interest to the world of children's books: the middle class? Isn't this the group who are neither the people who own the resources, from which they can benefit greatly by employing others, renting off vast swathes of property or plant, or from lending millions of dollars, nor the people who earn income solely through the sale of their labour power?

Well, to start off with, a lot of the people who are subjectively called 'middle class' are indeed people who live solely by selling their labour power – a lot of teachers, social workers and, if you like, educated employees. There may be a whole host of indicators that suggest these people see themselves as different from blue collar, less educated folk, but economically and structurally they're in the same boat. However, that said, there are some people who are, if you like, in a different boat – people who use small amounts of capital or property to generate income, people who employ a few people to generate profit, people who control sections of the workforce or make big decisions within the legal system and so acquire sufficient income to generate yet more income from property or capital. It is clear that structurally these people are neither substantial members of the owning class nor of the class that lives solely by selling its labour. Perhaps we can indeed call these people within this schema, 'middle class'.

When we look at the history of, and indeed the present state of affairs with, children's literature and education, we can see that it is from within the class that occupies either this middle position or those educated sections of the class that lives by selling its labour that the most writers have arisen. This group, then, has generated the outlook of most children's books and by definition, it provides the people who've done the most teaching and directing of children's reading.

As Bob Leeson showed us in 'Reading and Righting : The Past, Present, and Future of Fiction for the Young' (1985) the origins of what we call children's literature are full of struggles by those who thought they were upholding the values of this middle class against the low habits of the class below them reading their penny chapbooks and the like. The marks of these struggles can be still be found within the world of children's books, in something like the distinctions made between the 'Beano' comic and the 'picture book'. More seriously, we can see it at work in the nature of education itself.

In the 1970s, people began to ask what we might call 'class questions' about education. Are there ways in which we could say that class is built into education? I will suggest that I think this work of questioning is unfinished, and has an immense relevance to the world of children's books. We can ask: are there ways in which the very process of education, its language, its structures, its day to day goings on, its culture, is in some way or another encoded in ways that suit children of one kind rather than another? The coincidence of poverty and educational failure is based on what, precisely? That some children don't have enough food, or the right food, to eat? Enough time and space at home? That not enough time is given by hard-pressed parents?

Or is there something more subtle going on that is intimately linked to what we're about as educators? Pierre Bourdieu's theory of reproduction suggests that the educated, yes - middle-class, family creates what he calls a 'habitus', a linguistic and cultural disposition that matches the language, values and ideology of education. So, we know in this room, don't we, that there is in effect a private, informal, middle class curriculum that we offer our children -

in particular by choosing the 'right' mix of books, but also the visits to the museums and art galleries (with their guides for children - a kind of children's literature in itself), and of course by holding the kinds of conversation we have with our children about values, about their homework, about the place we live in, about the TV programmes we watch and the like. It is a potent mix of culture, values, abstract thought and outlook which matches perfectly what is on offer in school. There are historical and social reasons for this which can be spelled out and it's not a process that has gone on without struggles and resistance within the world

of children's literature. The argument over Leila Berg's reading scheme, 'Nippers' (1971) some years ago was precisely in this zone. I would suggest that a new hierarchy is emerging, exacerbated by the government's educational programme. That's to say, schools are being coerced into offering a bread-and-butter minimum literacy for all. The effect of this is that those children who would not in their lives easily or usually come across the full range of books on offer from the world of children's books (and there are economic and educational reasons for this) are now less and less likely to come across them in school, whilst middle class children will acquire the full range of books at home, thereby further enabling them to benefit from what I'll simplistically call the 'education code'. Children's literature has always been consumed hierarchically and by class. In the past there have been times when schools were places that tried to erode that hierarchy. I fear that the present situation restores it. A variety of writers, publishers, teachers and librarians have been contesting this for many years and in a variety of ways. I think there is a good deal of fruitful work we can do in this field, charting what's been done, what's been successful, what's failed, where we are now and the like.

Let's move on to 'base and superstructure'. For those who've read in this field, you'll know that there's a long and winding path of struggle with this concept. This is not going to be a review of the literature. I'll just make a few observations that I hope will be productive.

Firstly, the concept is a metaphor, not an abstraction. A better translation would have been something like 'foundations' and 'upper building'. What is being referred to here concerns an understanding of ideas and the whole field of institutions concerned with producing ideas and indeed putting them into practice institutionally. Both in idle usage and sometimes more theoretically, we often consider a process like education, or the work of an artist, or the operation of the law as if they exist in an autonomous world which is self-governing, influenced only by its predecessors and contemporaries within that field. Thus, we might say idly, 'Keats was influenced by Shakespeare'; 'Surrealism grew out of Dada'; 'The 1871 Education Act paved the way for the 1944 Education Act'. If that sounds too crude a representation of what gets said, then there is a modification that treats 'discourse' as if it too had this kind of autonomy. So, it is seen as legitimate by some to explain an artistic movement, the inspiration for a novel, or a legal judgment as if it is sufficient (I use that word advisedly) to treat these events simply and only as interventions within their ideological or discursive field. Thus, we might say that the work of Anthony Browne is 'in conversation with Magritte'; or that 'no anthropomorphic children's book of the twentieth century can quite escape the shadow of Beatrix Potter' or that 'Hans Christian Andersen was above all else part of Romanticism'.

Of themselves, these statements aren't, to my mind, wrong. The problem with them is when they become, as I've said, sufficient explanations. For that sufficiency, I suggest that we need something else.

So back to the Marxist metaphor: base and superstructure. The idea here is that human beings must organise themselves co-operatively in ways that enable them to satisfy their material needs: primarily food and shelter. The Marxist argument is that whatever structures a society devises for this to take place will in the final analysis (a phrase that may cause some of you to smile) shape and determine people's consciousness. In shorthand, the base will determine the superstructure. The material base or foundations of a society (economic arrangements) will shape its laws, its education system, the components of its dominant ideology, and its artistic output. However, in interpreting Marx's writings, and indeed the writing of many others since, people have been at pains to modify this schema and save it from what has been described as its vulgarity. Firstly, Marx himself spent some energy in pointing out one of the contradictions I referred to earlier; that in any given society there is often a mismatch between what the dominant ideology is saying and what developments might be taking place in the material base. So, for example, the ideological demands of the rising bourgeoisie in the sixteenth and seventeenth century (in relation to a lack of democratic representation in government, but also, say, with the representation of Hamlet as a prototype modern, secular, expressive, illusorily self-creating individual) were often in conflict with the economic arrangements of the time. It was, in Raymond Williams' terms, the 'emergent culture' coming into conflict with the material base of late feudalism.

So whatever determinations are going on, they can't simply be along the lines of formulaic statements like 'feudalism produced illustrated manuscripts', 'capitalism produced the Beach Boys'. And here we need to return to what we were saying about class. Class is, I suggested, a dynamic, changing relationship, full of conflict and contradiction. At any given moment, societally, there is some kind of uneasy balance of class forces. At any given moment, for any given individual, this balance of class forces is in some way or another played out in the consciousness and body of that individual. In other words, the foundations, or 'base', are not some rocky firmament but a shifting set of demanding forces acting on the ideational field and on individuals.

Take the case of the rise of the 'folk tale' and in particular someone like Hans Christian Andersen, born like the rest of us into a time and place not of his own choosing. He found himself in a Europe of immense turmoil but living in a backwater on a rural island in Denmark. Of all the writers to have ever produced children's literature, he is the one with perhaps the poorest origins. His father was one of those people we now see more and more clearly in the nineteenth century, European picture: the impoverished tradesman hungry for knowledge, eager for change, freedom and democracy. Many such people emerged as part of the American and French revolutions, events that broke as a consequence of the rise of a new class. Meanwhile, Hans Christian's mother, part-time worker and washerwoman was, it seems, embedded in the traditional ideology and so-called 'superstition' of the pagan, peasant culture of the previous several hundred years. When Andersen gets himself to Copenhagen he meets a world full of the old and new: the Danish fragment of Europe's aristocracy brushing shoulders with a local bourgeoisie. The form he is sometimes credited with inventing, the literary folk-tale, is in fact being invented simultaneously in Germany by such people as Clemens von Brentano, E.T.A Hoffman and of course the Grimms, with connections to the aristocratic French tales of Perrault, Mme. Aulnoy and the like. It is now clear that for the Grimms, the latent ideology behind their tales is the hope that they are producing a form that appeals to the whole society, the whole 'volk'. Meanwhile, Andersen, he of the humblest of humble origins, finds that his tales offer him a calling card in the most exalted of homes. Somewhere in all this, I detect the invention of a form that is concerned, consciously or not, with flying in the face of the social and economic upheavals and divisions going on all around: the creation of something unifying and consoling, that gives succour to the needs and desires of the lower orders for a better life whilst maintaining the institutional and structural status quo.

I'll also point out here that it's my view that we've reached a point in the writing about children's literature where some people are quite at ease conducting a discussion in this way without necessarily acknowledging that there is something Marxist about it. Jack Zipes's work on the Grimms *(The Brothers Grimm: From Enchanted Forest to the Modern World. 2002)* is full of this kind of observation and many more, but Zipes does not necessarily trace the reason *why* he is saying what he's saying back to quotes from Marx. Interestingly, Jackie Wullschlager's biography of Andersen (2000) is also a book that probes some questions of how the material stresses and strains of the time go towards shaping Andersen's life and work. Again, there is no acknowledgement that Marx and Marxism had ever existed.

There is another qualification to the 'base and superstructure metaphor'. Marxists of the non-vulgar kind have always understood that the ideological field is not without some impact on the material. Limits on human action are not only set by how you earn your livelihood. More satisfying is to understand this dialectically. That's to say, the material (with all its contradictions) shapes the ideological while the ideological is able to arc back on the material, to some degree. The law against homosexuality is a case in point. Here, in post-war Britain, was a law founded with all the practice of sustaining heterosexuality as the enforced norm, flying in the face of what was the day-to-day reality for a sizeable segment of society. The testimony of many gays from that period is that that law prescribed the shape and form of their lives, culture and, in some cases, their art. It was a law embedded in attitudes to the body which are in turn embedded in the ideologies that sustained the rising bourgeoisie in its assault on aristocratic power. It is these ideologies, also concerning family, childhood, gender specific roles and heterosexuality, that we find running right through the history of children's literature. Ideology, I suggest, has the power to affect and influence but will in the final analysis be traceable back to material interests and contradictions.

In recent years, it seems to me that several productive ideas have emerged that owe a debt to at least some of those I've outlined here. So, for example, of the many thoughts that pour forth from the mind of Frederic Jameson, his work on what he called 'the political unconscious' presents us with an interesting starting point. ('The Political Unconscious' (1982)). In fact, he borrowed and adapted the notion from Pierre Macherey ('A Theory of Literary Production' (1978)). If, as I've suggested, the contradictions of society are manifested within an individual, then we can also say that they are manifested in an artist or writer and so by continuation in that artist's work. One kind of contradiction I'm talking about here concerns what we might call 'positioning'. I think it was the writer Julius Lester who asked what was the historical difference between the field slave and the house slave. He suggested that if the slave-owner's house was on fire, the field slave said that the master's house was burning, whereas the house slave said that it was 'our' house that was burning. Though the two kinds of slave were materially in the same relationship with the owner, the house-slave perceived his or her position in a way that is in contradiction with that reality. If we take Hans Christian Andersen again, and one of the first literary folk-tales he wrote, if not the first, 'The Tinder Box', we see a story about a figure who strode across the European stage, the penniless soldier. He achieves what many folk-tales allow their penniless heroes to achieve, relief from his wretched state; upward social mobility through cunning and luck. However, his route to this involves bizarre scenes of sexual molestation carried out on an inert, prone upper class woman. No matter what these scenes tell us about Andersen's sexuality, it seems to me they also express the ambiguous contradictory position he found himself in: a member of the rural poor (who had in Europe been kept at subsistence level by the aristocracy for nearly a thousand years, occasionally relieved when the men were put in arms and received some cash and plunder if they weren't maimed or killed) but also someone who materially needed the attention of the middle and aristocratic classes if he was to sell his work. At one and the same time part of him yearned for that upper class to be prone and inert (or indeed flung into the air and dismembered by huge dogs) while another part of him yearned to be, how shall I say?, conjoined with it.

Another of the key contradictions to which Marx draws our attention is that the very methods the owning class uses, to further its own interests, creates the conditions within which it is resisted, and, Marx hopes, will be overthrown. Thus, for capitalism to work, it needs constantly to bring many people together in one place, in order to get them to produce the goods or services that will deliver up the profit. However, in order to sell these goods and services, it is necessary for the owning class to repeat over and over again how these goods will satisfy our individual needs, or, indeed, will construct our individuality. A particular hair-dye will make me look younger and I will have a better relationship with my lover as a result. I will also have my own bank account, my own mortgage and a choice of holiday, school, health provider and patio doors. However, as I've said, the process of production keeps bringing people together in large numbers in order to get things made, serviced and distributed. In those conditions people have often found that, as their needs are in contradiction with their employers', so are they in contradiction with the dominant ideology's way of dividing us up into castes, groups, cultures, and ultimately into seemingly individualised consumers, defined by what we buy. It seems to me that schools are also places which in some respects guy this process, bringing together in large numbers people (pupils and teachers) who some of the time appear opposed to each other, sometimes united, as the demands of the society keep trying to segregate and select those being educated. Teachers are often placed in the role of those who do the bidding of those who would have pupils divided in this way.

Some of you will be familiar with Robert Cormier's two 'Chocolate War' books ('The Chocolate War' (1975) and 'Beyond the Chocolate War' (1986)) which use the microcosm of a school, (in this case a Catholic Boys' School) to indicate what can and might happen when there is collaboration between corrupt power and popular thuggery in what one might call the 'masses'. As with all dystopias, and indeed, gothic horror stories, there is inevitably an onward momentum towards what I've jokingly called in the past the 'anti-Boris'; that's to say, someone, some thing, some force somewhere which will relieve us of the monster. If you saw 'The Blob' (1958) you'll remember the discovery that the blob didn't like cold, so members of the airforce dropped it on either the north or south pole.

Interestingly in the *Chocolate War* books, Cormier offers very little in the way of anti-Boris other than the growing awareness by the focaliser of what's happened. Powerful enough, you might say. However, the key speech at the end of *Beyond the Chocolate War* is made by the arch villain when he explains that in reality he is only what is inside all of us. What is this about? It seems to me that this expresses perfectly the contradiction born out of talking about a class-free notion of evil. In this denouément in the book, evil is de-located from time and place and person; made universal and in a way value-free. The implication is that evil just exists everywhere, unless you as an individual take up arms against the sea of troubles and vanquish it. However, this notion, which seems to suit the dominant ideology as it tries to explain everything, from Saddam Hussein to paedophilia via hoodies and Pol Pot, in the same way, sits in the *Chocolate War* books in contradiction with Cormier's brilliant exposé of the Machiavellian methods of corrupt power. It's Jameson and Macherey who offer us an insight into how such contradictions are manifested in literature through what they've called the 'political unconscious'.

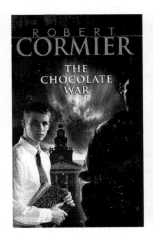

However, let me take a step back and make a cautionary comment. One severe challenge to these approaches has come to us from the critical field known loosely as 'reader-response' and its sister 'reception theory'. Put baldly, the problem is this. It's all very well me or you or anyone saying that this or that text says this, or shows this, or manifests this, but the truth of the matter, says reader-response theory, is that this is only my, or your, construction. A book's meaning, the argument goes, doesn't lie in some immanent way in the text. It lies in how the reader constructs that meaning. I have some sympathy with this. As Stanley Fish reminds us, *(Is There A Text In This Class' (1982))* writing is only a set of material squiggles on a page. We take those squiggles and turn them into words, ideas, concepts, plots, characters, meanings and values. This has given lots of fun to Fish who, he thought, had demolished the whole of criticism and critical theory with one stroke. Interestingly, he doesn't seem to have succeeded, as people, myself included, continue to talk about books as if we have unlocked key meanings from a text rather than simply saying that we have found stuff that interested or amazed us, given that we are prejudiced or biased or constructed in this or that way. In fact, a vast amount of what we call criticism continues to be little more than saying over and over again: 'the text I've just looked at reminds me of something else I read or something that happened to me ten years ago'. If not that, then you can get away with a series of intended-to-be engaging re-enactments of moments from the text. How do I know? I've done it many times. Perhaps it's not a particularly insightful activity but it is one of the ways in which we enjoy books.

However, Fish may be more than a spoilsport. He also stumbled on the fact that readers are not like random molecules bouncing around in boiling water. Certain groups of readers appear to respond to a given text in one way and other groups respond in other ways. Thus he gave birth to the notion of what he called 'interpretive communities'. I think we can and should take this further. Much further. Fish said that readers construct texts. We can ask, and I believe, should ask, what or who constructs readers and how? And indeed we are in a better position that many in academe to ask that question because we work at the very point at which people become readers and develop as readers. I think that it's possible to escape from

Fish's rather vague and elitist idea of 'interpretive communities' which is full of the suggestion that the main thing that defines readers is their reading. I think that some of the observations of Marx and Marxists would give us a far richer, far more complex notion of what a reader is, and what reading does for them. However, Fish and someone working in a related field, Tony Bennett, ('Outside Literature' (1990)) have put an important check on the kinds of statements that claim infinite certainty about meaning without reference to real readers. As any of us in this room know, this is particularly dangerous when it comes to interpreting books written for a young audience. In short, no matter what we think a book is about, or for that matter what its 'political unconscious' is, there is no certainty that any child will agree. Indeed, they might turn out to be that fascinating object, the reader who reads to the end of the book, refusing to be won over to what we might have thought were its ideological siren-songs; in short, 'the resistant reader'.

Which leads me neatly to questions of post-colonialism and gender because some of the most interesting work I've come across in relation to young readers reading across or against a text have been in these fields. Gemma Moss ('Un/Popular Fictions' (1989)) and Beverley Naidoo's work ('Exploring Racism: Reader, Text and Context', (1992)) come to mind. Now, it's quite possible to approach children's literature from the perspectives of race, gender, sexual orientation or physical ability without any acknowledgement that Marxism has got or should have anything to do with it. The question I'd like to raise though is whether some Marxist perspectives (as we've put it) can contribute something to these discussions.

At first glance, it might appear not. Classical Marxism places the dynamic model of class that I've represented here at the centre of its world-view whilst each of the areas I've mentioned here race, gender and the like, often appear to be talking of a world centred somewhere else: variously in, say, issues surrounding racial domination, patriarchy, heterosexuality or indeed the use (or the meaning of the use) of the human body. Hovering over and through all this is the use of the word 'power' particularly as used by Foucault who himself looked at most of these areas. Thus, very relevantly for us, Foucault brilliantly showed how one of the methods the modern period used in order for the bourgeoisie to seize and hold power is through what it did and does to contain and control the human body *('Discipline and Punish' (1975))* in particular the young human body in school. This offered us a viewfinder with which to look at a great deal of children's literature in terms of say, the libidinous desires it unleashes, or forbids; the transgressions it admonishes or appears to licence; the punishments it lends authority to, or undermines; the racial and sexual segregations it supports or resists; the idealisations of the human form it supports or subverts and so on. I find much of this kind of analysis fascinating and irresistible and raises important and troubling questions for us about children's books from, say, the imperial period; the construction of, for example, motherhood or the feminine ideal throughout children's literature; or indeed the support of certain kinds of masculinity through adventure books and so on. The other side of the coin is in my delight in reading books such as Benjamin Zephaniah's *'Refugee Boy'(2001)*, Mary Hoffman's *'The Colour of Home'(2002)* or David Levithan's *'Boy Meets Boy' (2005 UK)* all of which seem to be informed (at least partly) by a wish to break the power and certainty of such notions as nationhood, the dangerous 'other', and the heterosexual norm. But surely none of this can be simply subsumed under the heading 'Marxist perspectives'?

Well, I see that I've used the word 'power'. My first observation is a criticism of the criticism. Yes, indeed these Foucauldian approaches have been massively illuminating and part of that has been because they dissect in minutiae the means by which power and dominant ideology is sustained in society. But again, I'll ask, does it do so 'sufficiently'? I don't think so. The problem is that I don't think it is sustainable to suggest that power is wielded simply or only for its own reasons. I suggest this mystifies and reifies power. The most dominant power in all societies is what's wielded by those who own and control the resources and the means by which those resources are turned into useful things and in so doing, those people (a tiny minority) end up by owning the vast proportion of the wealth. Yes, it's absolutely true that down through society, through its groups, clubs, schools and on down to the most intimate relationships between two people and into the struggles within one's own head, there are indeed what we call 'power struggles'. The question we have to ask though is whether these smaller group and psychological questions of power are projected on to society or whether it's the origins, shape and determinations of power in society that reach down and into the groups, institutions and intimate relations we live in. Or perhaps both. Freud's model of the super-ego, ego and id was one way in which the reaching-down into the individual was conceptualised, though I've always thought his writing about totalitarian leaders suggests the reverse: the projection of psychology on to society. But there are others such as Wilhelm Reich and Erich Fromm who've struggled with it too.

Children's literature poses some interesting questions here. Children have very little power in any society and it could be said that children's literature, whilst appearing to support and sustain children over and beyond what they are often not allowed (identity, autonomous thought, culture, self, transgressive ideas, adult-free action and the like), is also a process by which adults in the form of writers, editors, publishers and critics wield some kind of ideological and emotional power over children. Children's literature might well be a form of nurture but it has historically been a suitable site from which it could apply torture. It has in its time offered a binary choice: 'nurture or torture'. In very general terms, I think we can say that its broad aim has nearly always been to improve the lives of its readers, but what if that was merely in order to make adults' lives more bearable? If any of this is true or only partly true, are different kinds, yes, different classes of children treated in different ways by children's literature? If so, to what ends? I've a feeling that it's possible to detect that power over children is wielded through children's literature and through the uses to which children's literature is put. However, and this links in part to Bourdieu's 'habitus', the power is wielded for a social purpose and that social purpose will in the end take us back to the dynamic, marxian model of class.

It seems to me that we have an area of fruitful discussion and debate here. Can we enlarge and demystify Foucauldian criticism by linking power to what classical Marxism would say is its function? After all, the very fact that we bandy about the term 'dominant ideology' stems from Marx's idea that the prevailing or dominant ideology of any time is in essence the ideology of the class that owns and rules. For much of the time, the criticism that I read looks at the dominant ideology but unhinges it from this class and has it hovering over us unattached. This doesn't make the criticism uninteresting or invalid. I just find myself wishing that it could do more.

Meanwhile, I hope we all have a fascinating and insightful day and that this is just the beginning.

REFERENCES

Bob Leeson, *Reading and Righting : The Past, Present, and Future of Fiction for the Young*. London: William Collins, Sons and Company Ltd, 1985.

Jack Zipes, *The Brothers Grimm: From Enchanted Forest to the Modern World*. Second edition. New York: Palgrave Macmillan, 2002.

Jackie Wullschlager, *Hans Christian Andersen: The Life of a Storyteller*. New York: Knopf, 2000.

Frederic Jameson, *The Political Unconscious: Narrative as a Socially Symbolic Act*. Ithaca, NY: Cornell University Press, 1981.

Pierre Macherey, *A Theory of Literary Production*. Routledge & Kegan Paul, 1978.

Robert Cormier, *The Chocolate War*. New York: Pantheon, 1974.

Robert Cormier, *Beyond the Chocolate War*. New York: Knopf, 1985.

Stanley Fish, *Is there a text in this class? : The authority of interpretive communities*. Cambridge, Massachussets: Harvard UP, 1982.

Tony Bennett, *Outside Literature*. London: Routledge, 1990.

Gemma Moss, *Un/Popular Fictions*. London: Virago, 1989.

Beverley Naidoo, *Exploring Racism: Reader, Text and Context*. Trentham Books, 1992.

Michel Foucault, *Discipline and Punish: The Birth of the Prison*. trans. Alan Sheridan. New York: Vintage, 1977.

Benjamin Zephaniah, *Refugee Boy*. London: Bloomsbury, 2001.

Mary Hoffman, *The Colour of Home*. London: Frances Lincoln, 2002.

David Levithan, *Boy Meets Boy*. New York: Baker and Taylor, 2005.

Richard MacSween

Fictionalising Fascism

NATIONAL INTEREST in the far-right will doubtless now shift to Barking and its eleven newly-elected British National Party councillors ('Welcome to Barking - new far right capital of Britain" ran the Guardian's post-election headline) but up till May 2006 the BNP had been most successful in the North. The decaying textile towns of Halifax, Keighley, Oldham and Burnley with their substantial Asian populations have suffered the attentions of the BNP for several years; their leader, Nick Griffin, who lives on the Welsh border, picked Oldham for his 2001 general election attempt and Keighley in 2005.

The riots in the summer of 2001, first in Oldham, then in Burnley and Bradford, received lurid, and predictably shallow, national media coverage. Images of torched cars and broken windows set middle England's moral panic bells ringing, and it was all given a decisively racist inflection by footage of young Asian men throwing stones at riot police. The far-right melted out of the picture leaving an "Asian problem". This was graphically confirmed in December 2001 by the Home Secretary, David Blunkett, who pre-empted the publication of the reports into the riots by blaming female circumcision, forced marriage and failure to learn English as root causes of friction between Asians and whites. Thankfully the Clarke Report on the Burnley riots went beyond Blunkett's victim-blaming diagnosis to include such mundane factors as industrial decline, poverty and bad housing - the Daneshouse ward in Burnley, where the Asian population is concentrated, is the eighth most deprived out of the 8,414 wards in England. The activity of the far-right is mentioned in the report too, though it is necessary to go to something like Nick Lowles' *White Riot*, an investigation into how the far-right fomented the riot in Oldham, to get a more complete picture.

Burnley's anti-fascists have campaigned against racism and the BNP for some years now, as a defensive but necessary activity; our aim, to isolate the fascists and prevent them gaining the support of a discontented, soft-racist constituency, as has happened in several other European countries. Hence the demonstrations; lobbying, town-centre stalls, leafleting, endless discussions and arguments - and the chance to have oneself pictured on a 'Red Watch' website.

Often our arguments have been with people who claim to be on the left and who argue the fascists should be ignored, that we are only giving them publicity, ignoring the fact that they are getting publicity anyway, and growing. Some people, though a shrinking number, urge us to merely laugh at the BNP: as a recent Labour leaflet fatuously put it: "Back in the 30s they were a joke – Hitler even had a Charlie Chaplin moustache". Some journalists, courting controversy, have been only too happy to give racists and fascists media space, invoking the right to freedom of speech with an ignorance of twentieth century history that, close up, doesn't seem farcical.

What we can't leaflet away is the profound disappointment with Labour. The BNP put up two candidates in Burnley in 1993, but with the Conservatives in power nobody was interested in the far-right and they scored a derisory vote. Now they have seven councillors here.

As I had just written my first novel for teenagers, the Burnley riots demanded to be the focus of a second. Riots and racism are hardly new subjects for fiction; *Huckleberry Finn*, *Absolute Beginners*, and *To Kill A Mockingbird*, to select some titles not quite at random, could all be claimed as teenage novels, but inevitably they are of their time and circumstances. Two recent books for young adults looked relevant - Alan Gibbons' *Caught In The Crossfire* and Malorie Blackman's *Noughts And Crosses* - but I decided to avoid reading them till after my book was written.

I had three main aims: to be faithful to what happened in Burnley and elsewhere within the limits of fictional realism; to give contemporary events a broader historical context; and to give the novel a clear anti-fascist angle. I came up with the following story:

The main character, Ellie, a 15 year-old girl, lives over a second-hand furniture shop in a mixed white/Asian part of the northern English town of Boltby, with her mother and younger brother. Next door is an Asian grocery shop and Ellie is friends with the son, Muzz, who attends the same school. Racial tension is growing in the town, fanned by the activities of a far-right group, the leader of which has a relationship with Ellie's mother. Ellie's older brother gets drawn into the nazi group, and an incident between him and Imran, Muzz's older brother, triggers a full-scale riot in which people are injured and Imran is killed.

An important aspect of the novel is that Ellie is an aspiring writer. The riot is told through a mixture of first-person and third person narrative, the latter being her version of events:

> This is what happened that day.
> Some is what I saw, some is what other people told me, some is what I read in the newspapers – and some is me trying to get into people's heads the best I can.
> You don't have to believe a word of what's written here if you don't want…

She also writes up the story of Mrs Pearl, an old woman who lives across the street and who turns out to have come over from Vienna on the kindertransport after Kristallnacht, and also the story of her best friend's stepfather who claims an Irish ancestry, twin brothers who came to the town in the mid-nineteenth century to escape the Famine.

In going beyond current British anti-Asian racism by pushing the geographical and historical boundaries in this way I was trying to make a simple point: migration is a historical fact, as a glance at the telephone directory will confirm, and new immigrants often suffer prejudice from an 'original' population whose origins are often not much older than the newcomers'. Nostalgia about a white working class, posited as though it existed since time immemorial but actually a mid-twentieth century construction, is likely to grow and the BNP success in Barking is an expression of this. Similarly Michael Collins in *The Likes Of Us* articulates an understandable discontent, but much of it is as suspect as the pearly king and queen which grace its cover.

If *Victory Street* were to connect at all with its intended readership, I felt it would have to include a wide range of characters. As an anti-fascist I can have a no-platform-for-nazis position but as a writer of fiction I am compelled to give them a voice, and if in doing that I were to create a simple caricature, no one would be convinced. The problem is summarised by Philip Roth: "Politics is the great generaliser and literature is the great particulariser...and they are in an antagonistic relationship." Now this comment probably applies to the novel rather than drama and poetry, and probably should be restricted still further to the nineteenth and twentieth century English-language novel with its focus on the domestic and on the psychology of individuals and their relationships, but it still has force for any writer of political fiction.

Hence in *Victory Street* there is a spread of fascists, from the slightly old-fashioned leader with a distaste for his more aggressive lieutenant, through to Ellie's brother who by the end of the novel has left the group. And in as much as fascism arises from an understandable frustration, I tried to articulate this too. Similarly with the Asian characters: I couldn't go along with the tradition in some anti-racist fiction of black characters who are decent to the point of invisibility - you sometimes wish Jim would punch Huck Finn on the nose, and I defy anyone to come up with the name of the black man on trial in *To Kill A Mockingbird* before they've finished reading to the end of this sentence. So Muzz is a rather troubled, slightly bitter, character and has a friend who Ellie describes as "a complete prat. He acts like he's got the contract for the whole area and it's not [Boltby] but the Bronx."

The idea that politics and literature are antagonistic might be true for some writers - Ian McEwan's *Saturday*, for instance, uses one of the great political issues of the early 2000s, the Iraq war, as background scenery, but has as a main character a liberal who vacillates between opposing and supporting the war, and the novel in the end collapses into the domestic and the private - but this isn't always the case. An early novel like *Robinson Crusoe* is both 'particular' and 'general', individual and political, and indeed Roth's own *The Plot Against America* creates individual characters who, while being products of larger circumstances, contend for what they believe.

Victory Street is a first-person, present-tense narrative (perhaps for capricious reasons - my first book had been third-person, past-tense) but that created the potential problem of a restricted viewpoint - not so much a problem if that viewpoint is Ellie's, a rather retiring narrator, but a huge problem if the viewpoint is mine, with designs on the reader! Breaking up the narrative with Ellie's 'stories' about Mrs Pearl and the Irish twins (in the third-person) provides narrative variety, and Ellie imaginatively extends the scope of the description of the riot by 'getting into other people's heads as best [she] can'. She includes, among others, sections told from the point of view of a riot policeman, a bus driver, and the Kapoors, an Indian family whose shop is burnt out. Whether the novel becomes 'heteroglossic' or 'many-voiced' in the Bakhtinian sense, others will have to decide.

At several points Ellie is revealed to be not a completely reliable narrator. Mrs Pearl reprimands her for inaccuracy in re-telling her story; we cannot resolve the truth of a rumour at school (rumour has a vital role in propagating racism); having been given the background to the Irish twins by an unreliable character, she then writes up their story as a kind of fairy story, using elements which have already appeared in the main narrative. For instance, a knife she finds in her writing desk becomes a murder weapon in the story she writes. Fiction figures throughout the book: Matilda, Romeo and Juliet, and Spot are mentioned at various points, and when Ellie gets a chance at school to contest the growing racism by telling Mrs Pearl's story her nerve fails and she concocts something based on Robert Cormier's *The Chocolate War*. My intention in using such metafictional devices was to open up the business of story-telling for the reader, and at a couple of points readers are invited to outsmart the narrator herself. The implicit extension of being critical of the narrator, I hoped, was to invite a critical approach to the whole novel.

The culmination, the riot, is problematic. A race riot in which white and Asian working class people confront one another as enemies is a political and social disaster, but as it happened in reality I could hardly avoid it in the novel. But if white people shouting racist abuse and giving Nazi salutes is deeply dispiriting, the action of Asian people in defending themselves rather than acquiescing, is a hopeful sign. (The courts of course didn't see it that way and handed down heavy sentences, halved on appeal.) And in some ways a riot is a form of celebration, of carnival; the assertion, however temporary, of a new order. Most recently the demonstrations by migrant workers in the US and those in France against new labour laws have been expressions of this spirit, and in my novel Mrs Pearl throwing the diamonds given to her by her father as insurance over sixty years previously into the broken glass of Victory Street is a small gesture from the same wellspring.

Five years after the Burnley riots there is an official desire to move on. Government money has been found for various schemes such as re-organising secondary schools, but this will not change the fact that this is a poor town. Until there is a rebirth of the left, the BNP's vilification of the Asian population will continue to find a ready audience. In this situation, and in the wider context of the vicissitudes of late capitalism, fiction is going to be something of a sideshow. Be that as it may. I decided to end the book with an optimistic section entitled 'A New Story'.

REFERENCES

Lord Clarke, *Burnley Speaks, Who Listens...?* ('The Clarke Report'), December 2001.

Richard MacSween, *Victory Street.* Andersen Press, 2004.

Mark Twain, *The Adventures of Huckleberry Finn.* New York: Exeter Books 1885.

Colin MacInnes, *Absolute Beginners.* London: Macgibbon and Kee,1959.

Harper Lee, *To Kill A Mockingbird.* Pennsylvania: Lippincott,, 1960.

Nick Lowles, *White Riot.* Milo Books, 2001.

Alan Gibbons, *Caught in the Crossfire.* Orion, 2003.

Malorie Blackman, *Noughts And Crosses.* Doubleday, 2001.

Mikhail Bakhtin, *Problems of Dostoevsky's Poetics.* 1963, edited and trans. by C. Emerson. Manchester: Manchester University Press, 1984.

Mikhail Bakhtin, *Rabelais and His World.* 1965, trans. Hélène Iswolsky. Bloomington: Indiana University Press, 1993.

Michael Collins, *The Likes Of Us: A biography of the White Working Class.* London: Granta Books, 2004.

Philip Roth, quoted by Richard Eyre, Guardian, 26.03.2005.

Ian McEwan, *Saturday.* London: Jonathan Cape, 2005.

Philip Roth, *The Plot Against America.* London: Jonathan Cape, 2004.

Robert Cormier, *The Chocolate War.* New York: Pantheon, 1974.

Spit Nolan

Spit Nolan was a pal of mine. He was a thin lad with a bony face that was always pale, except for two rosy spots on his cheekbones. He had quick brown eyes, short, wiry hair, rather stooped shoulders, and we all knew that he had only one lung. He had had a disease which in those

David Rudd

On Your Marks with Spit Nolan:
Childhood, Ideology and Taking Fantasy Seriously

MARX, IN SEEKING to explain why we are still moved by literary works from another historical epoch, such as those of ancient Greece, came up with the rather touching notion that they appealed to our sense of nostalgia, that they took us back to our collective childhood. Of course, this is remarkably similar to the reason that adults are said to like children's books in the first place - that is, literally in the 'first place' - in that they re-invoke what L.P. Hartley calls the 'foreign country' of childhood. In this conference we've given this an extra twist, seeing the study of children's books as - possibly - taking us back, not only to our childhoods, but to our Marx as well, in order that we may rethink our way forward.

But the two areas - Marxism and childhood - are more closely connected even than this, in that childhood is often figured as an Edenic time. As Mary Winn writes, "our myths of Paradise teach us the truth about childhood. There must be an Eden at the beginning, just as there is in every creation myth" (1983). It is seen as a utopian space preceding the fall - a time when Wordsworthian and Rousseauian children trail their clouds of glory. A number of children's literature critics have sought to make this link even more explicit, arguing that the key appeal of children's literature lies in its utopian leanings, its attempt to show us the good society. Indeed Fred Inglis (1981) uses Stendhal's statement that 'all great art holds out "the promise of happiness"' for the title of his study of children's literature. 'The best writers', Inglis declares, 'seek to create an ideal social order out of the values there are to hand ... the finest life he can imagine'. He even includes otherwise denigrated popular writers such as Enid Blyton and

Malcolm Saville within his compass (see also Inglis, 1997). Similarly utopian notions are central to Michael and Margaret Rustin's study, *Narratives of Love and Loss* (1987), and to much of Jack Zipes' work.

The point is that the child is a *figurative* being in all this: a given, a constant, a symbol of the good, of that to which society as a whole should aspire (even when figured by such unpalatable regimes as Nazi Germany, with the Hitler Youth - cf. Kamenetsky, 1984). A particular sort of child is thus constructed in much children's literature: one that is indeed special, that can redeem society. Ironically, although the child-within-the-text is seen to be relatively untouched by the socially degenerate adult world (e.g. Emil, Pippi Longstocking, the Famous Five, Peter Pan), child-readers-of-the-text are regarded in the opposite manner: as highly impressionable beings who must, therefore, be kept apart from the adult world and its literature, and for whom reading the wrong texts can be a serious matter:

> Fairy tales ...reinforce unhealthy and destructive images for the reader.
> .... Concerned parents and educators should work to liberate homes and schools from such potentially destructive materials and to provide children with more progressive and equally enjoyable fare.
> (Robert Moore, 1978)

Because children are symbols of the good, promising happiness, actual child readers are potentially a threat to this vision, and must therefore not be allowed to contaminate the utopian realm. In other words, the dialectic is not something that includes children: they stand outside the historical process.

In making this move, though, many social critics seem to forget their own history, what they themselves read as children; particularly as, given the generational slippage, one would expect it to have been far more explicitly racist, sexist, class-ridden, and so on. Not only have these critics survived such material but, more than this, see themselves as especially qualified to testify as to how harmful it will be for others. One could, of course, argue that many readers did not survive; that, for instance, the imperialist literature of G.A. Henty and others was responsible for readers 'playing up and playing the game' of the First World War. However, one might then want to point to all the other elements that led to that historical conjuncture, rather than scapegoat books; one would also want to know why and how conscientious objectors - A.A. Milne, amongst others - managed to read such material differently; and to know about those that read and enjoyed this material *after* the Great War. As I shall suggest later, there might be a need to consider literature in other than social realist terms; to take fantasy more seriously.

Jack Zipes is an interesting figure in this regard, trying to hold on to 'real' children while simultaneously mythologizing them within a Marxist framework. Thus adult children's literature critics are invited to see themselves as akin to Lenin's vanguard party, 'proletarians of the university' who 'working from marginalized positions ... take the side of the powerless, the children, to speak for them, to include them, and to fight for their rights ...to improve the manner in which we acculturate children' (2001). It is hard to see in what manner, apart from rhetorically, we, or indeed this collective, 'the children', might be 'proletarians'. Children, of course, are as cut across by divisions of class, gender, ethnicity, abled-ness (and so on) as adults. They are no more proletarians than they are the Golden Innocents that Mary Winn, from a very different perspective, champions when she argues for a return to that 'Golden Age of Innocence' when 'children read books about fairies and animals, or about other children engaged in the carefree pleasures of childhood' (1983).

This problem, of what children really want (whether it be fairies, animals, Barbie dolls, Harry Potter or Lemony Snicket) has proved problematic for many researchers. Karín Lesnik-Oberstein (1994) argues that finding 'the good book for the child' is the holy grail that children's literature critics are always in search of. Although Zipes does not specify exactly *what* children's needs are, he does believe that they are there and, through a dialectical process, tries to indicate what is working against the realisation of these needs. For him, such negative exemplars are works like the Disney versions of fairy tales, or Rowling's 'Harry Potter' series (2001). However, as we saw above, Zipes can only do this by making children into proxy agents of history - a pseudo-proletariat. And, as he also seems to suggest, this powerless group can only succeed in coming into their own with the help of some vanguard of adult intellectuals. The strains that this places on Marxism are considerable, as is apparent in the following passage:

> ...it was not possible for a broad range of books to be approved and to reach children in specific ways until the system of production, distribution and reception was instituted and became focused on how to socialize children through reading. Children's needs were not necessarily taken into consideration. It was and still is the need of the economic order that dictates how children will be formed and what forms are or are not acceptable.

Here Zipes attempts to historicise the construction of children ('how children will be formed') and their literature while simultaneously arguing that children exist independently, as a group with their own needs. Once again, the parallel with the proletariat is clear, with children's needs being supposedly obscured by the prevailing economic conditions, such that they are alienated from their species being (although given that many western children do not sell their labour in this manner, the parallel is rather difficult to sustain). Effectively, Zipes' move once again creates a loophole in the unfolding of the dialectic, in that children seem to be left relatively untouched. In short, we seem to be back with the powerful figure of the Romantic child, who somehow stands outside ideology, or could do so, with a little help from the community of adult children's literature critics.

Zipes is by no means alone in the way he figures children, of course. He just happens to be one of the best known and most eloquent critics in this area. Likewise, his treatment of fantasy is by no means exceptional. But just as children are figured as ciphers of some future utopia, so too is fantasy frequently read in terms of social critique, as offering alternative forms of sociality. Thus, for example, Zipes informs us that the fairy tale:

> opened up possibilities for children and adults to formulate innovative views about socialization, religious training, authority, sex roles, and art. For many late-Victorian authors, the writing of a fairy tale meant a process of creating an other

world, from which vantage point they could survey conditions in the real world and compare them to their ideal projections. (1999)

This tendency to see fantasy as, at worst, escapist and epiphenomenal or, at best, a blueprint for a more equable society, is fairly standard in Marxism. So too is a belief in some unproblematic 'real world' discernible outside ideology. Clearly, the main difference with writers more influenced by postmodernism is that the latter query our access to this bedrock of the real, which is - of course - to query Marxism's hold on the historical pulse, its millenarian trajectory.

Instead of the traditional 'grand narrative' of Marxism, Jean-François Lyotard and others prefer to talk less grandiosely of the 'little narrative' (Lyotard, 1984; 'little narratives for little hands', one is tempted to say, to adapt Beatrix Potter's aphorism). For these latter writers, the real world is not something that can so easily be detached from ideology. Instead, in the light of the 'linguistic turn' in theorising, we are all seen to be ideologically situated (or 'interpellated', as Althusser would put it), as – through language – it is ideology that structures our social world. There are a number of Marxist and post-Marxist thinkers who have tried to think this through while holding on to the basic framework of Marxism (e.g. Ernesto Laclau and Chantal Mouffe, 1985, and Fredric Jameson, 1991), but here I want to concentrate on the work of the Slovenian Marxist/ Lacanian, Slavoj Žižek.

Briefly Žižek argues for the centrality of fantasy, seeing it as far more embedded in our everyday lives. Indeed, we could not exist without it as, for Žižek, fantasy does not give us a *false* notion of reality, but is what structures reality in the first place, warding off that which lies outside. In other words, fantasy is synonymous with ideology. As Žižek phrases it, in slightly more powerful terms, 'The function of ideology is not to offer us a point of escape from our reality but to offer us the social reality itself as an escape from some traumatic, real kernel' (2004). Fantasy thus gives shape to our desires, providing us with a sense of coherence as a subject. So it is no good for some group of secure, white, middle-class, male intellectuals to proclaim, to more marginal groups, that they see through their fantasies, when the fantasies are the very thing that structure, or give meaning to their existence. For another example, consider the feminist who is highly critical of women wearing high-heels and make-up, accusing them of being mere pawns of patriarchy; rather than recognising that the pleasures these items deliver are more intrinsic to a person's identity, often giving the wearer a sense of power. (See, for example, John Fiske, 1989, on Madonna; or Kate Soper, 1990). In terms of literature, then, we should try to recognise more openly the multiple pleasures that texts and their writers offer us, without necessarily decrying them for being simplistically reactionary or progressive. As Jean-Paul Sartre (1963) sums it up, writing of the work of the French poet, Paul Valéry, he 'is a petit bourgeois intellectual, no doubt about it. But not every petit bourgeois intellectual is Valéry'.

In order to take this further in a more concrete way, let me now turn to Bill Naughton's famous and much anthologised story, 'Spit Nolan'.

Re-reading Spit Nolan

I have examined this text by Naughton (1968) elsewhere, and would like, quickly, to revisit that reading before taking it further (Rudd, 2000). Briefly, it's the tale of a one-lunged waif, Spit Nolan, who is a champion trolley, or soapbox rider. He rises to a challenge from Leslie Duckett, who has been given his own custom-built trolley. A friend sets them off and they race down one of the few tarmac roads in Bolton (it seems to be set some time after the Great War). Leslie just beats Spit but, in the process, sends him careering into an oncoming charabanc, causing Spit's death.

A Marxist reading would no doubt pick up on the class differences: Spit - thin and undernourished in his holey jersey, only able to be cured if he 'went away to Switzerland, which Spit certainly couldn't afford' - against Leslie, 'the plump son of the local publican' in his 'serge Sunday suit'. And not only class differences, for this thread is connected to one of nationality and colonisation: Spit Nolan is clearly Irish, up against the might of the plump English Duckett, whose father owns the pub, *The British Queen*, which gives Duckett's trolley its name (Spit's is named *Egdam* 'in memory of a girl called Madge, whom he had once met at Southport Sanatorium, where he had spent three happy weeks ...he had reversed the letters of her name to keep his love a secret'. One can detect a Marxist sense of owning one's labour here, or else of experiencing alienation. Thus Leslie's trolley, we are told, is 'specially made to measure ... by the gaffer of the Holt Engineering Works' - not even, note, by one of the regular workers. The narrator comments that 'nobody had ever had a trolley made by somebody else'; and Spit tells Leslie, 'it's got none of *you* in it ... you haven't so much as given it a single tap with a hammer'. He goes on, 'That trolley will be a stranger to you to your dying day.' - a statement heavy with irony, as it turns out.

In historical terms, then, Ireland can only lose, replaying contests that have run for centuries, with the victors holding most of the cards. Thus Spit, a craft-worker with his trolley, a *bricolage* construction, is set against Leslie's factory-made, precision *British Queen*, with its 'beautiful ball-bearing wheels, engineering made, encased in oil.' The wheels of British Empire are metaphorically turned on Spit, reinforced literally in the way that *The British Queen*'s 'heavy rear wheel' tips Spit's makeshift trolley into the equally 'heavy solid …wheel' of the charabanc. Spit's trolley thus ends 'smashed-up', transported away on the back of the victorious *British Queen*'

The story's ending is particularly interesting. It might be seen to reflect the historical situation of the Irish working-class in England (especially at this time) in the way that it re-inscribes the hegemonic power of the British. The opulent Leslie Duckett and his *British Queen* will therefore always win, albeit being saddled with the guilt over what they have done to the Irish. The final words of the story seem to endorse this:

> Then [the ambulance man] touched me on the elbow with his pencil and said: 'Where *did* he live?'
> I knew then. That word 'did' struck right into me. But for a minute I couldn't answer. I had to think hard, for the way he said it made it suddenly seem as though Spit Nolan had been dead and gone for ages.'

Spit's mythologisation at the end could thus be read as a subterfuge - religion, the opium of the masses, being the sop. Given that the Irish were also seen as more demonstrably (and Popishly) religious, this might give the story added poignancy for an English Protestant audience. The ambulance man's unanswered question, 'Where …?', perhaps endorses this sense of Nolan's displacement; what we might today discuss in terms of 'diasporic identities'. Spit's very surname, in fact, hints at this: 'No land'.

However, many will also be disappointed with this ending, wanting, against the odds, for Spit to win. Spit could then be seen to function more like a Brer Rabbit figure, a trickster underdog overcoming more mighty opposition thanks to his guile and skill, emphasising the importance of recognising and owning one's labour. In other words, readers could be presented with a working-class hero who might inspire others to fight against the system. Naughton's story would then fit Ernst Bloch's notion of a liberatory, utopian text. Naughton, however, himself an expatriate, working-class, Irish Catholic, chose not to have Spit triumph - which must make us cautious, especially as Naughton always declared a dislike for hack writing 'as a sin against the Holy Spirit - from which source all literature springs.' He continues: 'what a writer needed most was the impulse to tell the story or incident he had in his heart to tell' (1987) - a stance that has parallels with what Zipes terms 'genuine storytelling', that which sets out to expose 'sham and hypocrisy' (2001).

However, the dilemma over the ending arises only if we insist on making the socio-political context the *ground* from which the story has to make sense. Moreover, if we are to explain it in class terms, we have the added problem of dealing with the story's wider appeal - without, that is, resorting to notions about it invoking a nostalgia for some golden age of innocence, for lost childhoods, solid values, or whatever. Following Žižek's lead, we can perhaps see the story as fashioned out of a number of threads, which themselves circle around the staging of more basic issues of identity or - indeed, its lack - in death. Seen in such terms, we can take more seriously (rather than ideologically, epiphenomenally) issues of religion and, indeed, pleasure in general.

It seems to me that there are two other key discourses that frame this tale, which are themselves interwoven: love and religion. In order to make most sense of them some biographical information is also pertinent - not simply in the fact that Naughton grew up at the time and place of the story's events, but that, just as 'Egdam' encodes Madge, so 'Spit Nolan' encodes Bill Naughton (if we reverse the /t/ and /l/ letters, phonetically he becomes 'Spill Norton'). Naughton also called one of his volumes of memoirs *Saintly Billy*, in which he reveals (with some satisfaction) that he himself was often seen in this ascetic light. However, in this volume of memoirs we are presented with another Saintly Billy: Naughton's Uncle William, a soft, gentle Irishman, who committed suicide by slashing his throat, depressed as a result of the 1921 miners' strike. 'Uncle William, God rest his soul, ... was to die in the ambulance as it drove through the streets of Bolton on that sunny June morning' (1988).

In Spit's story, religious imagery is rife, with the hero sounding very much a Christ figure: he is described as 'almost godlike' on the Sunday when the race is to be held; his disciples round him, pulling his trolley up the hill (as Simon of Cyrene carried Jesus's cross), and the hill reminds one of Calvary, accentuated by the 'faint sweated glow ...over Spit's face', like a halo. He even rides 'belly-down ... lying flat on his trolley'; that is, on a 'piece of wood about five feet in length' with a cross piece of wood (for steering the front wheels) attached to it - a regular crucifix. His death is also foreshadowed, with the race being held ominously on 'Cemetery Brew', and with Spit being presented with a flower from the cemetery, described by Spit as having 'a 'eavenly smell!'. Even as he rides, 'gliding, as it were, over the rough patches', he is thought to be 'a bird that might suddenly open out its wings and fly clean into the air' - a veritable soul in ascension.

Yet there seems to be even more to it than this. The name 'Madge' signifies both Spit's lost love and his trolley (there are parallels with Citizen Kane's sledge, 'Rosebud'). But beyond this, the name 'Madge' literally means 'pearl', and there would seem to be parallels with the medieval religious poem of that name. In 'The Pearl', the main character bemoans the loss of his love: his precious daughter, Pearl. Lying on a 'flowery mead' (Spit, of course, ends up lying amongst 'yellow rose p etals'), we are told of how his 'spirit sprang forth in space' as he envisions her. She is described as a 'little queen' of heaven, not lost, but there awaiting him, in the manner of the 'Mother of Jesus, our Lady sweet' – just as Madge, Spit's Pearl, is presumably waiting for him. In these terms Spit can be seen to have won the bigger prize – a place in heaven alongside his 'little queen', leaving Duckett (whose name also suggests 'ducats', money – that which should be rendered unto Caesar) with his *British Queen* very much in second place (at the end Duckett actually defers to Spit, using, for the first and only time, a lower-class, Lancashire dialect: 'Thee! ...Tha just licked me.').

Of course, aside from the religious discourse there is the more amatory one of Spit riding 'belly-down' on Madge, giving the tale a certain sexual *frisson*; also her reversed name, 'Egdam', besides foreshadowing the doom of a chess 'endgame', more positively carries connotations of rebirth – of eggs, dams, damsels - or, of resurrection.

In this revised reading a number of discursive elements have been identified – intermixing class, nationality and colonialism with autobiographical, religious, sexual and amatory threads. It is suggested that, by taking note of all of these we are some way nearer to capturing the complex pleasures of the text, its sources of *jouissance* (by which is meant both its bitter-sweetness, its pleasure and pain); and, as I have suggested, at the centre of these lurks an omnipresent fear of death, of non-existence. This is an area where we all rely on ideological support, where we continually need to tell ourselves stories in order to ward off what Žižek earlier termed 'some traumatic, real kernel'. In more Lacanian terms, this kernel represents an intrusion of the Real; that is, a disruption of the order of the Symbolic, where signs give us a place and a name – where, in short, we keep ourselves pacified with stories.

For Lacan the Symbolic, despite the best attempts of any ideology, is always ultimately flawed; it is porous, and therefore the very place where the surplus of the Real will encroach. In Naughton's story, Spit has been shown in this tenuous light from the outset: marginal and one-lunged, he exists at the interstices of society's main discourses – a *bricoleur*, as I've described him – not even possessing a proper name ('Spit' itself suggests abjection, gesturing towards that most abject of all things: death). When, therefore, Leslie's wheel strikes Spit's and the charabanc appears, the Symbolic order is disrupted. But though Spit is seen to die in the Real, he is narrated, mythically, as living on in the Symbolic. He is what Žižek (1999) describes as being 'between two deaths'. For Žižek, such figures are seen to possess a 'sublime beauty'. They are paradoxical, representing that which is not normally representable: hovering, in this case, between the Symbolic and that which lies beyond it; the Real.

It should also be noted that this story is the *narrator's* fantasy (i.e. it is the story told by a homodiegetic character called 'Bill') – not Spit's. It is Bill who gives this tale its Imaginary glow; that is, who reads Spit's life and death in terms of a spiritual ascension, rising like Elijah in his chariot, the

'Imaginary' being that realm of wholeness, of plenitude, which we think we once enjoyed with the mother. Thus the relation of Spit to his Egdam, and to his little heavenly mother, helps suture this story into grander and more comforting cultural narratives. In Lacanian terms, this is the narrator's 'quilting-point', the point from which he stitches together the elements of a story in a particular way.

Fantasy, then, is essential to our being, helping us to live, to make sense of (or to quilt) a reality that is always flawed; in other words, that has parts which cannot be narrated without rupture because of historical circumstances; struggles of class, colonialism and nationalism, in this instance. Fantasies both show us the coordinates of our desire and also hint at the way our desires are fabricated, at how they might be otherwise. Spit Nolan is, thus, actually 'split' Nolan. The way he has been narrated might patch over some divisions while simultaneously revealing others - and ones to which we will continually return (they are the faultlines in our society, representing a return of the Real, as Fredric Jameson (1991) would say) and will continue to be worried over. However, this does not necessarily mean that we, participating in such pleasures, are ourselves seduced by these so-called opiates of the masses. Rather than reflect ideology, then, Naughton's story *reworks* it (Pierre Macherey's insight). Ideology is both restored and 're-storied' in the process, delivering a sense of existential pleasure (perhaps), while recognising the local, cultural coordinates of its satisfactions.

So, to return to matters raised at the beginning of this paper, I am suggesting that the tendency of Marxist writers to use the child as a symbol of the good society to come, or as a symbolic victim of a currently divisive and inequitable society (as is more the case with 'Spit') often loses sight of the more complex pleasures offered by texts - even if these pleasures sometimes seem worthless, crude and cheap; or, in more Marxist terms, expressing false-consciousness. This is especially a tendency amongst traditional Marxists, who feel that they hold the reins of history and, somehow, themselves stand outside the historical process; in never having had childhoods, for instance. The commonly used imagery of the midwife, giving birth to a new child /

society, is revealing here, in the way that it turns the child into a symbol once again. Some, more recent Marxist thinkers have relinquished this grand narrative, though, recognising the way that they, too, are subject to multifarious narrative threads, which should not be so readily dismissed by fiat. Equally so, the tendency to use children merely as convenient symbols of a former, or future, paradisaical state is slowly being challenged and unpacked.

REFERENCES

John Fiske, *Reading the Popular*. London: Unwin Hyman, 1989.

Fred Inglis, *The Promise of Happiness: Value and Meaning in Children's Fiction*. Cambridge: Cambridge University Press, 1981.

Fred Inglis, 'Enid Blyton, Malcolm Saville and the good society' in Nicholas Tucker and Kimberley Reynolds (eds), *Enid Blyton: A Celebration and Reappraisal*. London: NCRCL, pp. 127-33, 1997.

Fredric Jameson, *Postmodernism, or The Cultural Logic of Late Capitalism*. London: Verso, 1991.

Christa Kamenetsky, *Children's Literature in Hitler's Germany: The Cultural Policy of National Socialism*. Athens, Ohio: Ohio University Press, 1984.

Ernesto Laclau and Chantal Mouffe, *Hegemony and Socialist Strategy: Towards a Radical Democratic Politics*. London: Verso, 1985.

Karin Lesnik-Oberstein, *Children's Literature: Criticism and the Fictional Child*. Oxford: Clarendon Press, 1994.

Jean-Francois Lyotard, *The Postmodern Condition: A Report on Knowledge*, trans. by Geoff Ennington and Brian Massumi. Manchester: Manchester University Press, 1984.

Robert Moore, 'From rags to witches: stereotypes, distortions and anti-humanism in fairy tales'. Interracial Digest No. 2, pp. 27-34, 1978.

Bill Naughton, 'Spit Nolan' in *The Goalkeeper's Revenge and Other Stories*. Harmondsworth: Penguin, 1968.

Bill Naughton, *On the Pig's Back: An Autobiographical Excursion*. Oxford: Oxford University Press, 1987.

Bill Naughton, *Saintly Billy: a Catholic Boyhood*. Oxford: Oxford University Press, 1988.

David Rudd, 'Betwixt and between: the canonization of Naughton and Nolan', Signal 91, pp. 41-50, 2000.

Michael Rustin and Margaret Rustin, *Narratives of Love and Loss: Studies in Modern Children's Fiction*. London: Verso, 1987.

Jean-Paul Sartre, *Search for a Method*. New York: Vintage, 1963.

Kate Soper, *Troubled Pleasures: Writings on Politics, Gender and Hedonism*. London: Verso, 1990.

Mary Winn, *Children without Childhood*. Harmondsworth Penguin, 1983.

Jack Zipes, *When Dreams Came True: Classical Fairy Tales and their Tradition*. London: Routledge, 1999.

Jack Zipes, *Sticks and Stones: The Troublesome Success of Children's Literature from Slovenly Peter to Harry Potter.* London: Routledge, 2001.

Slavoj Žižek, *The Ticklish Subject: The Absent Centre of Political Ontology.* London: Verso, 1999.

Slavoj Žižek, 'The Sublime object of ideology' in *Literary Theory: An Anthology 2nd.* edited by Julie Rivkin and Michael Ryan. Oxford: Blackwell, pp. 712-24, 2004.

Anne-Marie Bird

A Journey to Utopia: A Marxist Reading of Russell Hoban's
The Mouse and his Child

IN AN INTRODUCTION to a collection of essays on Russell Hoban's work, Alida Allison claims that although Hoban is 'of the generation and general background... of writers such as Norman Mailer, Joseph Heller and Saul Bellow, unlike them, except for essays, he does not write about... politics and the big outside world in general' (2000). However, while it may be true that 'politics and the big outside world in general' are not overtly present in much of his work, I would add that there is the exception of his 1967 novel, *The Mouse and his Child*.

Hoban's text was published during a decade in which America had attained unprecedented levels of political, economic and military power on a global scale, yet the triumph of a capitalist world remained open to serious questioning and alternatives. In fact, the 1960s can be characterised as an era of social conflict - conflict between conformity and individuality, between tradition and innovation and between stability and disruption. This collapse of consensus in American politics saw a revival in utopian writing.

All these issues, most notably the conflict between the individualistic, capitalist ethos (the dominant American ideology that became progressively more prevalent during the Cold War years) and the other major twentieth century ideology - that of collectivist communism - are explored in Hoban's *The Mouse and his Child* as the clockwork protagonists journey through the landscape of consumerist America towards a communal utopian vision. Hoban's text takes the reader on a journey through the waste and rubbish of an affluent, technological, 'throw away' society, offering a larger vision of

America; illustrating how far it has journeyed from its Edenic origins and utopian dreams to its present materialistic values.

In addition to the physical and psychological journey through contemporary America, the journey the mouse and his child embark upon could be considered on other levels. In one sense it is the conscious search for a dream; a journey that parallels that of the original settlers who came to America - a vast unspoilt land of limitless opportunities - full of ideals, faith and optimism that they could begin again in America and create a nation built on the utopian concept of a radically different society. In another sense, the journey works on a more unconscious level, the nature of which they gradually realise as they travel, through war, art, and philosophy. It is a journey of psychological progress and development as the mouse and his child, through personal experience, grow in knowledge of the self and the world, and the relation of self to community or society.

It is important to consider, when discussing this journey and its significance, that the protagonists are clockwork. This attribute makes them extremely potent symbols of the human condition in contemporary society, entrapped as they are in a cyclical mechanical movement that propels them along; they are not in control of their own destiny, but are automatons controlled by others. This consideration raises the issues of individual subjectivity and freedom, and of course, the relation of these issues to a society that exerts such a tremendous influence over the individual as to produce serialisation or the loss of self. This is summed up in the text with the statement: 'all them windups look alike'. Their journey, therefore, naturally extends to and embraces an exploration of human possibilities and potential; also, inevitably, limitations.

The psychological journey of the mouse and his child begins in the toy shop. They awaken to consciousness and articulate the essential and eternal philosophical question: what is it, to be? or, in the words of the mouse child: 'Where are we?' immediately followed by 'What are we?' These questions, once expressed, effectively close down any route back to an unquestioning, unconscious existence. The answer is provided in harsh, realistic terms by the clockwork elephant:

> '...you are toy mice. People are going to buy you for children, because it's almost a time called Christmas.'

The clockwork elephant goes on to say:

> '...one simply goes out into the world and does whatever one does...One does what one is wound to do. ...And it is expected of this young mouse that he go out into the world with his father and dance in a circle.'

The answer emphasises that they are all trapped within a cyclical existence, not only in the literal sense, in that they are clockwork, but in the sense that someone else is doing the winding; secure in the knowledge that 'one' will do 'what one is wound to do', that 'one' will conform to expectations and keep the rules, such as, 'No talking before midnight and after dawn, and no crying on the job.'

The next step that must be taken is to violate the rules of an oppressive system. 'The mouse child was on the job and he knew it, but he began to cry'. This act breaks the limitations of rationality, resulting in their being smashed and cast out, thereby creating the possibility of a way forward. The notion of a 'fortunate fall' is a prevalent one that underpins much of American fiction. Hoban's text employs the parable of the fall in much the same way, suggesting that it is necessary to 'fall' - to overthrow 'the system' - however frightening the risks, in order to move beyond a state of debilitating innocence. This is evident in that the mouse and his child are reassembled by the tramp (who is also, in his refusal to conform, an outcast from society). They are reassembled in such a way that the father 'lurched straight ahead with a rolling stride, pushing the child backwards before him.' This constitutes significant progress as they no longer move in a cyclical fashion, but now move in a linear one.

However, although progress in the text is linear, it is also, paradoxically, cyclical; explicitly marked out by the changing seasons, and also in the framing of the narrative. The appearance of the tramp as the text opens and his return at its closure serves to emphasise the cyclical or 'clockwork' nature of the universe, and of an existence from which humanity is unable to escape. The physical journey that the mouse and his child embark upon is also circular, beginning and ending at the dump. The dump is a significant starting point for the journey. It is here that they first encounter the BONZO Dog Food can, whose label, depicting the apparently infinite regression of a 'little black-and-white spotted dog', is one of several motifs in the text. Indeed, the tin can, and the manner in which it is appropriated by various characters, is perhaps the most important motif throughout the journey of the mouse and his child. In some instances, the can itself is given practical application, being used during its first appearance at the dump by Manny Rat, as a container in which to store the mechanical parts extracted from broken clockwork toys. At other times, the label on the can is the source of philosophical speculation, its image of infinity growing in significance to the mouse and his child as their journey progresses.

More importantly, the dump is an appropriate place to begin their journey as they are forcibly thrust into reality in its most frightening form. Juxtaposed with the glittery consumer world - the toy shop in chapter 1 - and the description of the opulent dolls' house (representative of a bygone age of wealth and social hierarchy), the dump is a microcosm of contemporary American values: 'an evil-smelling huddle of gambling dens, gaming booths, dancehalls and taverns' presided over by Manny Rat, who significantly, has made his home in a 'gutted and screenless cabinet of a long-dead television set'. Manny Rat is the embodiment of the all-pervasive, ruthless face of capitalism, that 'once let in would never go away', but would continue to corrupt the landscape, turning it into a 'dumping ground'. This bears a striking resemblance to F. Scott Fitzgerald's 'valley of ashes' in his 1925 novel, *The Great Gatsby*; the valley of ashes being a spiritually desolate, grotesque hell created by modern industry and its values. This is itself evocative of T. S. Eliot's *The Waste Land*, published in 1922. The dump does not represent a significant point in their journey only because they encounter the physical results of a highly dubious form of 'progress' - the darker side of American affluence, as it were - but also because it serves to confront them with a far more frightening result; specifically, the distortion that resides within the psychology of its citizens. This distortion is conveyed by the vocabulary of the dangerously powerful advertising industry, prevalent in 1950s American culture, that resounds throughout the text, touting everything from food and household goods - 'Orange peels! Bacon grease! Scented soaps!' - to a way of life: 'WHAT FORTUNE AWAITS YOU? FROG LIFTS THE VEIL THAT HIDES THE FUTURE. CREDIT GIVEN'. The consumer attitude towards all facets of life is satirised at every opportunity in the headline style resumés of the news provided by the bluejay - 'RAT SLAIN IN BANK HOLDUP ATTEMPT' - and in the telegraphic headline-style warnings of the fortune-telling frog: 'DO NOT COMMIT THE TRAGIC ERROR OF SATISFYING PRESENT APPETITE AT THE COST OF FUTURE FULFILMENT'. This newsreel collage of data, headlines, reports and advertisements, captures and embodies the rhythmic mechanisation of life and the reduction of American citizens into mere functionaries in an ant-like collectivity.

The distorted psychology of the inhabitants of the dump is even more forcefully conveyed by their treatment of others. Here the mouse and his child are exposed to the fact that freedom is an extremely ambiguous and precarious concept; they witness other clockwork toys that have also been cast out, only to be 'salvaged from the dump' and subsequently recycled and adapted by the ever-practical Manny Rat - for movement that suits his purposes. These broken toys, described as 'the battered windups of the forage squad...[the] silent slaves', are exploited, and finally 'rested' when they are no longer productive:

[Manny Rat] picked up a heavy rock, lifted it high and brought it down on the donkey's back, splitting him open like a walnut. 'Put his works in the spare-parts can'.

According to Engels:

> [the] ravages of capitalism seemed to produce their own brutality, their own particular kind of savagery: the 'unfeeling' selfishness of the individual, a 'brutal indifference' to his or her fellow human being. It was the fragmenting culture of capitalism that destroyed the values of community, which divided labour on every front.... Individualism, the ideology of the liberal bourgeoisie which promoted the virtues of private enterprise, hard work and non-state interventionism, concealed beneath the trappings of civilisation, a crude barbarism (quoted in Wolfreys and Baker, 1996).

Margaret and Michael Rustin refer to the dump as 'a fascist world of tyranny and sadism'; as 'a parody of industrial organisation' (1987). At the dump, then, the truth concerning the huge gulf between the rhetoric and the reality of the American Dream, between the left-wing and Marxist attitudes of the 1930s and the capitalist ideology of post war America, is revealed as the mouse and his child begin to learn, through personal experience (having to take part in the bank robbery, for example), that they too lack any form of agency. All the windups are figures of alienation; like the Marxist conception of the proletariat, they are victimised, dislocated, and ultimately dehumanised, their individual identities being dissolved into 'the system'.

John Stephens, in an essay addressing the contexts of meaning and identity in *The Mouse and His Child*, refers to a formulation by Levi- Strauss: 'Being human signifies, for each of us, belonging to a class, a society, a country, a continent and a civilisation' (in Allison, 2000). The desire to belong (the mouse child's impulse for community) and to possess a degree of self-agency (the mouse father's opposing impulse for individual autonomy) is evoked during the territorial war of the shrews. Again, this stage of the journey proves to be an essential consciousness-raising episode for the mouse and his child. The mouse father is told about, and thus is made aware of, the idea of territory:

'A territory is your place... . It's where everything smells right. It's where you know the runways and the hideouts, night or day. It's what you fought for, or what your father fought for, and you feel all safe and strong there. It's the place where, when you fight, you win'.

This in turn provides him with knowledge of what he later refers to as 'our placelessness'. Later in the text, the notion of a territorial war takes on a personal significance when the mouse and his child 'must fight for [their] territory'. The realisation of the importance of territory is significant in that it leads to the mouse father's growing awareness of the extent to which he lacks any kind of personal freedom:

He saw now that for him and his son the whole wide world was someone else's territory, on which he could not even walk without someone to wind him up.

His actual physical involvement in freeing the captive wood mice or 'rations' (reminiscent of Manny Rat's captive foragers in chapter 2) becomes emblematic of his growing disillusionment with 'the system' and, 'for the first time in his life [he] knew what it was to strike a blow for freedom'.

The journey proceeds from the theatre of war - which, although it has created the desire for, and an understanding of, the concept of territory, of belonging somewhere, has not ultimately provided a solution for the protagonists - to a parody of the theatre of existential art. This stage of the journey sees the BONZO Dog Food can being appropriated in a very different manner. The label provides the inspiration for the Beckett-like play, The Last Visible Dog, to be performed by the 'Caws of Art Experimental Theatre Group'. The play consists essentially of a contemplation of infinity. It is 'a play with a message', and, even if the actual message evades all understanding, it is suggested that meaning or truth is entirely related to an individual's confrontation with either limitless possibilities, or, as in a nihilistic perspective of infinity, the limitations of nothingness. 'It just goes on and on until it means anything and everything, depending on who you are and what your last visible dog is'. The former perspective of infinity is immediately appropriated by the mouse child as being the correct 'place' in which to seek his utopia, that is, his dream of home and family. Thus, like the exploration of war, an exploration of existential art has merely sustained an impulse: as the mouse father says, 'we're brave and clever - but not clever enough to wind ourselves up'. Therefore, although existential art may lead to some kind of awareness, the suggestion is that it is the perspective and concrete experience of the individual that is of paramount importance, as opposed to the artistic endeavours of the detached, objective observer.

Not only existential art is rejected in the quest for an understanding of their lives. So is the empiricism of the Muskrat. His philosophy veers between logical atomism and logical positivism. Like Manny Rat, Muskrat does not use the BONZO Dog Food can as a source of metaphysical speculation, but uses it as a container in which to store things, specifically, 'all the neglected apparatus of past experiments in applied thought'. Muskrat and his theories, however, are totally myopic. They can provide no insight whatsoever in contrast with the practical skills and application of the beavers who, although lacking 'in intellect', have 'got method'. Moreover, Muskrat does not intend to personally fell the tree; instead he harnesses the labour of the mouse and his child, who once again find themselves in a position of servitude 'going in a circle again', the mouse child 'follow[ing] his own footsteps going nowhere', and 'no closer to self-winding than before!' Like the proletariat, the mouse and his child are exploited and alienated - they are unable enjoy the fruits of their labour.

Juxtaposed with Muskrat is the existentialist turtle, C. Serpentina, whose philosophy echoes the early work of Jean-Paul Sartre (1957, passim). According to C. Serpentina:

> 'Each of us, sunk in the mud however deep, must rise on the propulsion of his own thought. Each of us must journey through the dogs, beyond the dots, and to the truth, alone'.

The 'truth' emerges when the journey is brought to an abrupt halt and the mouse and his child find themselves stuck in the mud at the bottom of the pond with Serpentina. The turtle's predominant occupation consists of a contemplation of infinity. He will not, or cannot, tell the mouse and his child how to get out of the pond. Rather, their freedom must be gained by accepting personal responsibility for their position, hence, they must choose between inaction and action. To this end the mouse and his child 'must contemplate' infinity, or, in existentialist terms, must confront the ultimate meaninglessness of life in order to gain access to some kind of personal truth:

> 'Nothing,' said the mouse child. 'I can see nothing between the dots. Nothing at all, coming and going. Nothing is what is beyond the last visible dog...' .
> 'Nothing!' said the mouse father. 'What about the ultimate truth?' 'That's it,' said Serpentina. 'Nothing is the ultimate truth'.

However, while Serpentina is entirely satisfied with the nihilistic result of the mouse child's contemplation, and the mouse father ready to accept the fatalistic answer, the optimistically-minded and proactive mouse child himself will not accept it, but 'want[s] to see what's behind it'. With the help of Miss Mudd, who chews the paper label off the can, the mouse child discovers, in a climactic moment that is evocative of the Lacanian infant contemplating itself in the mirror (Lacan, 1977), what for him, is the ultimate truth:

> ...the shiny tin...became visible, and the child saw a beady eye looking at him from the surface of the can. ...he saw his own face and his out-stretched hands holding his father's hands. ...he had never seen himself before, but he recognised his father, and therefore knew himself. 'Ah,' he said, 'there's nothing on the other side of nothing but us'.

Seeing his image represents a turning point. He experiences himself as a whole and unified being and thereby gains a sense of identity; he is, or so he believes, capable of anything. 'There's nothing beyond the last visible dog but us', therefore becomes, 'Nobody can get us out of here but us'. This positive statement not only demands concrete action, but confirms that what they had been searching for on their journey was there all the time, and that it is, as always, their own skills that will free them. And, although the text has displayed a strong identification with existentialist principles in its advocacy that the individual 'alone' must choose between action or inaction, it is at this juncture - optimism or defeat - that the text departs from the nihilistic doctrines of existentialism that are represented in Serpentina's statements. Serpentina, therefore, is stuck in the mud precisely because his answer or 'truth' is 'nothing', hence, there is 'nothing' to do, and thus, 'there is no way out'. The fact that the mouse child has found the truth that provides the impetus for action and change, through a revelation that is not a direct result of philosophical investigation, suggests the ineffectiveness of philosophical attempts to provide satisfactory answers to the fundamental issues concerning existence. As Marx writes: 'The philosophers have only interpreted the world in different ways; the point is to change it' (Bottomore and Rubel, 1967).

In addition to emphasising the limitations and inadequacies of existential art and various philosophies when attempting to seek satisfactory answers and bring about change, what is significant about each stage of their journey so far is that every time the mouse and his child have successfully negotiated the various stages, it has been as a result of their own actions and the concrete, practical help of others. This serves to emphasise what, at this point in the narrative, appears to be two opposing concepts; namely, the importance of the self and the importance of community. Indeed, an awareness of these two concepts has been steadily growing throughout their journey:

> '...look how far we've come!' said the child. 'And think of all we've done! We got out of the dump; we came through the war safely; we saved the Caws of Art.' 'We escaped after the attempted bank robbery and survived the war only because we had Frog to help us,' said the father. 'And we saved the Caws of Art by making animals laugh at us'.

Individual action, or autonomy, therefore, is repeatedly shown to be less important and less effective than that of the community. The insight gained at the bottom of Serpentina's pond by the mouse child undoubtedly provides the impetus for positive action, but it is not enough. The protagonists are freed from the pond and reassembled and resurrected as two separate individuals only with the help of others.

The notion of 'community' continues to grow in importance, until the opposing concepts - individualism and community - begin to converge as the journey reaches its completion. The desire to be self-winding, though, is an impulse that does not disappear immediately. As the mouse father says:

> 'It's the principle of the thing... . A mouse wants independence. Having fought for and won our territory, are we to be helpless to patrol its boundaries unassisted?'.

It does become less important to the mouse and his child once they have their new family installed in the dolls' house. In Frog's view, it 'scarcely seems necessary... [when] you have good friends to wind you up'. Nevertheless, the impulse continues, resulting in what turns out to be only a temporary period of self-winding. However, by this stage of the narrative, the text has effected a complete shift from the importance of individualism in favour of the importance of community, stating that no one is 'ever completely self-winding', which suggests that total freedom, or autonomy, is an unattainable condition. The clichéd statement: 'That's what friends are for' develops this suggestion, further serving to emphasise why the establishment of a co-operative community, or a collective is of vital importance.

The concept of community is finally realised in the utopia that is created, significantly, at the dump where the journey began. Before this, the dolls' house, almost destroyed by fire, thrown away, and then appropriated by Manny Rat, is symbolic of the fact that the old order has ceased to exist, and that a new order now prevails; that of rampant capitalism and ruthless individual ambition:

> The ambitious rat, as he expanded his operations...had become a considerably more important personage than before: he now commanded squads of rats as well as windups, and he had begun to think about the dignity of his position. ...Manny Rat resolved on a dwelling appropriate to his rank, and a location a little removed from the hurly-burly, where he might relax after the cares of the night while yet keeping an eye upon his business interests. ...[He] devoted his ingenuity to the relocation and restoration of his new property. Press gangs of smaller, weaker rats had toiled to raise up and repair the house...the elephant had been harnessed to the crane and windlass so that she might help to put in good order for her master the house she once had called her own.

The house, when run under this regime, could be read as an indictment of the ethos that creates a society in which a feeling of community has been dramatically and drastically eroded, a society in which only individual values and success are recognised. This extreme form of individualism, represented by Manny Rat, is finally overthrown in preference for a return to some kind of communal values. Thus, the house, when won as a result of the combined efforts of the mouse and his child and their 'family', is not allowed to remain in its present condition, nor is it restored to its former status of bourgeois, material comfort. It is restored in such a way as to reflect its different purpose. Specifically, it is the 'place where the scattering is regathered' - the family for which the mouse child had been searching - and has an extended use as a communal gathering place, as 'an inn or hotel' for travellers and migrants.

Thus, the concept of community is widened to embrace all those who live on the margins of society. The tramp's return effectively signifies the end of the journey, not only for the mouse and his child and their newly created extended family, but for America itself. In this communal utopia, inhabited by a multitude of species, the creation of the type of society envisaged by the original settlers who came in search of freedom and equality is finally realised. Underlying the journey's conclusion, then, is an ideal of America based on past myths and collective hopes and desires. However, the fact that this idealised community is situated high up on a pole above the dump, effectively not occupying any 'real' space, renders it the same as any other utopian vision; that is, nowhere to be found. In other words, the original American dream (the dream before it became debased by wealth and material values) was too fantastic to be realised; it could not be fulfilled, and a journey through contemporary American society only serves to confirm that the utopia that was once dreamed of is nowhere in evidence.

To finish on a more positive note, Hoban's utopia is, in many ways, similar to Fredric Jameson's conception of 'a Utopia of misfits and oddballs'. Jameson notes how most utopias are founded in violence, by an 'act of disjunction and/or exclusion', for example, Thomas More's original was founded by having a trench dug between it and the mainland. Therefore, when people are all happy together, it is because they are suppressing all their antisocial behaviours. Hence, Fredric. Jameson's more realistic, diverse version of a Utopia of misfits and oddballs, in which the constraints for uniformization and conformity have been removed, and human beings grow wild like plants in a state of nature: not the beings of Thomas More, in whom sociality has been implanted by way of the miracle of the utopian text, but rather those of the opening of Altman's *Popeye*, who, no longer fettered by the constraints of a now oppressive sociality, blossom into the neurotics, compulsives, obsessives, paranoids, and schizophrenics whom our society considers sick but who, in a world of true freedom, may make up the flora and fauna of 'human nature' itself (1990).

Alternatively, we could compare the text's utopia, raised high up above the dump, with that of the Stylites (sometimes referred to as the Pillar-Saints), who removed themselves from society, or the 'real' world, perching themselves high up on pillars in the Syrian Desert. In other words, existing nowhere, in no place, aiming, presumably, to be more in touch with God or 'Truth'. However, for the Stylites, contact with society was kept to an absolute minimum, whereas Hoban's idealised community differs slightly in that his utopia is more in touch. The dump is visible and the community up on the pole is continually being renewed, remade and recycled - migrants are welcome. Once again there are parallels with the American experience; with the Inn or hotel being akin to Ellis Island, which was the gateway for more than half of the immigrants entering the United States in the late nineteenth and early twentieth century.

Finally, I would just like to draw attention to the Tramp's closing remark. 'Be happy', he says. As Lois Kuznets notes, however, this remark is no guarantee of a happy future. Rather, 'this relatively happy ending acknowledges the necessity of an endless remaking, virtual recycling of the world to meet human desires' (1994). In this sense, the community in the dolls' house, in which migrants are welcome, is an endless remaking of, or recycling of the community. 'Be happy' is not the same as 'and they all lived happily ever after'. What Hoban's text suggests is that utopia, in whatever form it is envisaged, has to be constantly striven for, constantly made and remade.

REFERENCES

Alida Allison (ed), *Russell Hoban / Forty Years: Essays on his Writings for Children*. London: Garland, 2000.

T.B. Bottomore. and M. Rubel (eds), *Karl Marx: Selected Writings in Sociology and Social Philosophy*. London: Penguin, 1967.

T.S. Eliot, *Collected Poems: 1909-1962*. London: Faber and Faber, 1974.

F. Scott Fitzgerald, *The Great Gatsby*. London: Penguin, 1994.

Russell Hoban, *The Mouse and his Child*. London: Penguin, 1976.

Frederic Jameson, *Late Marxism: Adorno, or, The Persistence of the Dialectic*. London: Verso, 1990.

Lois.R. Kuznets, *When Toys Come Alive: Narratives of Animation, Metamorphosis and Development*. New Haven: Yale University Press, 1994.

J. Lacan, *Écrits: A Selection*. London: Tavistock Publications, 1977

Margaret Rustin and Michael Rustin, *Narratives of Love and Loss: Studies in Modern Children's Fiction*. London: Verso, 1987.

Jean-Paul Sartre, *Being and Nothingness: An Essay on Phenomenological Ontology*. New York: Washington Square Press, 1957.

J. Wolfreys and W. Baker (eds), *Literary Theories: A Case study in Critical Performance*. London: Macmillan, 1996.

the Catholic church, particularly depicting [...]
...hardson RSCJ (1903-1983) Prolific output of saints' lives; school sto[...]
...nal references, etc

...r, WF Tales of 'Wopsy' a guardian angel

...ographer, especially of Newman; several children's books, fantasy &

*Evelyn Waugh and Bruce Marshall were probably the best known
...for adults during this period- none wrote significantly for children. Fr.
...l, wrote fiction in pamphlets largely for adults.)

...known to be a convert to Catholicism- this may also be the case [...]
...the representation of the aristocracy in the [...] period, and clergy [...]
...or action throughout, is of note)

dumbing down

by David Harrold

(Extract - headmaster's speech from the start of Act 2)

It is school assembly.
A, as the Head, is on stage settling the audience / pupils

A: *(Solemn, disapproving.)* As a result of your disgraceful conduct just
before the break, we will keep everyone behind afterwards. No one is to
complain about this or display any challenging behaviour.
(To audience members)
DAVID PERKINS, CHARLOTTE GRANGE, PETER LAUD - STAND UP!!
WHAT HAVE I JUST BEEN SAYING? (Beat) YOU DON'T KNOW, DO
YOU? THAT'S BECAUSE YOU WERE TALKING! DON'T ARGUE! YOU
WERE. I SAW YOU. *(Beat)* THERE IS NOTHING TO SMILE ABOUT.
THIS ISN'T FUNNY FOR ANY OF US. OFSTED will be here soon. Do
you remember the last inspection? And the headlines in the local paper?
Some of us remember living week after week hearing everyone in the
area refer to us as a rubbish school. Some of us felt our lives had been
wrecked. And that's not funny. *(To the three audience members)* You may
sit down. *(Beat)* So this time we aim to be "good and improving". It is no
longer satisfactory to be satisfactory. To be good is to be satisfactory
and to be satisfactory is to be unsatisfactory. That should be clear to
everybody. We are going to present OFSTED with an aspiring and happy
school. In a manner of speaking. We have spent hundreds of pounds on
potted plants for the classrooms and we expect you to blend in nicely
with the décor. We want the Inspectors to experience a calm and orderly
environment. And so, the following students will be going on Work
Experience: Angela Bulge, Kevin Macorielli, Rufus Hicks, Michelle Canning,
Shane Duran, Wayne Tug. Under no circumstances are you to be seen in
school that week. Now, following our assemblies on Sacrifice,
Commitment and Fear, I want to talk about Rebellion. Rebellion is just a

defect of the brain. It is a stage one passes through. What <u>you</u> people
are passing through. The adolescent brain, scientists now tell us, is
"...an explosive package..."

A begins to walk backwards out of the scene. It is a theatrical dissolve......

down with skool!

Geoffrey Willans
and
Ronald Searle

36

-1983) Prolific output of saints' lives; school
a guardian angel
of Newman; several children's books, fantasy &
Bruce Marshall were probably the best known
period- none wrote significantly for children. Fr.
largely for adults.)
also be the case
period, and clergy

Pat Pinsent

Catholicism, Class and Cultural Identity in British Children's Fiction

THE CLASS MAKE-UP of the Roman Catholic church in Britain has often fascinated sociologists studying religion, differing as it does from that of Anglicanism on the one hand and non-conformity on the other. Traditionally it has been wider in its membership than either the Church of England or the Free Churches, and has embraced both the aristocracy and the working class, though increasingly today the majority of church-goers are middle-class. It is scarcely surprising therefore that literature written for or about Catholic children over the last one hundred and thirty years should reflect something of this variety and complexity. In this paper I hope to show how, from having been written in the early part of this period by upper-class authors whose didactic intentions were very explicit, British books featuring Catholic characters have come to display a kind of 'cultural Catholicism' with a largely working-class setting and cast list. I shall focus on three periods: the 1870s-1880s, the mid twentieth century, and the last ten years or so.

Background

At the Reformation, with the imposition of the penal laws, Catholicism in Britain virtually went 'underground' for about two hundred years. Its adherents, who were largely members of old recusant families and their retainers, often lived in areas remote from London such as North-West England, and kept their religion very much a private matter. During the eighteenth century, the advent of workmen from Ireland to build the canals, and later the railways, changed the demography. As a result there was in the nineteenth century an increasing body of working-class Catholics, who remained something of a puzzle to their upper-class co-religionists. Nevertheless, the Catholic aristocracy in many cases endowed, mostly for the lower classes, some quite splendid churches - no doubt partly with the idea of competing with the Church of England, which was seen as having stolen the gems of medieval architecture. A third group, which came to prominence in the nineteenth century, comprised converts, with greater claims to intellectual eminence than either of the foregoing groups. These were more likely to be of comfortable middle-class origin, Cardinal Newman being the best known example. There was also a smaller number of incomers deriving from continental Europe, often as a result of persecution there; some orders of French nuns in particular took refuge in England, and their convents came to supply part of the bed-rock of the Catholic school system.

With the Catholic Emancipation Act in 1829 and the restoration of the hierarchy in 1851, all these groups gained greater confidence and began to realise the necessity of being involved in the provision of Elementary Education. Concomitant with this was the need for books for Catholic children which would be free of the bias and falsehoods which were all too often to be found in evangelical fiction and in the little religious magazines for children. (In a single issue of *The Gleaner*, for instance, I found three instances of the claim that people had to pay to have their sins forgiven in confession.)

Mid to late Victorian

Realisation about the importance of educational material led some publishers, priests, and aristocratic ladies towards a mission to provide edifying religious tracts and short novels for young readers. The Catholic Truth Society was set up in 1884, partially in response to the work of the largely Evangelical Religious Tract Society. Among its early publications were several pamphlets of stories for young people of the generation we should now call 'Young Adults.' Some were written by aristocratic ladies and addressed to working-class girls going out into service. Others were written by high-ranking churchmen. These literary gems often portray members of the working class as shiftless and unreliable, beset by the demon drink, and only saved from immorality by an early death.

Typical of the Catholic Truth Society pamphlets of the period is *The Story of Mary* (c.1888) by Lady Herbert. We are told that, 'In a large workroom of an orphanage in London a group of elder girls was sitting... "I hope I shall be going to service soon," exclaimed a tall, fair girl.' Our heroine is the fifteen-year-old Mary 'a ... modest-looking girl' who 'has always borne a good character, is also a beautiful needlewoman and very handy with children,' though Sister Agnes is a little afraid that she may be weak enough to fall in love with 'some unprincipled man.' Mary goes to work for Mrs Bristowe, 'a pleasant-looking lady of about thirty, accompanied by a little boy of six,' who wants a good Catholic girl. The family go to Australia, where Mary fulfils the nun's fears when she meets a young man of gentlemanlike appearance, and becomes 'restless and unhappy whenever a day passed without their meeting.' Despite the opposition of her mistress and the young man's hostility to religion, Mary marries him, and he takes her to New York. All too soon he is unfaithful. She throws herself into the river in desperation, but is rescued and taken in by the Sisters of Mercy. Her husband repents and becomes a Catholic; they return to England but again he leaves her, this time to marry another wife, at which point Mary tries to kill herself with rat poison. She recovers and repents, realising that 'her ill-regulated passion for this man had been the root of all her misfortunes - how in her mad love, she had forgotten her Lord and sacrificed even her religion to please him.' Giving up the idea of family life, she obtains an excellent situation and 'is loved and respected by her employers for her conscientious discharge of every duty.'

The upper-class author displays a characteristic suspicion of someone of lower-class birth, whose lack of moral fibre, accurately recognised by the nun (whose religious profession, in this kind of writing, seems automatically to admit her to the higher ranks of society) leads her astray. Her only salvation lies in abjuring family life and sexual relationships altogether, with her development of character qualities that her employers can justly praise being put forward as a more than adequate substitute.

Another example, *Molly's Prayer*, is by Monseigneur Cologan (high-ranking churchmen seem to be seen as somewhat similar in social position to the nobility). It is of a similar date, and tells how a little girl, Molly, is praying for the amendment of life of her father, a drunkard who seems incapable of mending his ways. Her last words as she dies are 'Make father good.' Soon after this, Molly's father attends a temperance meeting and decides to reform and practise his religion. On his way back home, he sees a house on fire and hears a cry, 'Molly is in the top room.' The coincidence of the name with that of his beloved daughter leads him to rush in and rescue the child, but before he can descend with her, the fire destroys the staircase, so that he has to jump out of the window. The child is saved but the father is fatally injured in the fall. He asks for a priest, and: 'The prodigal son is received into his father's arms.' More dissolute in his ways than Mary, the father here can only be redeemed by death!

The audience envisaged by the founder of the Catholic Truth Society, James Britten, was the labouring and semi-educated poor, who may of course have needed the text to be mediated to them by their more literate class superiors. These pious works, written by people who may be presumed to have little immediate knowledge of the classes and characters they depict, have a clear didactic aim, and are very representative of their period and class. These cautionary tales - and many others could be cited - generally seem to imply that the poor are incapable of helping themselves but need the support of the those better off to enable them to lead moral and religious lives.

The Mid-Twentieth Century

Some of these pamphlets and little books remained in print for a long period, being reissued as late as the 1930s. In the intervening period a number of more entertaining Catholic works in genres such as the school story and historical fiction were also published, but these too have the very clear aim of influencing their young readers' beliefs and behaviour. By the 1930s, the Catholic community had gained some confidence in literary endeavours, particularly as a result of the work of G.K. Chesterton and

Hilaire Belloc, whose novels and polemical writings made no secret of their Catholic convictions - a phenomenon later also to be observed in the 'Catholic novels' of Graham Greene and Evelyn Waugh. The influence of these writers for an adult audience on authors addressing a younger audience is to be detected in a number of mid-century children's writers, most of whom seem almost totally forgotten, judging by the evidence of their omission from the standard reference works on children's literature.

The comfortable middle-class world that some of these authors inhabit is very evident - whereas beforehand the working classes were at least there to be admonished, now they seem only to exist as dutiful hangers-on. The children in Cecily Hallack's books of the between-the-war period are generally blessed with a large retinue of retainers; the indoor and outdoor servants, as well as the governesses who are on the fringe of gentility, are frequently excellent exemplars of prayer and devotion to the children. The didactic message is as clear in her books as it was in those of an earlier period. In *All about Selina*, from the mid-1930s, the central character, aged nine, whose mother is dead and whose father is in the army, is being brought up in the country by a governess, Miss Brown, working for Selina's aunt Edith, who is distant (in more ways than one) in London. The household also includes Cook, Rumbold the housemaid and Rose the parlourmaid. Miss Brown herself is of good family and by the end of the book has inherited enough money for her to have Selina living with her in a house sufficiently near to a church for them both to attend Mass each morning.

One of the most telling incidents is when Selina becomes so ill that she is in danger of dying. Miss Brown ponders with her charge the possibility that God may intend to make her worse, 'Either to take you home to have you all to himself, or else to cure you in such a way as to show that it was he who cured you and not the doctor.' This gives Miss Brown the chance to tell Selina a story about heaven, to the effect that when the child recovers she finds it disappointing that she won't be going there yet. Hallack uses warm and comforting human relationships with the saints as a way to make heaven appealing, and indeed to reflect Selina's lack of such relationships in her daily life. This leads effectively to the climax of the book, when the child's emotional needs will be supported by a closer relationship with Miss Brown.

Even Meriol Trevor, a writer of scholarly biographies, seems to view her children's novels as vehicles for explicit ideology, including in them a strong message about Catholicism being 'the old religion.' Other than the historical realism of *Light in a Dark Town* about the work of Cardinal Newman among the poor in Birmingham, her books are usually fantasies set in large country houses. In *Sun Slower, Sun Faster*, Cecil, a non-Catholic girl from the twentieth century, time-travels to various periods in the history of the church. In the seventeenth century she meets Dom Placid, an elderly priest, in the house of a recusant Catholic family. He is in secular clothes as a result of dangers concomitant with the period of the 'Glorious Revolution'; Cecil observes:

> Dom Placid was not dressed like a monk. He wore ordinary clothes and looked like a rather shabby clerk of some kind. From an inner pocket he now pulled out a string of wooden beads and put them in Cecil's hand ... 'Come, learn how to say the mysteries of the holy rosary,' he said gently. 'I will say the prayers and you say them after me, and we will think of the sorrowful mysteries of Our Lord's Passion, when Our Lady had to stand by and see Him suffer.' ... She watched the old man's fingers moving slowly along the beads, his lips slowly repeating the words of the prayer, while his kind old eyes rested on her, and she felt herself grow quiet. She was still anxious but she felt as if a little circle of peace grew round them by the fire and that in its centre she was no longer impatiently fighting inaction but was caught into another kind of action. This doing is being, she thought.

A little later in the book (the time-travel seems to work in a reverse direction to the chronology of the text), Cecil travels to an earlier period, Elizabethan England. She meets an elderly nun who has had to leave her convent at the dissolution of the monasteries, and contents herself in doing beautiful embroidery. Then her hostess, Lady Morne, explains to her about the Mass, before going off to attend to the needs of the poor. The didactic tone of the book is clear. Just as Cecil, who hasn't been brought up as a

Catholic, is being instructed, so is the reader. The explicit religious instruction here about prayers and sacraments, as well as the message that Catholicism preceded Protestantism as the national religion, means that it is quite surprising today to realise that this book was not published by a specifically Catholic publisher. It is also apparent that our perspective as readers is firmly middle-class - which is probably an accurate judgment of Trevor's actual audience.

Generalising from these and a number of other writers of this period, I would claim that 'Catholic' fiction was generally marginal to the mainstream, and produced by members of the middle class with the implicit idea of influencing readers from a similar social background. I ought perhaps at least to mention two very significant children's authors of this period, who were also Catholic, J.R. Tolkien and Elinor Brent-Dyer. I would not see their books as 'Catholic' fiction in the sense in which I am considering it, but even so they do not represent any exception from the class aspect. It's also of note that nearly all the authors I've either mentioned or included in generalisations so far, with the exception of Tolkien, were converts to Catholicism.

Perhaps as a result of the ecumenical movement just as much as of any literary factors, in the latter part of the twentieth century, there seems to have been a very clear decline, within all areas of Christianity, in the kind of writing for children which seeks to persuade them towards a specific denominational position - with the possible exception of some evangelical novels such as those by Patricia St John. There has been a fairly general tendency to eschew realistic portrayals of denominational belief and practice in favour of a more generalised 'spirituality', often conveyed in a fantasy mode. This trend may well have been triggered off by the 'Narnia' books. Despite C.S. Lewis's own orthodox Anglicanism, the message conveyed by his books seems for most young readers to consist rather in a combination of moral behaviour, such as fair play and consideration for others, and a recognition of a kind of 'connectedness' to other people and to the universe, which relates to what might be termed 'spirituality' rather than to denominational religion.

Realism, 'Cultural Catholicism' and Working-Class Fiction

Despite what I see as a general trend towards books with a 'spiritual' message being fantasies, and a general lack within 'gritty realism' of any explicit mention of religion, it is interesting to observe a recent resurgence within the work of a few writers of the attention to religion as a social signifier. Several children's writers feature characters with a background of working-class 'cultural Catholicism,' a background which echoes that of the authors concerned. Unlike 'other world' fantasy, in which denominational aspects are largely irrelevant, such books generally involve a largely realistic setting, sometimes tinged with elements of what has been termed 'fantasy realism.' The authors exemplifying this feature are David Almond, Frank Cottrell Boyce, Catherine Forde, and Theresa Breslin, who have all written novels which reflect the Catholic environments in which they themselves grew up. Unlike the texts I have mentioned earlier, these books, set respectively in Tyneside, Liverpool and for the last two writers, Glasgow, do not seem to be portraying Catholicism from either a polemical or a didactic point of view, but merely as a solid background for the characters, just as it seems to have been for the authors themselves when young. It is particularly worth note that, unlike so many of the earlier writers, none of these four are converts who have come to the Catholic religion in later life and thus inevitably bring a different agenda to their writing. I would also suggest that all of them can be seen as 'mainstream' children's writers in a way in which those I have mentioned earlier are not.

It would probably be fair to say that Hallack, Trevor and their predecessors certainly had very explicit ideological intentions vis-à-vis Catholicism in their novels for the young. While the contemporary writers I have named equally possess and express their own ideologies in their work, these ideologies bear relatively little resemblance to those of their predecessors. Contemporary authors may indeed want their young readers to imbibe the moral and spiritual values of integrity, connectedness to other people and to the natural world, self-confidence and care for others and the environment; they don't in any way convey the idea that adherence to the Catholic church is the best way of attaining these values, or that their characters, by going to church, are performing an action that readers should emulate.

66   FROM SLAVERY TO FREEDOM

David Almond

Almond's first published children's book, *Skellig*, certainly offers much to a researcher with an interest in children's literature and spirituality, but has little direct reference to Catholicism. It seems, however, that as Almond's confidence as a writer has grown, he has felt able to incorporate elements from his own childhood in a devoutly Catholic family - a fact confirmed by the writer himself. His background is portrayed in the largely autobiographical collection of short stories, *Counting the Stars*, while his most recent novels, *The Fire-Eaters* and *Clay*, show working-class Catholicism as an unquestioned part of the characters' backgrounds, just as it was to Almond himself as a child. The behaviour of his young male protagonists is certainly not offered as a model, even if they are regular church-goers, nor is it presented as a warning. While some issues relating to the supernatural do indeed occur in *Clay*, they are in no way used as instruments towards persuasion of the readers towards an explicitly 'religious' view of life. That the plots and characterisation of these books involve deeper issues which themselves relate to Catholic theology is also evident, but this is not my focus in this paper. I have chosen rather to exemplify instances of how Almond uses devotions of Catholic origin to make concrete his characterisation and setting; he shows how these, far from idealized, children from a working-class background are steeped, in a totally non-pious way, in the practices of their religious culture.

In *The Fire-Eaters*, for instance, there is a scene where the central character, Bobby, is using all the resources of his Catholic education to pray for his father:

> I said a string of prayers: Hail Marys, Our Fathers, Confiteors. I touched Mary and Bernadette in their plastic grotto ... 'If he gets better,' I said, 'I'll always be good. I'll always fight evil.'(2003)

It is natural for him to pray, and, in effect, to use statues of the saints as a kind of talisman in a way that might justly be termed superstitious, though Almond does not in any way apply a negative perspective here.

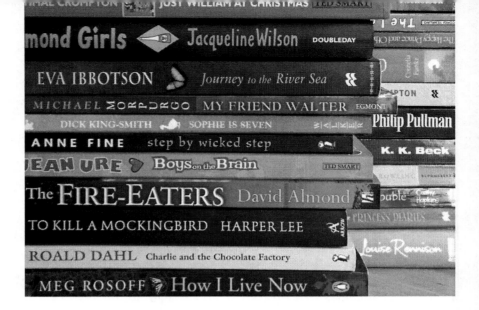

Almond's most recent novel, *Clay*, is set in a period the same as its author's own childhood, and the narrator, perhaps significantly named Davie, quite unselfconsciously reveals Catholicism to be an essential part of his identity. At the beginning of the book Davie is reflecting on the arrival in the village of the mysterious Stephen Rose, who figures large in the subsequent plot:

> He arrived in Felling on a bright and icy February morning. Not so long ago, but it was a different age. I was with Geordie Craggs, like I always was back then. We were swaggering along like always, laughing and joking like always. We passed a Players back and forward and blew long strings of smoke into the air. We'd just been on the altar ... We were on Watermill Lane when a red taxi rattled past us. Black fumes belched from it. The sign at the top said it was from down at the coast.
> 'What's that doing up here?' said Geordie.
> A bit of communion wafer was still stuck to my teeth. I poked it free with my tongue and swallowed it, then drew on the cigarette again.
> 'God knows,' I said. (2005)

The collocation of religious practice - having served on the altar and received Holy Communion - with their smoking (not quite so reprehensible then, perhaps, but scarcely approved) might seem incongruous but certainly signals that we do not have here two overly pious youths (unlike the ones sometimes found in earlier Catholic children's novels).

A little later we see Davie at his regular fortnightly confession, a scene which seems to be intended to have the effect of establishing Davie's childish innocence:

> Saturday evening, the same week. I went to St Patrick's. I knelt in the dark confessional. I could see Father O'Mahoney's face through the grille. I wondered if I should try to disguise my voice, but I knew, like always, it would be no good. Of course he'd know who I was. And did it matter? There was nothing unusual about me. There was nothing unusual about my sins... I started with the words I'd been taught when I was a little kid.
>> 'Bless me, Father, for I have sinned. It is two weeks since my last confession.'
>> 'Yes, my son?' he said.
>> He sighed and waited.
>> It was always best to get the worst out first.
>> 'I drank some altar wine, Father.'
>> 'Did you now? This is both theft and blasphemy.'
>> 'Yes, Father. I understand. Sorry, Father.'
>> ...'And I stole some cigarettes from my dad.'
>> 'And smoked them?'
>> 'Yes, Father. And the cigarettes of somebody else's dad. And I have coveted other people's goods. And I have called people cruel names. And- '
>> 'Have you now? What kind of names?'
>> 'Fishface, Father.'
>> I heard his little snort of laughter.
>> 'Yes, Father.'
>> 'That is terrible. What else?'... (2005)

The priest's initial near boredom, and later his barely concealed amusement, reveal how far from 'terrible' he regards Davie's sins. The very ordinariness of the routine serves to present the easy relationship between the protagonist and the rituals of the church.

Frank Cottrell Boyce

Millions, which was a successful film before becoming a novel, is not explicitly set in a Catholic milieu, though this is revealed by factors such as the obsession with saints that besets the protagonist Damian (a very Catholic name, an aspect later to be discussed in more detail in relation to another novel). When I asked the author recently about his own Catholic background, he talked of having as a child been fascinated with saints, citing a book then well known to Catholic children, Joan Wyndham's *Six O'Clock Saints*. The central theme of *Millions* is the money that seems literally to drop out of the sky when Damian is praying, though we soon learn that its immediate origin was from a robbery rather than from heaven. Another important strand is the way in which a third world charity is featured as one of the ways in which Damian seeks to find a way to spend this windfall. Themes of honesty, morality, and the need to help those worse off certainly feature, but Boyce's message is not for readers to copy Damian's rather eccentric devotion to the saints nor his attempt to imitate some of them by building himself a hermitage.

After Damian's near obsession with the saints has been established, we see him trying on God the technique that he and his brother use for getting out of trouble, which is to recall their mother's death:

> Then I started to think about the saints, and how Dad didn't seem to like them any more and maybe they weren't all they were cracked up to be and it was just all a big misunderstanding. Then I thought that these doubts were just another temptation, so I tried to say a prayer, but all I could think of to say was, 'In the name of the Father and of the Son and of the Holy Spirit, Amen. My Mum is Dead. Amen.'
>
> Even that little prayer took me about five minutes to say because my teeth kept chattering. God must have heard me, though, because he answered it. And you know what? He did the same thing as everyone else. He gave me something. (2004)

The explicit mention of a character saying a prayer is relatively rare in mainstream children's fiction today, but the absence of any didacticism addressed towards the reader is also evident. Damian goes on to enlist the saints in his personal campaign:

> I did manage to get to the repository shop at the back of St Margaret Mary's. I got statues of St Francis, St Martin de Porres, the Little Flower, Gerard Majella and the Child of Prague. I got miraculous medals of St Benedict, St Bernadette and St Anthony. They had a St Christopher, but I don't count him as a proper saint personally. They had colourful cards of all the above plus St Michael the Archangel with a burning sword. They all fitted on my windowsill. (2004:68-9)

The humour of this passage, resulting from the excessive number of purchases Damian makes, amounts to a kind of gentle 'sending-up' which prevents it being seen as instructive to readers, but at the same time suggests some degree of authorial identification with his behaviour. What is very evident throughout the book is that prayer, and images of the saints, are part of Damian's life, something which could well seem strange to many readers, yet they are clearly not incorporated in any attempt to persuade them to behave in a similar manner.

Catherine Forde

The main character of *Fat Boy Swim* is Jimmy, who is bullied because of his obesity, and as a result feels unable to admit to his schoolmates the fact that he is an excellent cook. He is given self confidence by a priest who is also a football coach: GI Joe is a good character but in no way 'a plaster saint'; as well as bringing out Jimmy's talent for swimming he helps him unravel the mystery of his home background (that the woman who he thinks is his aunt is really his mother) and makes him aware of the needs of the third world. This novel is located in a setting in which prayer and church-going are assumed to be part of the characters' background, but in no way is this seen as any kind of ideal to be imitated. In conversation, Forde said that the background in the novel was one which was natural to her from her own upbringing and from her subsequent working experience. This novel clearly conveys the wrongness of bullying, the potential abilities possessed by everyone, and the need to have confidence in and be honest with oneself. It certainly doesn't have a denominational didactic aim.

Early in the novel, Jimmy, who has encountered GI Joe at school as a demanding football coach, free in his language, is astonished when his mother introduces him as a priest.

> How the heck was Jimmy supposed to know GI Joe was a priest?
> Divine telepathy?
> He'd appeared from nowhere in the PE department one day after Easter. Call me Coach, he'd said. Added: 'I'm gonna kick ass.' Hardly an ecclesiastical starter for ten. 'Been watching you jokers.' He'd paced the gym like a hungry rotweiler, eyeballing the team one by one.'
> ...None of them would ever have guessed GI Joe was a priest. Jimmy didn't believe it himself, yet there he was - 'Father Joseph!' as Mum snapped - holding out his hand for Jimmy to shake. Even dressed as a priest. Jimmy had been in too much shock at the sight of the crewcut at first to notice the dusty black suit you only ever see priests wearing. GI's neck bulged from the stranglehold of a dog-collar.
> At least in his holy gear, Coach seemed smaller, less musclebound. When Jimmy shook GI's hand, he was surprised: the grip, though firm, wasn't the bonecrushing testicle-shrinker that he would have expected.
> 'Call me Joe,' Coach pumped Jimmy's arm... (2003)

Catherine Forde told me that the character of GI Joe was largely based on a priest she knew, but that she had no direct intention of trying to rehabilitate the image of priests from the somewhat bad press some of them have recently received. In his combination of concern for Jimmy and the kind of language generally seen as more appropriate to a football coach than someone of ecclesiastical profession, the character rings true. A little later in the book, we again see the priest again rejecting the 'holier-than-thou' image with which some clergy are all too easily identified:

Jimmy was sneaking out of Mass before the end, tiptoeing as best he could down the front steps of St Jude's when GI Joe caught him... During Mass, Jimmy had been vaguely aware of Father Patrick's usual dronesville sermon including something about fundraising to help our less fortunate brothers and sisters overseas. Blah. Blah. Blah. His brain had pressed the off button at that point...
'You mean you didn't hear the sermon? I'm disappointed.'
Jimmy squirmed...
'Hey, lighten up, Jim.' GI Joe's hand circled Jimmy's elbow, shook it playfully.
'Kidding. I don't listen to that old codger, either...'   (2003)

The priest's active charity, as revealed in his being an instrument in Jimmy's gaining of self-esteem, and his work in Africa, is seen as far more important than what happens in church; GI's admission that he too finds little of interest in the sermon is calculated to appeal to the young reader.

Theresa Breslin

Divided City is set in Glasgow, a city which even today displays sectarian violence, most notably through the Protestant Rangers / Catholic Celtic antagonism (which seems to survive even when neither team includes many (if any) players of local origin. The book has some affinities with Joan Lingard's 'Kevin and Sadie' chronicles (1970-1976), largely set in Belfast, and I suppose Lingard's five books could also be seen as reflecting cultural rather than spiritual aspects of denominational affiliation. Like Breslin's book, they are set in a largely working-class environment.

This novel also mentions prayer and church attendance, largely as cultural signifiers and without any element of didacticism. In particular, and based on her own experience, Breslin (who admits that her own origin is indicated by her name, 'Theresa') has a good deal to say about social signifiers such as names, faces and geographical locations. Like the other books mentioned, this book has a strongly moral message, but it certainly isn't one of 'say your prayers, go to Mass, tell people that the Catholic church is best.' Two boys, one Protestant, Graham, and one Catholic, Joe, play in a non-denominational football team, and also become involved in helping an asylum seeker, who is, of course, neither Protestant nor Catholic. Thus they come to realise the stupidity of the divides between them, and to feel critical of many of their own relatives who perpetuate hostility between people who have in fact so much in common. Here the Protestant boy is confronted by some Catholic youths:

> 'What school do you go to?'
> 'None of your business.'
> The boy took in Graham's face and his clothes. 'You don't belong here.'
> 'Aye I do,' said Graham shortly, and tried to walk away.
> The older boy grabbed his sleeve. 'I don't like the look of you,' he snarled.
> 'You've got a Protestant face.'
> 'What does that mean?' Graham said. 'A Protestant face?'
> 'I can tell.' The older boy shoved his own face up against Graham's. 'Your wee beady eyes are too close together.'

Graham opened his eyes as wide as he could and tried to laugh it off, but he was taken aback. It hadn't occurred to him that Catholics might think that Protestants looked different from them. He knew that some Protestants regarded Catholics as a separate race. He hadn't realized it worked the other way. His Uncle Maxwell believed absolutely that Catholics had definite physical characteristics that were not the same as Protestants. Graham had heard him say it often enough, especially at the New Year, when his uncle had too much drink in him. 'They're a different breed, the Tims. I'm telling you. In a way I feel sorry for them. 'Cos the thing with the Cathlicks is, they cannae help being taken in by aw that mumbo-jumbo their priests tell them. It's because they're mair stupit than us, see? Their brains are actually smaller…(2005)

Breslin is consistently even-handed in exposing the mindless prejudice of both factions; here having shown one group judging on physionomy, she allows Graham to articulate the other group's parallel prejudice. Another signifier of religious identity that she highlights is that of names. Firstly Graham is 'examined' by Joe's cousin about his name:

'What's your name, then?' Jammy came forward and inspected Graham.
'Gra-'
'Gregory,' Joe cut in. 'His name's Gregory. After a pope. See?'
'What?' said Graham.
Joe whacked Graham in the ribs. 'Your mammy called you after a pope. Isn't that right, Gregory?'
'A pope?' said Graham.
'A pope?' repeated Jammy. The scowl left his face. 'So he's no a Hun?' (2005)

This passage is set in parallel with another when Graham is confronted by his arch-Protestant, 'orange' grandfather who asks him about his friend's name:

'What's his name?'
'Joe,' said Graham.
'His second name?'
'Flaherty,' said Graham reluctantly.
'He'll be a Roman then?'

Graham shrugged. 'Dunno,' he said.

'You can bet your boots on it.' His granda spoke bitterly. 'Theyre everywhere. You can tell by their names if nothing else. Reilly, O'Connell, Doyle. They're not Scottish names, are they? Incomers. That's what they are. And see what they've done. Corrupted us with their false doctrine. Intermarried and polluted the race…' (2005)

Having established the stupidity of prejudice, Breslin presents Graham being confronted by some of the externals of Catholicism when he unwillingly visits a church:

'Are you scared to come inside?' Joe challenged him.

'No,' said Graham. He followed Joe into the interior of the [church] building and hung back at the door as Joe went over to a stand of candles…

'What are you doing anyway?'

'Putting up a candle,' said Joe.

'What!'

'It's for my ma,' said Joe. 'Since she died a few years ago I always do it if I pass this church. Right?' he added belligerently.

Graham glanced around. He'd seen pictures of Catholic churches, with all their decoroations and ornaments, but he had never actually been inside one before. There were statues everywhere… 'There's too much…stuff in your churches… crosses and candlesticks and crucifixes and altars and wee coloured lamps here and there.'(2005)

The conversation that ensues allows Joe the opportunity to explain to Graham something about the saints and about prayer, but we never see this as an instance of Breslin trying to persuade the reader towards a particular form of behaviour. Rather she uses the incident as a means to indicate the mind-set of an ordinary boy in working-class Glasgow.

Conclusion

That the characters in all the books exemplified have a Catholic background results from the authors' own upbringing. None of them derive from the intellectual middle class of the earlier converts, still less the aristocracy. Perhaps even more significantly, none of these writers were converts to Catholicism, so none of them had thus taken on a set of beliefs and values as mature individuals, together with, quite frequently, the desire to convince the world of the validity of an ideological position. All come from areas where there is an 'endemic' Catholicism among the working classes: North East England, Liverpool and Glasgow. Perhaps as a result of these aspects, their books display less self-consciousness about the religious adherence of the characters, which seems a natural part of their being. It seems to me that books like these have something also to say about the situation of minority religious groups which have yet to become as fully integrated as have the descendants of Catholic working-class immigrants from earlier centuries.

people took the water they had drawn for their Sheep.

o-
ht
se
in

ed
he
ad
or

as
of
et
so

he

Moses had been sitting still, thinking deeply.

REFERENCES

David Almond, *Counting the Stars*. London: Hodder, 2000.

David Almond, *The Fire-Eaters*. London: Hodder, 2003.

David Almond, *Clay*. London: Hodder, 2005.

Frank Cottrell Boyce, *Millions*. Basingstoke: Macmillan, 2004.

Theresa Breslin, *Divided City*. London: Doubleday, 2005.

Mgr. Cologan, *Molly's Prayer*. London: Catholic Truth Society, c.1888.

Catherine Forde, *Fat Boy Swim*. London: Egmont, 2003.

Cecily Hallack, *All About Selina*. London: Burns Oates & Wahsbourne, n.d., c.1935.

Lady M. Herbert, *The Story of Mary*. London: Catholic Truth Society, c.1888.

Meriol Trevor, *Sun Slower, Sun Faster*. London: Collins, 1955.

Writing the Future Red:
Writers on Science Fiction

Farah Mendelson

Writing the Future Red

IT IS NOW a truism that the default position of UK science fiction is 'leftish', but this did not used to be the case with SF written for the teen market. I am uncomfortable with the term *young adult*, because the social values of young adult science fiction of the 1980s are so very different from the social values of Juvenile science fiction of the 1950s. "Teen" seems a more generic descriptor. In the 1970s, although the counter-culture influenced the genre greatly - most of John Christopher's work, for example, operates on the assumption that anything parents or elders say about the world is wrong - most authors continued to generate tales of individual exceptionalism, hierarchical governments and hereditary leadership.

At the end of the 1990s, however, a number of new SF writers began writing for children and teens. Some, such as Stephen Baxter and Ken MacLeod, came into the field from the adult genre, as had been typical before the 1970s. Others, such as Philip Reeve, Conor Kostick and Rhiannon Lassiter, write only for children. One of the new elements many of these writers brought into the field was a distinctively leftish stance, a willingness not simply to challenge the opinions of authority but to challenge the construction of that authority and the ideologies which supported it.

At the liberal/anarchist end are writers such as Philip Reeve, whose *Mortal Engines* sequence (2001 - 2006) has sought to challenge unthinking martialism, ecological devastation and entrenched hierarchies. His character Tom Naisworthy, a lowly apprentice to the historians, breaks from his destiny, helps to destroy his world and by the third book, *Infernal Devices*, has settled for the life of a pastoralist. The post-city future which Reeve depicts at the end of the sequence is high-tech pastoralism, but with little sense of the "getting from here to there" - which, I think it fair to say, is one of the distinctive elements of Marxist literature. Where the books do reflect a Marxist sense of history, however, is in their grand canvasses. Although Tom and Hester - the principal protagonists in the first two books - are important, always there is a sense that they, and later their daughter Wren and her friend Theo, are swept up in a movement in history in which it is the mass of people, their choices *as a group*, which will unseat the entrenched interests of all sides.

Written for an older audience, perhaps mid-teens and above, the late Jan Mark's *Useful Idiots* (2004) comments on the nature of imperialism and takes a dig at the well-meaning liberal. When a skeleton is found on the beach, Merrick Korda's attempts to help the minority indigenous population (the Inglish) support a *kulturkampf* undermine his own 'assimilation' (he is third generation assimilated). His attempts are repudiated and exploited by the people he set out to "help" without ever having actually discussed with them what they wanted.

For younger readers, Rhiannon Lassiter offers a masterly critique of imperialism in her *Borderlands* portal fantasy/science fiction sequence. Across three books, *Borderland* (2003) *Outland* (2004) and *Shadowland* (2005), Lassiter discusses the true likely impact of four westerners arriving in a foreign land with all the assumptions of (even liberal) western imperialism.

In *Borderland*, Laura and Alex go through into another world and in their attempts to take it over (Alex thinks of himself as another Alexander the Great, Laura is more subtle) manage to bring the entire political edifice down around their ears, killing several thousand people. Jzhera, a desert warrior woman in love with Alex, comes to realise that he has feet of clay, and that she can't remember what her tribe were going to do with the wealth of the desert city had they won it anyway. In *Outland* and *Shadowland* the protagonists meet the Library between Worlds, with its factions, and plots and lessons on imperialist interference and economic imperialism. The doctrine of non-interference comes under some severe scrutiny, but without offering any easy answers, and the protagonists discover that they can be *manipulated* as well as *manipulator*. All the destinarian, imperialist assumptions of portal fantasies are overturned as they come to realize that the worlds they enter are not customized play-grounds.

Surprisingly, economics has become the science most of interest to the new generation of SF writers in this market. Although K.A. Applegate's *Remnants* sequence is mostly concerned with the dynamics of survival in a hostile universe, it begins with a space ship setting out from a ruined earth, full of people who have fought or bought their way on. Much of the matter of the first three books focuses on the "false consciousness" endemic in capitalist societies where status is presumed to relate to worth. Similarly, Julie Bertagana's *Exodus* destroys any sense of superiority on the world stage, with a consideration of British refugees in a flooded world. In *Exodus*, values which made sense in the old world are undermined by new economic imperatives and readers get to see how much of our sense of commodity capitalism is a construct. Oisin McGann's *Small Minded Giants*, set in the middle of an ice-age, offers a rare example of a working class protagonist and manual labourers as role models. In this race-against-time thriller, the pleasures of the book are in the growing awareness of the economic and physical complexity of any large city. Exploitation of labour is here presented, not as an inevitable consequence of natural hierarchies, or as a necessity of survival, but as a calculated element in the political and physical construction of the domed-in world.

Perhaps the most interesting (for Marxists) of the new writers is Conor Kostick. In his first novel, *Epic*, a group of colonizers on an unnamed planet play at the interface game of Epic. Once a mere pastime for bored star-travellers, over the centuries Epic has come to be the arena of the economy and of law. Prizes and monies won, given or traded, transfer as points accumulated in the real world. Victory in the graduation tournaments can bring a university place. Armour bought with the pennies stolen from kobolds become tractor allocations or books for a school. Presiding as referee over the system is Central Allocations. Made up of the most prestigious and victorious players, this Committee ensures fairness in

everything, from hip replacement operations to luxury goods.
The difficulty is that over the years, the colony seems to be doing worse, although Central Allocations is forever talking about improvements in the future. Equipment is degrading, people's lives are getting harder, and the gap between the rich and poor in the game seems to be growing. However, Central Allocation decisions may be challenged in the arena, and when Erik's parents feel their village has been treated unjustly in the allocation of solar panels they decide to give it a go. Unusually, they succeed in reducing the Central Allocations team to a draw. This one act sets off a chain of political events as Central Allocations becomes increasingly repressive in order to hold in place the economic system they think preserves society.

But there is also another chain of events. Dead once again in the game, Erik, in a flash of bravado, creates a new character very different from the norm. The emphasis in the political system on accumulation of prizes and powers as the route to economic success has led to a game world in which avatars are attributed loaded grey pixels, and almost all action takes place in the arena. Erik flippantly assigns almost all his start up points to beauty and wit. In response, the game offers him more opportunities to interact. Kostick begins to argue that the game itself has been subverted. The more it is tied to a crude capitalism, the less interactive, rich and joyous it becomes. By part way through, we as readers learn that the game itself (an Artificial Intelligence) is pretty unhappy. As we get further into the game, the political complexity of the novel extends. One of the things Kostick uses it for is to present a critique of meritocracy. The graduation games, for example, which are supposed to test the mettle of the young, are lies. Not because anyone cheats, but because it is well within the rules of Epic to gift powers and spells, weapons and potions, so that some young people enter the arena with a rich inheritance of armour while others enter with the small pieces of plate that their folks grubbed together penny by penny. In the game of Epic, accumulation is compound not hierarchical, so that the richest have the opportunity to get richer. Not unreasonably, one character advocates violent surgery.

Social and political speculation in children's science fiction is clearly getting richer. The assumption that social norms will persist appears to be dying away; the sense that the economic superstructure and its accompanying ideology is fragile is becoming clearer. The empires of commodity capitalism no longer extend unthinkingly into the future.

REFERENCES

K. A. Applegate, *Remnants*. New York: Scholastic, 2001-2003.

Neil Arkasy, *Playing on the Edge*. Harmondsworth, Puffin, 2000.

Stephen Baxter. *The Web; Gulliverzone*, London: Orion, 2007.

Julie Bertagna, *Exodus*. Picador, 2002.

Conor Kostick, *Epic*. Dublin: O'Brien Press, 2004.

Rhiannon Lassiter, *Outland*. Oxford: Oxford University Press, 2004.

Rhiannon Lassiter, *Shadowland*. Oxford: Oxford University Press, 2005.

Ken MacLeod, *Cydonia*. London: Orion, 1999.

Jan Mark, *Useful Idiots*. London: David Fickling Books, 2004.

Oisin McGann, *Small Minded Giants*. London: Doubleday, 2007.

Philip Reeve, *Mortal Engines*. London: Scholastic, 2001.

Philip Reeve, *Predator's Gold*. London: Scholasic Point, 2004.

Philip Reeve, *Infernal Devices*. London: Scholastic, 2005.

Philip Reeve, *A Darkling Plain*. London: Scholastic, 2006.

Conor Kostick

Error! Bookmark not defined

CHILDREN'S LITERATURE is much more laden with politics and philosophy than is perhaps commonly realised. A well known example would be C. S. Lewis's *Narnia* books, at the heart of which is an extended interaction with Christian theology. This observation is not meant as necessarily a critical one; sometimes the philosophy inherent in a work is precisely what makes it so valuable. The *Moomin* books of Tove Jansson are possibly the greatest works of existentialism in fiction, and the strength of characters like Snufkin and Little My is rooted in their fierce independence from any kind of obligation. In so far as they form relationships they do so freely, and not because it is required of them.

Lewis's works are wonderful and the escape they offer from our humdrum world of competition and stultifying rules into one of fantasy has quite rightly been appreciated over the generations. The theology working through them does, however, emerge from time to time in a problematic way. The biggest difficulty is probably in the character of Aslan. If Aslan is as powerful as we later see him, the creator of the world, then why must he die in *The Lion The Witch and the Wardrobe*? The rather contrived answer is that his death is required because the forces for good have accepted into their ranks a traitor, Edmund, and this contravenes ancient laws.

The 'Harry Potter' series by J. K. Rowling is, for the large part, extremely positive in the implicit politics it contains. Bravery is celebrated, as is multiculturalism, in the persons of Harry's friends, and in a refusal to bow down before bullying. But it is worth being aware of some problem areas.

Overweight people are generally portrayed in a very negative light; Dudley Dursley, for example, or Vincent Crabbe. The reality of the experience of overweight children at schools is, however, that rather than being the bullies, it is they who are more likely to be unhappy and picked upon.

Perhaps a deeper issue in the Harry Potter books is the relationship between magicians and non-magicians, the 'muggles'. The central issue of the books is whether the muggles will be governed by the outright dictatorship of the dark wizard Voldemort or by the subtle invisible government of the good magicians. In either case, the muggles are passive inferiors towards whom we are invited to feel mild amusement at their quaint ways. This schism is an elitist one that contrasts very strongly with, say, Ursula Le Guin's much more sophisticated portrayal of the relationship between magicians and non-magicians in the *Earthsea* series. For Le Guin, the goatherd, the sailor or the farmer are dignified, respected, individuals and wizards have to earn their trust. For, quite rightly, the non-magical population has seen a lot of harm as well as good come from those who have power.

My own book *Epic* is set in a world where everybody on the planet has to play a certain online game to determine their income, their job and where they are to live. Judicial challenges are resolved by battles between game characters in the arena. The game, however, has become unfair, with a small elite controlling the most powerful weapons and magic in the game to ensure their decisions are always victorious, or go uncontested. Into this structure I set loose various characters who, without being conscious of it, based their outlook on the thinking of Hobbes, Marx and Machiavelli respectively. Not only was this great fun, but I think it helped avoid an overly crude 'evil versus good' set up and, therefore, one of the greatest weaknesses of children's fantasy - the lack of a convincing motivation for those characters representing the dark side.

Rhiannon Lassiter

The Edge of the Possible

SCIENCE FICTION, like politics, is the art of the possible. To dream of another world is the task of idealists and escapists - to make that world a reality that of the revolutionary. The role of writer as revolutionary is a well-known theme. Shelley wrote of poets that they are the unacknowledged legislators of the world and the poet Arthur O'Shaughnessy, in a flawed but oddly memorable ode, that "the dreamers of dreams" are "world-losers and world-forsakers" and yet also "movers and shakers" who can build an empire or overthrow it with prophesies of the future.

The worlds of science fiction are prophecies of a future that exists only in the imagination of writer and reader. Here, on the edge of the possible, we build our visions of future societies and cultures. And, for all that children's authors mostly attempt to avoid didacticism; we consciously or unconsciously imbue those worlds with our own values. Post-holocaust fictions and other dystopias are born of a fear of authoritarianism in the world today. Futurist utopias are often the result of imagined economic and political revolutions, giving birth to a brave new world.

We inhabit these worlds only briefly. The message that the reader takes away from these writings may be as fleeting as a dream. However, there is that power in fiction to make an imagined world more believable than reality. As a reader of science fiction, I sometimes find the troubles of the real world disorientating, as I have the memories of these same problems solved and surpassed in a future that never existed. Science fiction opened my mind and it is to fiction, both my own and that of other authors, that I turn for answers to the problems that perplex me. In raising these possibilities, these worlds of 'might have been', are we also raising consciousness? All prophecies carry the seeds of their completion. Marx would find our world strange indeed - one in which his dreams have built and overthrown empires. Perhaps our messages to the future will someday be written in the stars.

Jean Webb

Swash-buckler with a re-fashioned sword?

The model of the hero in contemporary adventure stories

THIS PAPER TAKES THE position that the model of the hero in nineteenth and early twentieth century adventure stories for boys can no longer exist in contemporary writing, since such heroes were based on values which contributed to a model of heroism conducive to imperialism and embedded in adventures which furthered such causes.

The construction of the nineteenth century hero, in works such as Charles Kingsley's *Westward Ho!* (1855), R.M. Ballantyne's *The Coral Island* (1858) and the adventure stories by G.A. Henty, such as *With Clive in India* (1884) draw on the ideals of Muscular Christianity, imperialism and colonialism. In the dedication which prefaces *Westward Ho!* Kingsley addressed The Rajah Sir James Brooke, K.C.B., and George Augustus Selwyn, Bishop of New Zealand, who represented imperialism and the Church of England. Kingsley nominated the values he admired and revered in these figureheads, which he traced back to an idealized essence of Englishness embodied in Elizabethan times. The dedication reads as follows:

> That type of English virtue, at once manful and godly, practical and enthusiastic, prudent and self-sacrificing, which he (Kingsley) has tried to depict in these pages, they have exhibited in a form even purer and more heroic than that in which he has drest it, and than that in which it was exhibited by the worthies whom Elizabeth, without distinction of rank or age, gathered round her in the ever glorious wars of her great reign. (Kingsley 1855, Preface)

Kingsley is representing an essence of English manliness which he would want his young readers to espouse; that is, being manful, godly, practical, enthusiastic, prudent, self-sacrificing, moving across class barriers and dedicated to the furtherance of English interests through war. In *Westward Ho!*, for example, Kingsley is able clearly to identify the enemy as the Spanish, since Drake was defending England against invasion by the Spanish Armada. Similarly, on discovering that they 'have an island all to themselves', Ballantyne's patriotic boy heroes in *The Coral Island* are in no doubt that they will 'Take possession in the name of the king' and will 'rise naturally to the top of affairs' for 'White men always do in savage countries.' (Ballantyne 16). Henty's heroes are equally confident. Doubt does not cloud their patriotically driven minds, for the quest is to defend the homeland or further interests abroad in the name of England and the British Empire. Equally, heroes of war stories of the First and Second World War, such as W.E. Johns' Biggles (e.g. Johns, *The Camels Are Coming*, 1932) know that the enemy is the German and continue on their course of heroic and patriotic action with impunity.

However, this model, based on patriotism and defined notions of Englishness, is no longer viable in the contemporary adventure story. The 'old enemies' no longer exist within the contemporary world of the European Union, where the iniquities of the First and Second World wars are part of cultural consciousness and conscience. The crimes of imperialism and colonialism are documented, not only historically, but also in fiction for children, as for example in the work of the Australian author Gary Crew (see, for example *Crew, Strange Objects* 1991), in this post-colonial multi-cultural contemporary context.

Furthermore, the First and Second World Wars produced clearly marked boundaries in British social history. Following both wars there was considerable social and cultural change. After World War One, the previous social hierarchies of the aristocracy and the working class were dislocated. Beliefs in patriotism and heroism came into question when men returned from a war that saw the reduction of humanity and ideals to the seemingly senseless destruction of a generation in the trenches and on the battlefields of France. The high ideals of heroism founded in the nineteenth century in Muscular Christianity, propounded by writers such as Thomas Hughes in *Tom Brown's Schooldays* (Hughes, 1857) and Henty in his tales of imperialism and conquest, could no longer remain inviolable. One might suggest that the consciousness of the working classes had been irretrievably altered; that is, the model of 'heroism' for the ordinary man was no longer of high ideals - of Dulce Et Decorum Est - when so many had died for reasons they did not understand in situations beyond their control.

The adventure story circulating about patriotism and war has, therefore, become outmoded and confined to particular historical and cultural moments. Writers of war stories, such as Robert Westall, have taken the position of bringing together those who were previously divided through common understandings of the depravities of war.

The work of Michael Morpurgo takes this particular focus, questioning such outmoded ideals, producing different models of heroism and exhibiting a set of attitudes towards war different from those of the swash-buckling heroes of yore. In particular, Morpurgo demonstrates that even in the most difficult of circumstances there is an interconnectedness which goes beyond class and nationality; that humanity can cross boundaries despite circumstances in which, in the words of Robert Burns, 'Man's inhumanity to man makes countless thousands mourn'. Morpurgo's *Private Peaceful* (2003) which I wish to discuss in this context, ironically takes what was deemed as an act of cowardice on the battlefield as an exemplar of heroism.

Private Peaceful (2003) explores the trust between brothers. Brought up in a rural community prior to the First World War, with their widowed mother working for the local landowner, the Colonel, the two Peaceful boys have a relationship which is close but also subliminally threatened by the love they both have for the same young woman, a childhood friend. Morpurgo sets his story within the historical context of pre-War Britain, where rural working class freedom and pride has to negotiate with the restrictions of limited education and working opportunities bounded and controlled by the demands and conventions of a dominant landed gentry. The Peaceful family, despite their name, are not subservient. In addition to the dramas of the battlefield, the family, headed by the mother, must fight to maintain their sense of 'self' and not be swamped by the power of their landlord. Mrs.

Peaceful demonstrates bravery and determination, battling against poverty and authority to bring up her family of three sons, one of whom suffers from a mental disability. The story is both a domestic drama and one about the experiences of young men who volunteered to fight for their country and are then caught in the inhumanity of an horrific war.

The power of storytelling is enhanced by the narrative form. The reader enters into the voice and mind of the younger brother who 'writes' as it were a live journal for his readers, telling his story. The novel begins:

> They've gone now, and I'm alone at last. I have the whole night ahead of me, and I won't waste a single moment of it. I shan't sleep it anyway. I won't dream it away either. I mustn't, because every moment of it will be far too precious.
>
> > I want to try to remember everything, just as it was, just as it happened. I've had nearly eighteen years of yesterdays and tomorrows, and tonight I must remember as many of them as I can.   (Private Peaceful 7)

The weight of time, of personal and political history, is powerful, reverberating throughout the novel, setting up puzzles and possible pathways for predicting what might happen, or has happened, which emphasizes the growing drama. The teenagers leave their rural home, full of pride, idealism, patriotism and duty, to join the conflict-locked armies in the trenches. Shortly they become disillusioned marionettes caught dangling on the rack of war; entrenched both physically and mentally. They are adolescents caught in the world of men. Charlie, the elder brother, has always demonstrated a strong sense of self; caring for his younger sibling, Tommo, and battling against the control executed by class dominance. The potential division between the brothers over the love of a woman, who becomes Charlie's wife, is overcome by the strong and deeply loving relationship they hold between them; the younger brother sublimating his potential jealousy and desires, yet able to express such through the intimate relationship he has with the reader through the form of the novel. On the desolate battlefields of France, Charlie finally sacrifices himself for his brother by disobeying orders, adamantly and staunchly insisting on staying with his injured brother, rather

The engagement began with great fury.

than leaving him for the exterior demands of imposed duty - his duty is one of love and true brotherliness over the 'love' of country. These deep human bonds are stronger than comparatively flimsy patriotic ties, and demonstrate the inanities into which the ordinary person was, and sadly is, trapped by war, particularly with the absurd stalemate experienced in the trenches. Charlie's decision to stay with his brother, rather than obey orders to leave, is deemed an act of cowardice and results in a court martial and execution by firing squad. It is, in fact, heroism, where one man is prepared to sacrifice his life to save another for brotherly love. Michael Morpurgo concludes the novel with a short documentary postscript recording the fact that:

> 'over 290 soldiers of the British and the Commonwealth armies were executed by firing squad, some for desertion and cowardice, two for simply sleeping at their posts. Many of these men we know were traumatised by shell shock. Courts martial were brief, the accused often unrepresented.
> To this day the injustice they suffered has never been officially recognised. The British Government continues to refuse to grant posthumous pardons.
>
> (Private Peaceful 186)

In many ways this is an emotionally searing novel to read, recreating the experiences of warfare at the time, combined with the other stream of 'ordinary' life running beneath. Tommo is not present at the execution, creating the awful event in an imagined scenario for his readers before marching potentially to his own death on the Somme. His name, 'Tommo' is also emblematic of the Tommies who relinquished their individual identities for King and Country. If we are to educate our children into an abhorrence of war, then an emotionally convincing and 'true' representation through sensitive and carefully crafted, intelligently written and well-researched literature is far better than sending them onto fruitless battlefields in the name of a 'false' heroism.

Michael Morpurgo's concern with educating his readers against the atrocities of war and thereby re-shaping notions of heroism is also reflected in his latest collection of short stories by other authors starkly entitled *War* (2005). The collection brings together a range of stories about war from highly skilled and respected authors such as Michelle Magorian, Robert

Westall and Jamila Gavin. The stories variously re-situate the war story within the experiences of children, soldiers and the civilian population caught up in battle. The acts of heroism are those which demonstrate humanity; hiding a child from the soldiers rounding up villagers for execution, for example, or entering into the minds of young men who bitterly discover that the war zone of the Gulf is a place of devastation rather than heroism. Michael Morpurgo's preface to this collection records his meeting with a Spitfire pilot who was badly burned during the Second World War. The pilot subsequently became one of Professor McIndoe's sadly famous guinea pigs as McIndoe carried out pioneering plastic surgery to save their faces and their exterior social identities. Perhaps some of the reasons which lie behind war and such associated images of heroism are 'saving face'; the negative side of national pride which leads to lust for power, dominance and territory. Rather than raise humanity from the ashes of a city, the post-war ruins of Munich, London or contemporaneously Baghdad, for instance, we are far better to battle on the cricket field confining any Ashes symbolically to an urn where the conflict hurts no one and everyone has to obey the rules.

Overall, Morpurgo's stories are not the heroic tales directly out of the mould of nineteenth century Englishness, the boys' adventure story where no feat was too great. They are stories which are set in, and draw upon, a very particular context both in terms of landscape and history. They are, however, stories about a different kind of heroism which is drawn from this nineteenth century model, a modified form applicable to a world still torn by conflict. The ethical and personal values are of stoicism, courage, trust, crossing boundaries and coming to understanding through personal interaction, caring, an humanitarian approach and listening to each other. These are the values which supersede the limitations of nationalism; which contain an ethical wisdom which transcend the immediacy of the everyday, which will translate into the future in an unpredictable world. Morpurgo takes the best from the past, humanises heroism and introduces such, both to the contemporary protagonists and contemporary readers. In a number of his novels the adventure is observed by the child protagonist who travels back in time - in particular, to that of Arthurian legend - to a period less trammelled by the complexities of internationalism, when there was an ethical code clearly demarcated - the code of chivalry.

In *Arthur, High King of Britain* (1994), a boy is cut off by the sea, and threatened by drowning. He wakes, unsure of whether he is alive or dead, in a strange room in the presence of an aged King Arthur, who recounts the story of Camelot, of bravery, heroism, love and betrayal. The protagonist in *The Sleeping Sword* (2002) is a young boy blinded in an accident, who finds the sword of Arthur and, again, re-visits the heroic and chivalric past through the stories of an elderly member of the Arthurian court. Kevin Crossley-Holland also returns to Arthurian legend in his trilogy, the first of which is *The Seeing Stone* (2000). The story is a *bildungsroman*, following the life and adventures of Arthur, who has been given a piece of obsidian, his 'seeing-stone', by Merlin, his mentor. Arthur can experience both past and present and inform his future by looking into his seeing-stone where he observes the young King Arthur. His life is interconnected with the adventures of this kingly hero, yet in the first part of the trilogy he does not know if he is watching a premonition of his own life, or whether this will be but observation of another's. What he does learn is that there are important moral and ethical virtues which are applicable to king and peasant alike, such as befriending and respecting the peasant girl, Gatty, despite the differences in their status. He also learns of the harshness of law which is meted out irrespective of the circumstances of ordinary folk, when the taxes demanded by the new king threaten the livelihood of the peasants. Whether Arthur does become an heroic king, or remains a member of the ordinary populace, as the hero of the trilogy, through him the reader learns of the humanitarian and social values essential to a civilised society. Arthur is also a scholar, a reader and a writer; an observer both of the execution of harsh law and that which is governed by sensibility to the realities of peasant life. He is a thinker and a problem solver. This is symbolised by his relationship with the seeing-stone in determining the course of his life relative to that of the legendary king. What he does share with Arthur, King of England, is his engagement with a quest. For the boy, the quest is the discovery of his parentage, his place in life and, in the wider realm of matters, by engaging in the Crusades.

History has made the Crusades 'safe' for a contemporary story teller such as Crossley-Holland, for outside of Arthurian legend, the pen of the historian has sealed action, event and enmity within the vaults of time. Crossley-Holland has created a 'traditional' hero with humanitarian values which translate into and are applicable to contemporary society.

Michelle Paver's trilogy, *The Chronicles of Ancient Darkness,* the first of which is *Wolf Brother,* is set in the Stone Age. Torak, the young male protagonist, lives close to nature, since apart from the hunter-gatherer lifestyle he has been partially brought up by wolves and is a member of the wolf clan. He, again, is a chosen one; given the responsibility of solving the problems and puzzles. His quest will lead to the eradication of the evil which has invaded the various clan peoples; an evil conjured up in the name of greed and desire. In a novel of learning and maturation, the heroic Torak has to adhere to the values of the clans overall, and to accommodate their various differences, in order to fulfil his destiny. He learns the crafts of survival, and pieces together the histories of the peoples amongst whom he moves and lives. Torak is a hero who has to survive, yet in doing so he respects the humanity of others, albeit in the harsh Stone Age world. Centuries away from this technological age, Torak represents the contemporary values of heroism, which are derived from those nominated by Kingsley. He demonstrates manliness in his fearless and selfless confrontations of dangers and through physical trials. He is godly, although these are the spirits of a pre-Christian era. He is practical, else he could not survive. Enthusiasm, for Torak, is translated into determination and a resistance of failure, for he holds the future of his peoples in his actions or his failures. He is therefore prudent and self-sacrificing, moving across 'class' barriers, which are for him the boundaries of the various clans with whom he interacts. He is a Stone Age fictional creation who embodies the highest values of heroism, without the political and imperialist stigmata attached to the hero of the nineteenth century.

As Lord Byron wrote 'What I want is a hero'. However, one may question why contemporary readers need heroes today. Heroes are desired, else they would not be created by writers of fiction in the attempt to satisfy a particular cultural psychic need. That need is evident in our culture - the success of Harry Potter being testament to such. Potter fights the dark forces of evil, operating in a parallel world which is removed from contemporary political complexities. There are magical powers available to him which will solve the seemingly insoluble. His personal solution is the quest for defeat of the powers of darkness, whilst also dealing with the 'real' world problems of the Dursley's capitalist greed and selfishness. One of his battlegrounds is the Quidditch field where injuries can be rectified. Potter is the 'playful' hero with magic at his wand tip, so that the reader, or viewer, is confident from the beginning that whatever else happens, Potter will be there at the end as the winner, ready to solve all problems another day.

Perhaps that is why we need heroes. To give hope that what is seemingly insoluble can be solved; that the greatest difficulties and most malignant powers can be overcome and 'right' win out. Although the nineteenth century qualities of heroism are outmoded for a contemporary society which (one would hope) abhors war and imperialist attitudes (although that is highly questionable in some quarters) the heroes do, however, embody a number of values and attitudes which travel across time and cultures. Fortitude, courage, perseverance, problem solving, humanitarian values and engagement with a quest - this last is the precept of life itself, as Crossley-Holland notes on the end paper of *The Seeing-Stone*:

Each of us needs a quest, and a person without one is lost to himself.

The heroes created by contemporary writers as discussed are imbued with those values which, hopefully, will take the next generation into the continuation of that great quest to produce a safe, peaceful, productive and humanitarian society for all - where all are heroes and heroines, swash-bucklers with swords re-fashioned into ploughshares.

REFERENCES

Charles Kingsley, *Westward Ho!* 1855.

R.M. Ballantyne, *The Coral Island.* 1858.

G.A. Henty, *With Clive In India.* 1884.

W.E. Johns, *The Camels Are Coming.* 1932.

Gary Crew, *Strange Objects.* Melbourne: Heineman, 1990.

Thomas Hughes, *Tom Brown's Schooldays.* 1857.

Michael Morpurgo (ed.), *War: Stories of Conflict.* Macmillan Children's Books, 2005.

Michael Morpurgo, *Private Peaceful.* Collins, 2003.

Michael Morpurgo, *Arthur, High King of Britain.* Pavillion, 1994.

Michael Morpurgo, *The Sleeping Sword.* Egmont Books, 2002.

Kevin Crossley-Holland, *The Seeing Stone.* Orion Children's, 2000.

Michelle Paver, *Wolf Brother.* Harper Children's, 2004.

J.K. Rowling, *Harry Potter and the Philosopher's Stone.* Bloomsbury, 1997.

"How goes the work?"

Victoria de Rijke

The Revolutionary Quack

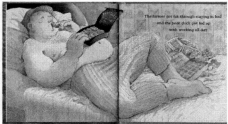

'There was once a duck who had the bad luck to live with a lazy old farmer.
The duck did the work, the farmer stayed all day in bed.'

Lev Davidovich Bronstein, born the son of a hard working Jewish famer from
the Ukraine, became an intellectual, arrested for his political activities and
deported in 1900, changed his name to Leon Trotsky when he escaped from
Siberia and met Lenin in London. In *Literature and Revolution*, 1917, Trotsky
argued our greatest responsibility would be to throw light on the origins and
social significance of the works of art & literature. He foresaw a new art and
self-consciousness, promising:

'This new art is incompatible with pessimism, with scepticism, and with all the
other forms of spiritual collapse. It is realistic, active, vitally collectivist, and
filled with a limitless creative faith in the Future.' (Trotsky:51)

He was murdered on Stalin's orders in 1940. This paper draws its structure from a Marxist dialectic: the struggle of opposites; what Lenin called 'the study of the contradiction within the very essence of things'.

> 'The duck fetched the cow from the field." How goes the work?" called the farmer. The duck answered "Quack".'

1 in 10 of all employees in the UK are migrant workers, 2.6 million in total, but many go unrecorded. 5000 gang-masters or labour contractors (apparently typically white British, Russian and Pakistani men) supply up to 100,000 workers a year to British farming industries. Migrants often cannot bring their families with them, arrive in debt for their journey, have to repay loans at high interest and with what they earn find they cannot leave. Anti-slavery groups call this bonded labour. In 2004, the Home Office increased the number of seasonal workers allowed into Britain from 10,000 to 25,000 every year. One of the UK's largest strawberry growers uses 1000 migrants a season from E. Europe, S. Africa, China and South America, housed in tiny mobile homes.

> 'The duck brought the sheep from the hill. "How goes the work?" called the farmer. The duck answered: "Quack."
> The duck put the hens in their house. "How goes the work?" called the farmer. The duck answered: "Quack."

18 million ducks are slaughtered every year in the UK. Factory farmed duck conditions - famously supplying Marks & Spencers stores - are kept indoors 10,000 at a time, given no access to swimming and have their bills and penises trimmed to avoid the aggressive behaviours factory conditions produce. Due to action in 2005, the Co-op cleared its shelves of factory farmed duck but not all supermarkets have followed suit. (Do you know what duck you may be eating?)

> 'No animal in England is free. The life of an animal is misery and slavery: that is the plain truth.
> ...Why then do we continue in this miserable condition? Because nearly the whole of the produce of our labour is stolen from us by human beings. There, comrades, is the answer to all our problems. It is summed up in a single word- Man. Man is the only real enemy we have.
> ... Man is the only creature that consumes without producing. He does not give milk, he does not lay eggs... Yet he is lord of all the animals. He sets them to work, he gives back to them the bare minimum that will prevent them from starving and the rest he keeps for himself... Only get rid of Man and the produce of our labour would be our own.
> That is my message to you, comrades. Rebellion!' (Orwell:3-4)

Later, the pigs call upon the hens to surrender their eggs, just as Stalin tried to collectivise the peasant farmers of Russia, followed by their bitter revolt, where millions were starved into submission. In *Animal Farm* the hens at first smashed their eggs rather than turn them over, but the pigs still get fat.

> 'The farmer got fat through staying in bed and the poor duck got fed up with working all day'

> And I've always thought: the simplest words of all
> Must do. When I see how things are
> Every heart must bleed.
> You'll go under if you don't fight back,
> But you must see that.

> Bertolt Brecht, *And I've Always Thought.*

Bertolt Brecht was born Eugen Brecht in 1898 and was a published poet by the age of 16. A playwright who developed theatre as a social form, attacked bourgeois respectability and discouraged audiences from involvement, wanting them to think with critical detachment, Brecht went into exile from Germany in 1933 as not enough of a socialist, then got into trouble in the US for being too much of a socialist in 1947. He died in 1956 in East Berlin, as much a socialist as ever.

Born Ernesto Guevara in Argentina, Che Guevara completed his study to be a doctor but became a legend in his own lifetime as a leader of the Latin American Revolution 1956-1958 which liberated Cuba. He was murdered on the CIA's orders in 1967. Though many people have posters, carry bags or wear clothes with his picture on rather than read his writing, Che is not just a fashion icon but a hero. His face is used both to market consumer capitalist commodities and to keep up revolutionary spirits in the last remaining communist countries.

Farmer Duck is used throughout British schools for recommended reading in the literacy hour, as well as for pleasure. There are also big books, mini books and story sacks for sale.

> *The hens and the cow and the sheep got very upset. They loved the duck. So*
> *they held a meeting under the moon and they made a plan for the morning.*
> *Moo! Said the cow. Baa! Said the sheep. Cluck! said the hen. And that was their plan.*
>
> *It was just before dawn and the farmyard was still. Through the back door and*
> *into the house crept the cow and the sheep and the hens.*
> *They stole down the hall. They creaked up the stairs.*

They squeezed under the bed of the farmer and wriggled about. The bed started
to rock and the farmer woke up and he called: "How goes the work?" and Moo!
Baa! Cluck! They lifted his bed and he started to shout and they banged and
they bounced the old farmer about and about and about, right out of the bed
And he fled with the cow and the sheep and the hens mooing and baaing and
clucking around him.

'Rumours of a wonderful farm, where the human beings had been turned
out and the animals managed their own affairs, continued to circulate,
inspiring other animals.'

George Orwell was born Eric Arthur Blair in Bengal, as his father worked for
the Government of India. During the 1930s Orwell became a journalist and
socialist and travelled to Spain to report on their civil war. He took the side of
the United Workers Marxist Party militia and fought alongside them. It was
this war that made him hate communism and favour the English brand of
socialism. Orwell wrote *Animal Farm* in 1945, which if you read it as a child is a
story about unfair pigs and then later, when you're older, teachers tell you it's
a really obvious allegory of Stalinism. Orwell died of tuberculosis in 1950.

The duck awoke and waddled wearily into the yard expecting to hear "How goes the
work?" but nobody spoke!
The cow and the sheep and the hens came back. Quack? Asked the duck. Moo! Said the
cow, Baa! Said the sheep, Cluck! Said the hens. Which told the duck the whole story.
Then mooing and baaing and clucking and quacking they all set to work on their farm.

Will there be equal distribution of wealth; each creature happy in their work? Like Orwell's *Animal Farm*, doesn't *Farmer Duck* hint at the possibility of the overthrow of the oppressor supplanted by a new leader? Socialism perverted into oppressive militarist totalitarianism?

This paper has argued the case for Orwell's influence on *Farmer Duck*, drawing on the Marxist revolutionary ideas of Che Guevara and Leon Trotsky. I throw in some of Brecht's poetry, too; I can't help myself. *Farmer Duck* directly shows the effects of class struggle, from the point of view of the proletariat duck. But - in order for it to be a truly Marxist text - have its authors directly participated in lives similar to those described?

Helen Oxenbury grew up in Ipswich, spent her childhood in the Suffolk countryside, went to art school, married John Burningham another eminent children's book artist, had children and worked from home. She says with each new project she tries to push back the boundaries.

Martin Waddell grew up in Belfast. His mother and an uncle and aunt are actors. Waddell usually writes about how political unrest affects the lives of ordinary people. He says he found a drawing of a duck by his cousin at the age of 4 or 5 and 'So I wrote Animal Farm for Teeny Weenies'.

An illustrator who does not work the land herself but paints it as an unspoiled pastoral idyll, and a writer who belittles young comrades as 'teeny weenies'. It is not enough to interpret the world; it must be transformed.

No! to publishers who place white middle-class illustrators with white middleclass writers to make profits on their success and fame. *No!* to the price of the book. *No!* to how much children's literature costs and *No!* to children not earning a living wage and *No!* to children never writing or publishing any literature they write and illustrate themselves.

No! In *Farmer Duck* the farmer represents the oppressor, the adult and also the capitalist world that eats up world markets, fattening on the profits based on the hunger and exploitation of the dependent world. *Farmer Duck* leads proletarian 5 year olds to recognise their role in the class struggle, as they identify with the oppressed and the revolution required to overthrow it.

> When I was small, I went to school
> And I learnt what was mine and what was yours
> And when I'd learnt all they had to teach
> It didn't seem to be all to me.
> For I had no breakfast to eat
> But others, they had some;
> And so I learnt all again, all
> About the nature of the class enemy.
> And I learnt the whys and the wherefores
> Of the rift that runs through the world,
> Dividing us just as surely as the rain
> Falls down from above.

> Bertolt Brecht, *Song of the Class Enemy.*

In 1917 Trotsky called for new proletarian literature with new language, new forms to express emotions and ideas. Could we have found one at last, nearly a century later? What better new form than the picture book? What better new language than the quack?

So, is this all 'duckspeak'? (George Orwell's word in the novel *1984* for preaching to the choir), or is anyone converted?

Che Guevara said the people climb history on the feet of farmers. In *Farmer Duck* the duck climbs history with the hooves and webbed feet of the farmyard animals from *Animal Farm* half a century earlier. Our next battle in this century is to create the conditions where children can write, publish, critique their own literature themselves, and do me out of a job.

Che's last letter, *To my Children*, reads: 'Above all always be capable of feeling deeply any injustice committed against anyone, anywhere in the world. This is the most beautiful quality in a revolutionary.' (Guevara:388)

* Born in Devon of Dutch parents (one from aristocracy and the other peasant stock), Victoria's first job was as Primary School teacher in Brent, North London. She is now Reader in Arts & Education at Middlesex University and works collaboratively with colleagues, publishing on children's literature and pedagogy.

Victoria is also on the Editorial Board of the journal *Children's Literature in Education*.

REFERENCES

Bertolt Brecht's poetry from Martin Hoyles, *Changing Childhood*. Rochester: Readers & Writers Publishing Cooperative, 1979.
David Deutschmann (ed), *Che Guevara Reader*. New York: Ocean Press, 2003.
George Orwell, *Animal Farm: A Fairy Story*. London: Longmans, 1964.
Leon Trotsky, *Literature and Revolution*. London: Redwords, 1991.

Illustrations copyright 1991 Helen Oxenbury,
From *Farmer Duck* by Martin Waddell & illustrated by Helen Oxenbury.
Reproduced by kind permission of Walker Books Ltd, London SE11 5JH.

Beverley Naidoo

How Do I Tell You This Story?

Children's Literature - Some Marxist Perspectives

MICHAEL WAS ON THE PHONE. He was saying something about a conference idea... something about 'Marxist perspectives in children's literature'. Was this a time-trip? Past or future?

> 'But I'm in the middle of writing a novel, Michael. I've grounded myself.'
> 'Why not come and read us some work-in-progress?' Then, adding the writer's bait, Michael asked what my novel was about...
> 'Aah, interesting! Just half-an-hour?'

I was introduced to Marx in early 1960s South Africa as a student in an underground study group. We discussed his then banned books, unaware that an undercover Special Branch officer had rented the flat next door and was recording everything through a secretly planted microphone! While I never came to think of myself as a Marxist - I could never conform to any singular political identity - those discussions offered a set of lenses through which to examine the world of apartheid with its divisions and fractures more sharply than any others. I began to consider aspects of 'race', class and ideology for the first time. Even if I was not always convinced by some over-neat answers, I learned then that Marx's lenses raised questions otherwise ignored.

Over forty years later, as those of us in the children's book world are swept up, under, along or aside by powerful global market forces, what are the questions we *haven't* been asking? What do we understand about what is happening to us? When I throw my characters near the edge of rapids, in their struggles to avoid extinction, they usually open their eyes! Needless to say, I was hooked by Michael's bait.

Six months after the conference, my novel is complete. It has a title now. *Burn My Heart*. However, most of the opening page that I read on the day did not survive to the final draft except for the opening questions of my unidentified narrator:

> *'How do I tell you this story? Do I tell you the truth, the whole truth and nothing but the truth? Do I tell you my side or his? What if I had been born on his side and he on mine? We were both only children...'* (1)

The novel is indeed two stories, two sets of eyes in the same place and time. Two boys in 1950s Kenya and a story of friendship and betrayal during the State of Emergency that saw the most violent end of empire in one of Britain's African colonies. 55,000 British troops were sent to crush the Kikuyu 'Mau Mau' movement that led the resistance to the white settlers - *wazungu* - who had taken their land. While Britons at home were gripped (especially through the popular press) by gory Mau Mau attacks on white settlers and Kikuyu 'loyalists', most of them averted their gaze from the draconian and frequently bloody actions of the authorities. The numbers are telling. 32 white settlers were killed and over 1800 African 'loyalists' by Mau Mau. The colonial forces killed at least 12,000 Mau Mau fighters and suspects. With the death penalty extended for a wide range of offences, 1090 Kikuyu men were hung, with courts prepared to accept even very weak evidence. At least 150,000 Kikuyu men and women were detained without trial, many just on suspicion of being Mau Mau supporters. David Anderson in *Histories of the Hanged* (2005) estimates that at least one in four Kikuyu adult males were imprisoned or detained between 1950 and 1958. Whole communities were subjected to 'collective punishment'. Kenya was a prime example of colonial occupation and anti-colonial rebellion with massive civilian suffering and what amounted to a civil war among the subjugated. Sound familiar?

This is the background to *Burn My Heart*. My novel takes readers into the lives of imagined individuals, not statistics. I have set it at a specific point in time: a few months before and after the declaration of the State of Emergency. The viewpoints are those of a thirteen-year-old Kikuyu boy, Mugo, and a slightly younger British settler child, Mathew. Mugo works as a 'kitchen toto' for Mathew's family, the Graysons. When not on duty in the kitchen, Mugo acts as a playmate and reliable minder for the lonely Mathew on the Grayson's farm in the highland bush below Mount Kenya. Forty years earlier, the Grayson's land belonged to Mugo's grandfather.

As ever, I hope that as readers engage with the personal dramas, they also discover a prism through which to glimpse my characters' wider world. I dislike the term 'social realism' for works of fiction. The phrase has connotations that appear not to recognise the role of imagination in exploring reality. When pushed to describe the genre to which I am most drawn, I quote Nadine Gordimer when she writes of 'witness literature'. She records how, even as a child, she tried to find the meaning in what she saw by transforming it into stories based on everyday incidents of ordinary life. This involved a dialogue with herself:

> 'Time and published books confirmed that I was a writer, and witness literature, if it is a genre of circumstance or time and place, was mine. I had to find how to keep my integrity to the Word, the sacred charge of the writer. I realised, as I believe many writers do, that instead of restricting, inhibiting and coarsely despoiling aesthetic liberty, the existential condition of witness was enlarging, inspiring aesthetic liberty, breaching the previous limitations of my sense of form and use of language through necessity: to create form and use it anew.' (2002)

Gordimer is talking about literature that is 'umbilically' connected to society. Stories are a way of making sense for oneself as a writer, as well as for others. Furthermore, if one can find the truths in a specific human situation, the meaning will carry across time, place.

My own experiences of reading literature as a young adult - with writers like Peter Abrahams, Es'kia Mphahlele and many others, including a host of excellent writers in the Heinemann African Writers' Series - were part of my own journey as a white South African in crossing racialised borders, so deeply embedded through apartheid. Literature became part of the ongoing process that I call 'deracination'. I still recall the shock of reading Mphahlele's *Down Second Avenue* (1962). He took me into his childhood in Marabastad. It was not too far from where I had grown up in Jo'burg. It could have been on another planet. But that is the generosity of writers. They invite you in. Of course, writers are not neutral. They may also deceive you, as Chinua Achebe put so aptly:

> 'Stories are not innocent. They can put you in the wrong crowd, in the party of the man who has come to dispossess you.' (1990)

Indeed many of the stories that I had uncritically consumed as a young child in my whites-only school and home had also put me in the wrong crowd!

This is the first novel I have set in Kenya but my own colonial upbringing in apartheid South Africa spurred my desire to research and explore the world that Mathew and Mugo share in their completely fractured way, separated by 'race', culture, class. The aesthetic quest, to which Gordimer refers, led me to interweave each boy's story into a larger narrative whole. Despite all the fractures of their experience, there is something these boys share at a human level that drives their relationship and the tragedy of the story they hold in common.

Writing fiction within this genre that involves the 'existential condition of witness' is for me also a way of reflecting, exploring, questioning. It is not simply a matter of telling 'how it is'. Entering the world of Lily in 'One Day, Lily, One Day', in Out of Bounds, was a journey for me even though Lily was a white child growing up in my home town, Johannesburg, with not many years between us. Her parents' politics, however, were very different from my own. I set the story in 1960, the year of Sharpeville Massacre, a watershed for South Africa and for Lily too. The story opens with a terrified Lily watching the security police take away her father. Her parents have been holding secret meetings in her father's study. Lily has heard the typewriter tapping. Most white children were brought up calling white adults 'Aunty', 'Uncle', 'Mr ---' or 'Mrs ---' but black adults were either 'the boy' or 'the girl', or known only by an easily pronounced European first name (John, Jim, Jane were favourites). Lily, however, has a family friend 'Uncle Max' who is black. Lily remembers begging him to take her to the park and her frustration when he declines. Uncle Max has tried to explain:

"'One day, little Lily, one day. When we have freedom, you and I will go to the park."
His voice was so grave that I calmed down but I still didn't understand that Uncle Max
wasn't allowed to take me - a little white girl - to the park because he was black.
When the police took Daddy away, I didn't understand that too.' (2001)

Her father's arrest is enough to stir gossip and a comment from a girl at school:

"'My mom says your parents are Commies. She says they have native friends. Is it true
they sit and eat with you?'" (2001)

In the story Lily, who is desperate to not to be friendless, tussles with the consequences of her parents' choices in a racist, police state. I have a fascinating piece of writing by a Scottish boy whose identification with Lily clearly stems from having a white South African grandfather who, like Lily's father, was arrested for his political involvement with Mandela and the African National Congress. But while only a tiny minority of readers will share Lily's unusual family background, the universal desire of a child to have friends hopefully allows other readers to make an imaginative identification with Lily. I hope that they can imagine themselves beyond their own class, colour, culture, gender etc. as they engage with Lily's experience and her journey of discovery. Might this imaginative identification enable some loosening of the confines of the reader's own frames of reference and an opportunity to question deep and unexamined assumptions? I still want to think so although it is a complicated matter, as I learned in my doctoral research project and wrote about in *Through Whose Eyes? Exploring racism: reader, text and context.* (2002) Just as stories 'are not innocent', neither are readers' eyes.

The majority of letters I receive are from readers who express surprise and sometimes shock at what they have experienced in the imaginative journey they have made with my characters. It is beyond the world they know. I am constantly asked 'Is this true?' I want to end with a recent letter from an eleven-year-old boy in a London primary school where his surprise was of a different nature. 'K' had just finished reading *Web of Lies* (2004). At the core of the novel lie questions of power and how to respond to those who use might as right and who exploit cultural dislocation. My character

Femi has just begun secondary school and is swiftly drawn into a frightening gang, ostensibly for protection. Femi's vulnerability on London's tough streets is inextricably linked with his family's history. He and his sister Sade have been smuggled into London - we first meet them in *The Other Side of Truth* (2000) - because their father, an outspoken journalist, has fallen foul of General Abacha and his military regime in Nigeria. The children have witnessed the killing of their mother in an assassination attempt on Papa. At the beginning of *Web of Lies*, they are still awaiting the decision of the Home Office as to whether they will be given refugee status and allowed to stay. Their spacious middle-class house in Lagos, with its large garden where Femi played football between pawpaw and flaming forest trees, has been exchanged for a cramped London council flat. While Papa holds steadfastly to his cultural and moral compass, his children's grip is much more tenuous. It was clear from K's letter, that some aspect of Femi's situation reflected his own:

> '...I have always felt no enjoyment when I have had to read in the past but your book was incredibly inspiring. The similarities between the lives of Femi and myself left me wondering. Wondering how two people can be so similar, wondering how you know so much about what young boys are going through and wondering where you got your inspiration? Thank you for making me understand a little more about myself and for understanding that it is not easy (something that adults far too often forget)....'
> (Private letter to author, London, 2 February 2006)

Behind these words (music to an author's ears) I am sure that there are more disturbing questions of identity, class, culture, relations between generations, and an expression of the pressures under which this young person feels expected to make sense of the fractured world. In addition, his name reveals that his family is Muslim. His strong identification with Femi suggests to me that, like Femi, he is walking on a tightrope. He writes of not enjoying reading. How much literature is there to speak to this boy and other child 'tightrope walkers' who do not live safe or charmed existences?

The reality of children's publishing is that although over the last few decades we have made chinks in the walls that have traditionally surrounded the children's book world, the industry remains overwhelmingly white and middle-class and the majority of published books reflect this. However the struggles of the 1970s and 80s - to challenge racism, sexism, false depictions of working class characters and other stereotypes and silences - were critical in developing awareness. The movement helped to stir and support demand, particularly through schools and library services, for books reflecting the diversity of experience of young people in Britain today. There has been change and young readers of all backgrounds have been the beneficiaries of the much richer, livelier, more diverse range of books on most school library shelves. Nevertheless, when you go into W. H. Smith's in Lewisham, South London, for instance, and find that there is only one black author - Malorie Blackman - on the children's bookshelves, you are bound to question just how far that change goes.

As Michael outlined in his opening paper, new forces threaten the attempts to assert humanism and diversity in children's literature. At the same time as government policy in schools has reduced literature to the *"handmaid to literacy"* (11), global corporation bulldozers are at work inside the children's book industry. Books and their authors are scrutinised more closely for their commodity value than ever before. Globalisation does not implicitly mean an increase in diversity. It means that a children's bookshop in Delhi or Johannesburg looks largely similar to one in London, offering almost the same diet to mainly middle class children everywhere. As the old book world's walls are replaced by nouveau glass, concrete and steel, stories told by those outside the walls remain mostly unheard. The majority of young people, wherever they are, still do not see themselves reflected within the world of books.

A luta continua.

AUTHOR'S NOTE
I have constructed this piece out of scribbled notes and what I might have said on the day if I had not been 'mid-novel' and had more time to prepare!

REFERENCES

Chinua Achebe, *'African Literature as Restoration of Celebration'*, in K. Holt Peterson & A. Rutherford (eds) *Chinua Achebe: A Celebration*, New Hampshire: Dangeroo Press, p 7, 1990.

D. Anderson, *Histories of the Hanged*. London: Weidenfeld & Nicolson, 2005.

Nadine Gordimer, *'Testament of the Word'*. London: The Guardian Review, 15.06.2002.

Es'kia Mphahlele, *Down Second Avenue*. Berlin: Seven Seas Books, 1962.

Beverley Naidoo, *Out of Bounds*. London: Puffin, 2001.

Beverley Naidoo, *Through Whose Eyes*. Stoke on Trent: Trentham, 2002.

Beverley Naidoo, *Web of Lies*. London: Puffin, 2004.

Beverley Naidoo, *The Other Side of Truth*. London: Puffin, 2000.

Beverley Naidoo, *Burn My Heart*. London: Puffin, due 2007.

Private letter to author, London, 02.02.2006.

Michael Rosen, Keynote address at conference on Children's Literature - Some Marxist Perspectives, University of Hertfordshire, 23.03.2006.

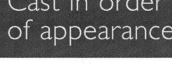

Cast in order of appearance:

Michael Rosen
is a writer, broadcaster and tutor on MA in Education Studies at London Metropolitan Studies and MA in Modern Literature at Birkbeck College, University of London. He has written many successful books of children's poetry and prose, some on difficult issues. Extensive broadcast material includes *Word of Mouth* and programmes on writers of children's stories. (www.michaelrosen.co.uk)

Richard McSween
lives in Lancashire and is a writer, teacher and political activist. He has published two novels for teenagers and his most recent play, *Rockingham's Coat*, is set in the English Civil War.

David Rudd
teaches Children's Literature in the Dept of Cultural and Creative Studies at the University of Bolton, England. He has published some 80 articles on the subject and two books: one on Roald Dahl, *A Communication Studies Approach to Children's Literature* (1992) and one on Blyton, *Enid Blyton and the Mystery of Children's Literature* (2000). He is currently working on the issue of animals and toys in children's books.

Anne-Marie Bird
is a former research student and part-time lecturer at The University of Bolton and has published several articles on children's literature. Her most recent publication was on Philip Pullman's '*His Dark Materials*' trilogy.

David Harrold
made his debut in professional theatre in 1998, playing opposite Judi Bowker's Hedda Gabler at Pentameters Theatre. This was followed by a leading role in an Edinburgh Festival production, five short films and a T.V. documentary. Since 2002, he has been writing and performing for Cadco Productions, and in 2006 produced and starred in *Dumbing Down*, a play about schools and teaching.

Pat Pinsent
is Senior Research Fellow at Roehampton University. She is editor of IBBYLink (the journal of the British section of the International Board on Books for Young People) and of The Journal of Children's Literature Studies. Her books include *Children's Literature and the Politics of Equality* (Fulton 1997) and the Proceedings of a number of the annual IBBY conferences.

Dr Farah Mendleson
is the editor of Foundation: the International Review for Science Fiction, and the author of several books, including one on her favourite fantasy writer, Diana Wynne Jones. She has a forthcoming book on the rhetorics of fantasy.

Conor Kostick
is the author of the young adult fantasy novel *Epic*, and its sequel *Saga*. *Epic* was awarded a place on the 2006 Honour List of the International Board on Books for Youth and has become an international bestseller. Conor teaches medieval history at Trinity College, Dublin, reviews for the Journal of Music in Ireland and is a member of the editorial board of the Irish Socialist Worker.

Rhiannon Lassiter
has published ten novels, a non-fiction book about the supernatural and co-edited an anthology of war poetry and prose in addition to several short stories. She co-edits Armadillo Magazine, a quarterly children's books review publication (www.armadillomagazine.com) and maintains her own website (www.rhiannonlassiter.com). Her first three novels, the Hex trilogy, have been translated into many foreign languages. She is currently working on a horror novel *Bad Blood* forthcoming from Oxford University Press in 2007.

Professor Jean Webb
is Director of the International Centre for Research in Children's Literature, Literacy and Creativity, the University of Worcester, UK. She is also programme leader for the MA in 'Children's Literature: An International Perspective'. Her research interests include 19th, 20th and 21st century

children's literature from an international perspective. She was a founding executive member of the Nordic Children's Literature Research Network and is an International Committee member of the Children's Literature Association. Publications include *Text, Culture and National Identity in Children's Literature:* (ed. Jean Webb; 2000), *Introducing Children's Literature: Romanticism to Postmodernism*, Cogan Thacker, Deborah and Webb, Jean (2002) and *The Sunny Side Of Darkness: Children´s Literature in Totalitarian and Post-Totalitarian Eastern Europe*, Webb, Jean (ed) 2005.

Dr. Quack & Dr. Victoria de Rijke
are Reader in Arts & Education, and work at Middlesex University in North London. Victoria publishes regularly on children's literature, often in collaboration with young readers and old colleagues. She and Dr. Quack have collaborated on several projects, including www.Quack-Project.com and *The Grain of a Duck's Voice* for Performance Research Journal. They are working towards a forthcoming book on 'duck' for Reaktion Books.

Beverley Naidoo
joined the resistance to apartheid as a student in South Africa. After detention without trial she came to England into exile. Her PhD explored teenagers' responses to literature and racism. Her writing includes novels, short stories and plays and has won many awards, including the Carnegie Medal. Her forthcoming novel *Burn My Heart* is a story of loyalty and betrayal set in 1950s Kenya. (www.beverleynaidoo.com)

If you enjoyed this one.....

University of Hertfordshire
School of Education

The Story and The Self:
Children's Literature
Some Psychoanalytic Perspectives

a two-day conference
Friday 13th and Saturday 14th April 2007, 10am - 4pm
at the Fielder Centre, Hatfield, Hertfordshire

Speakers include:
Margaret Rustin and Michael Rustin
The Regeneration of Dr. Who

Rosemary Stones
editor Books For Keeps
Stories with Meaning
Throughout Our Lives

For further information contact: **Lisa Garner**
telephone: 01707 285695 email: L.A.Garner@herts.ac.uk

....see you there!